When Children
Are Disobedient They Cannot Escape
Punishment Unless Their Parents Exert Compassion
And Forgive Them. We Are All Sinners and Need
God's Mercy. If You Believe You Are Not a
Sinner You Do Share Satan's Pride
Stop Right Here! Do Not Read
This Book!

666

MYSTERY REVEALED

THE NEXT WORLD CONFLICT

CLAUDE FLEURY

LEIDE JESSE LLC
Orlando, FL

For information regarding special quantity discounts for bulk purchase for sales, promotions, premiums, fund raising and educational needs, visit the following Web sites: www.leidejessellc.com

www.666mysteryrevealed.org

Copyright © 2008 by Claude Fleury

Unless otherwise indicated, all Scripture quotations are from the Holy Bible, English Standard Version, copyright © 2001 by Crossway Bibles, a division of Good News Publishers. Used by permission. All rights reserved.

Scripture quotations marked (KJV) are from the King James Version of the Bible.

Scripture quotations marked (CEV) are from the Contemporary English Version Copyright © 1991, 1992, 1995 American Bible Society. Used by Permission.

Scripture quotations marked (EMTV) are from the Holy Bible, English Majority Text Translation, copyright © 2000 by Paul W. Esposito. Used by permission of the Copyright holder. Courtesy of Stauros Ministries.

Library of Congress Control Number: 2008910764

666 Mystery Revealed: The Next World Conflict / Claude Fleury
ISBN 13: 978-0-9790043-0-8

Printed in the United States of America

TABLE OF CONTENTS

PREFACE

Dear brethren, I, the author of this book, am a sinner chosen by Jesus to bring you His message. I struggle daily to remain on the narrow path to heaven, not on my own strength but by relying on His Holy Spirit after accepting His gift of salvation for an assured victory. To the Romans Paul wrote, "For all have sinned and fall short of the glory of God, and are justified by His grace as a gift, through the redemption that is in Christ Jesus, whom God put forward as a propitiation by His blood, to be received by faith. This was to show God's righteousness, because in His divine forbearance He had passed over former sins. It was to show His righteousness at the present time, so that He might be just and the justifier of the one who has faith in Jesus" (Romans 3:23-26).

When Jesus returned to Capernaum, He invited many sinners and tax collectors along with His disciples to His house, which did not please many religious teachers. The Bible says, "And the scribes of the Pharisees, when they saw that He was eating with sinners and tax collectors, said to His disciples, 'Why does He eat with tax collectors and sinners?' And when Jesus heard it, He said to them, 'Those who are well have no need of a physician, but those who

are sick. I came not to call the righteous, but sinners' "
(Mark 2:16-17).

This book is written to unveil certain biblical mysteries,
and to share with you messages I have received from the
Lord.

This is also an epistle to the Church, a collection of letters to the body of Christ.

This book is not a plan of mine; it has been the Lord's.
He uploaded images, sentences, and words; I would wake
up with a specific sentence that was to be corrected, a subject that needed revision, or a biblical passage to use.
Around February 2004, as I was still emailing His second
message to Church leaders one by one, I was also recording
visions I had before and since the death of Pope John Paul
II. I was contemplating the problem of emailing a letter that
was getting longer day by day as I was given new messages. Little did I know where the Lord was leading me!
Three months later, I knew that it was to be made available
to the Church, not just to the leaders. Then a new challenge
arose: I was to find the right way to make that happen. Because I never take any step in life without requesting direction from the Lord, I did just that. During the time when I
was completing this work for distribution by mail, with the
Lord's guidance it finally became obvious that it must become a book. With the advantage of being durable and

more appealing to many, it was the best medium.

In 2003, when I was to write "The Lord's Rebuke" as He was urging me to do, I questioned Him to make sure that I understood what He expected of me. I finally went to work fervently, and after two months, I knew that I had written down the complete message. As I delayed sending it out, one day He let me know that I was late in doing so in a manner that we all know. It's like that look we get from our dad that tells us that we'd better obey quickly—or else. The following morning I started emailing it to Church leaders worldwide. Over a period of several months, thousands of them received it, including the deceased pontiff.

MESSAGE TO CHURCH LEADERS

Wake up! The Beast Is About to Rule the World: This is a last minute message to Church leaders.

Message to Cardinals before the Papal Election: This is a message sent to warn Cardinals that they were to elect a pontiff who would guide the Catholic Church away from idolatry.

A Judas in Your Midst: This is a strong warning against the practice of promoting John Paul II, who worshiped a queen of heaven and the dead in the tradition of the Catholic Church, and who has caused many to commit idolatry.

The Anchored Galleon: This is an introduction to the quick unfolding of End-Time prophecies.

The Lord's Command: To warn that the time of the last tribulations is at hand, remembering that during World War II, many, especially Jews and Christians, suffered at the hands of Satan.

Rise, Church leaders, head-on! This is a challenge to leaders, mainly those who are spiritually dead, to shake off complacency and to rise up.

"The Lord's Rebuke," which has been circulating only among Church leaders (Protestant, Catholic, and others) all over the world since 2003, is being released for the first time to all Christians. (Those who have received it have probably repented of their sins but still remain sinners [Romans 3:20, Romans 8:7, James 2:10], but they will be saved if they accept Jesus as their personal Savior [Romans 10:4]).

NEW MESSAGES TO THE WHOLE BODY

"False Teachings and Practices" addresses the destructive power of idolatry in today's Church.

"Visions of the Beast" is a collection of dreams and visions that covered the period before and after the funeral of

John Paul II, unveiling the true nature of the beast and its destructive work inside the Church.

REPENT OF YOUR SINS, THE DAY OF THE LORD IS AT HAND

We all sin occasionally and when we do we become overwhelmed with remorse right away, which causes us to repent almost immediately. A sinful lifestyle causes us to remain unrepentant because we come to accept it as a fact of life. Many will perish because of it.

In this very book you are holding in your hands, the identity of the antichrist is being revealed, which means that before long, the man of lawlessness will propose peace and many great nations of this world will be eager to accept his offer. He will be trusted to the point that finally he will become the supreme ruler of the planet.

Beware, once this come to pass, an angel of the Lord will be sent to appose the seal of God on the forehead of the 144 virgins mentioned by John in Revelation and of those that he will find repentant of their sins. They are the believers whose names are written in the book of life. Those who do not receive the seal will be afflicted by the plagues and will surely die in a sinful state and go to eternal damnation in the lake of fire. The Bible says, "Then from the smoke came locusts on the earth, and they were given power like the power of scorpions of the earth. They were told not to harm the grass of the earth or any green plant or any tree, but only those people who do not have the seal of God on their foreheads. They were allowed to torment them for five months, but not to kill them, and their torment was like the torment of a scorpion when it stings someone. And in those days people will seek death and will not find it. They will long to die, but death will flee from them" (Revelation 9:3-6).

AN ALMOST TWO-THOUSAND-YEAR-OLD-MYSTERY AND MANY MORE FINALLY REVEALED

The Beast—The Next World Conflict: 666, the number of the beast, and the number of its name were revealed to me by the Holy Spirit, that you may believe who I say I am, because the glorious coming of the Son of Man is at hand.

The unveiling of this mystery was foretold in a vision I had on the morning of February 15, 2005, succeeding another one in which it was revealed to me the meaning of a certain end-time mystery; then I became aware that the knowledge I was given was being erased from my memory, and I struggled to access it but could not. It was revealed in successive steps: The number of the beast (on July 7, when the G8 Summit was being wrapped up, the same day terrorists blew up two trains and a bus in London), and the number of the beast count.

The number 666 is an ancient one, the number of the beast, the call sign of the Antichrist. But what does it mean to you now? What are the whereabouts of this man? I reveal all to you through the story of a life lived in prophecy.

What is the sprit of Antichrist? The bible says, "And every spirit that does not confess Jesus is not from God. This is the spirit of the antichrist, which you heard was coming and now is in the world already" (1 John 4:3). John, one of the twelve apostles wrote, "We are from God. Whoever knows God listens to us; whoever is not from God does not listen to us. By this we know the Spirit of truth and the spirit of error" (1 John 4:6).

Who is an antichrist? John to the faithful wrote, "Children, it is the last hour, and as you have heard that antichrist is coming, so now many antichrists have come. Therefore we know that it is the last hour. They went out from us, but they were not of us; for if they had been of us, they would have continued with us. But they went out, that it might become plain that they all are not of us" (1 John 2:18-19).

Who is the Antichrist? John asked the same question to

answer it for us: "Who is the liar but he who denies that Jesus is the Christ? This is the antichrist, he who denies the Father and the Son" (1 John 2:22).

Is he already here? In this volume, his identity and his modus operandi are revealed for the first time. God has also revealed the protagonists of the Next World Conflict, which, unlike previous wars, will be different because Satan and his fallen angels, the demons, will fight side by side with the beast's armies to help them win.

Called by the Lord when Saddam Hussein was about to plunge the world into a nuclear conflict, this messenger, the Lord's forerunner, was witness to the development of a plan that would culminate in the September 11, 2001 (9/11), World Trade Center attack. He was called again when Al-Qaeda was about to launch an economic war against the U.S. Now, he is revealing end-time mysteries that have never been unveiled before, as well as the identity of the Antichrist.

Who will the beast side with in the coming world conflict, and what does his coming mean? Find out in 666 MYSTERY REVEALED: THE NEXT WORLD CONFLICT.

By November of 2005, I really thought that the message the Lord gave me concerning the Vatican, on October 26, was the last one I would receive. As I took steps to publish this book in 2006, the Lord kept giving me new ones and I realized then that I could not say that I was done until it is in print.

The comments, concerning China, Iran, Russia, and the other member nations of the now defunct U.S.S.R., were penned in 2005. I had to rewrite the prophetic ones as they were being fulfilled, mainly those concerning the Russian President Vladimir Putin, and followed closely the deterioration of his antagonistic position towards the U.S. as the Lord showed me.

I would suggest that you keep a pen or a highlighter handy as you read this book; do not hesitate to underline what is of interest to you and to write your remarks in the margins or in the "Notes" (page 341), making it an interesting journey into biblical truths.

I have to thank those who have encouraged and helped me in many ways, especially with kind words and love, even when the Lord kept me secluded to receive most of His messages.

The Lord in heaven for whom there is no secrets will reward them in this world and the next.

VISIONS OF THE BEAST

My mother who, during a very long and arduous parturition had consecrated me to the Lord, told me of little Jesus in the manger and sang Christmas songs to me, all of which introduced his Father and Him to my young mind. When I was a child, my grandmother and mother were unaware of my gifts. When they saw me at home several times while I was supposed to be in school or in church, they thought that a ghost was responsible for this phenomenon, but I was aware of them and God kept me silent. Even when some of the neighborhood children witnessed me vanish in front of their eyes, at a distance to reappear among them; even as a teen, when fishermen came out in droves to watch me fishing with a slingshot as my pail filled up fast; even when, at one hundred thirty five pounds, the strongest man would not be stronger than a baby in my hands; even when a flower, a vine, or the winds were obeying my commands; even when my enemies, devil worshippers, were trembling in my presence and hiding from me, escaping through the closest side street or door; even when they wanted my life as I was treating them with compassion, poisoning my food and drink, and I did not die, the Lord kept me silent. But now He has loosened my tongue and untied my hands.

THE WITNESS

I am the one Jesus has sent to precede His coming; this I am not saying to impress you but because God through signs, miracles, dreams, and visions finally convinced me that I was the forerunner Jesus spoke about. Two embroideries, one at the bottom of a robe I saw myself wearing in recurrent dreams, and another one on attire shown to me by angels in 2001, were Jewish motifs I saw side by side five years later in a picture of the floor in a room at the house of the high priest Caiaphas in Jerusalem. Recently it was revealed to me that they meant "A prophet of old and I were one." A vest, which is part of the attire, is the color of the red sand I walked on in that ancient village I used to cross in those dreams.

When the Lord gave me the first of several messages for Church leaders in 1998, He had me quote a verse concerning my being His harbinger, even though I could not yet relate my work to that of Elijah, whom I did not know much about. God spoke to the prophet Malachi, announcing, "Behold, I will send you Elijah the prophet before the great and awesome day of the LORD comes. And he will turn the hearts of fathers to their children and the hearts of children to their fathers, lest I come and strike the land with a decree of utter destruction" (Malachi 4:5-6).

God also sent an angel to a priest named Zechariah to announce to him the pregnancy of his barren wife Elizabeth and the birth of a son, John the Baptist, whose ministry was to prepare the way for the coming Messiah, saying, "And he will turn many of the children of Israel to the Lord their God, and he will go before him in the spirit and power of Elijah, to turn the hearts of the fathers to the children, and the disobedient to the wisdom of the just, to make ready for the Lord a people prepared" (Luke 1:16-17).

Jesus, speaking of John the Baptist, said, "What then did you go out to see? A prophet? Yes, I tell you, and more than a prophet. This is he of whom it is written, 'Behold, I send my messenger before your face, who will prepare your way before you.' Truly, I say to you, among those born of women there has arisen no one greater than John the Baptist. Yet the one who is least in the kingdom of heaven is greater than he. From the days of John the Baptist until now the kingdom of heaven has suffered violence, and the violent take it by force. For all the Prophets and the Law prophesied until John, and if you are willing to accept it, he is Elijah who is to come" (Matthew 11:9-14). But when John the Baptist was asked who he was, "He confessed, and did not deny, but confessed, 'I am not the Christ.' And they asked him, 'What then? Are you Elijah?' He said, 'I am not.' 'Are you the Prophet?' And he answered, 'No' " (John 1:20-21).

When I was writing the second letter to Church leaders, I read more than once the following passage: "He answered, "Elijah does come, and he will restore all things" (Matthew 17:11), which Jesus straightforwardly told His apostles who wanted to know about the coming of the prophet Elijah. I understood He meant one forerunner.

To those who might argue that I act on behalf of Beelzebub, I would simply mention the following verses when the Pharisee tried to falsely accuse Jesus of being Satan's servant: "But when the Pharisees heard it, they said, 'It is only by Beelzebul, the prince of demons, that this man casts out demons.' Knowing their thoughts, he said to them, 'Every kingdom divided against itself is laid waste, and no city or house divided against itself will stand' " (Matthew 12:24-25).

When Jesus' ministry had started, after John the Baptist had baptized Him, John was removed from the scene, as it will become of me, His forerunner, before His coming, which is near.

Around mid-September 2005, a sign, shaped as an upside-down flame, which would sometimes become quite bright in the center of my forehead, had faded away, but briefly reappeared on the evening of August 22, 2006, on the eighth anniversary of the revelation of the 9/11 event; my maternal grandmother had always described it as being a star that the nurse who had assisted the attending doctor when I was born saw and alerted her to.

As a young man, when I was ready to start my professional life, I spent a few months in training at my father's import and retail operation before I landed an administrative position with a medical research institute. After working for them a few years and for other firms, I moved with my wife and two-year-old son to a mountain resort, leased lands and hired locals, and grew vegetables and potatoes. A few years later, the Lord showed me how to hand-weave a certain intricate pattern while He prevented anyone else from duplicating a sample with which I was presented and I had left several days in the hands of all master-weavers I could reach. He showed me in a dream, similar to the first half of the one Joseph had interpreted for Pharaoh, that for seven years He was going to prosper me greatly; this became my first ministry, because what He laid in my heart then was to provide jobs to those in need; thousands of men and women were trained on how to make this product. In 1981, when He let me know that He needed me elsewhere, I was not a theologian; I was a manufacturer expecting large orders from several parts of the world for my products after they were presented at a merchandise show in Germany. In obedience I had accepted this calling; but since then, my life has suffered the destructive force of many storms because Satan has asked God permission to test my faith, tearing into pieces my family, using the people closest to me, whom I was always good to, using lies, jealousy, and treasons. One of those loved ones went as far as discarding every piece of my personal property that he had his hands on, even the complete documentation for a product I had invented. Others have called me a thief even though I never committed theft, robbed, or defrauded anyone, even while I was sharing my meager income with them. When Jesus began to preach at the synagogue of His hometown, those there who knew Him said, "'Is not this the carpenter, the son of Mary and brother of James and Joses and Judas and Simon? And are not his sisters here with us?' And they took offense at Him. And Jesus said to them, 'A prophet is not without honor, except in his hometown and among his relatives and in his own household'" (Mark 6:3-4). Those who tried to hurt me were not aware that they were builders of challenges that I was to overcome to receive, in this world and the next, riches that the Lord showed me He had reserved for me. I am grateful to them and never ceased to love them; to the contrary I forgave them and pray for them everyday, asking the Lord to draw them near Him and to give them wisdom that they may repent and that they may be saved; Jesus said, "Blessed are you when people hate you and when they exclude you and revile you and spurn your name as evil, on account of the Son of Man!" (Luke 6:22).

The enemy, which is Satan, has also tried to erode the love I have for my eldest son, testing my patience and forgiveness by pitting him against me, but the Lord has strengthened my heart and enlarged my wisdom, and I keep forgiving and blessing him seventy times seven as He commanded, even though I suffered violence at the hand of Satan. Through the challenge, my son showed me that he loves me, because I keep proving to him that I will always love him unconditionally, reminding myself how much my father in heaven loves me.

If I had not been tested as strongly as I was, I could never say to you with assurance, "You too can overcome whatever stands between you and your loved ones, even though Satan keeps trying to pit them against you." We must always forgive those who envy and hate us. While Jesus was teaching, "Then Peter came up and said to him, 'Lord, how often will my brother sin against me, and I forgive him? As many as seven times?' Jesus said to him, 'I do not say to you seven times, but seventy times seven'"

(Matthew 18:21-22), and Jesus later said, "And whenever you stand praying, forgive, if you have anything against anyone, so that your Father also who is in heaven may forgive you your trespasses" (Mark 11:25).

We cannot say that we love God if we cannot love our enemies; to this effect Jesus commanded, "You have heard that it was said, 'You shall love your neighbor and hate your enemy.' But I say to you, Love your enemies and pray for those who persecute you, so that you may be sons of your Father who is in heaven. For he makes his sun rise on the evil and on the good, and sends rain on the just and on the unjust. For if you love those who love you, what reward do you have? Do not even the tax collectors do the same?" (Matthew 5:43-46).

When I felt that I was almost through emailing the second message to Church leaders, I thought of going back into business, but the Lord had His own plan and had an angel urge me to leave town to go spend time with my son and to meet with a certain man who was selling his store. It was an act of obedience on my part to go acquire his firm, even though I had eyes on another one that I felt was a better deal. I faithfully tried to make the acquisition without love for it. I had preferred to sell fast food than run a tire shop. But willing to find out if it was just another test of my faith, I invited a brother, who was never eager at taking financial risks, to become my business partner, and sent him accounting statements to prove that the business was no more profitable to the owner. When he called me to let me know he would not, I was elated because I had an acid-test result then that the Lord just wanted me to prove to myself again that I was a faithful servant.

I nevertheless kept sending His message to Church leaders, and a year had passed as I was waiting for a word from the Lord to know when to return to my wife. After several months of pleading with me to come home, she finally lost hope of seeing me back and moved on. I spent my days between four walls, at my PC, listening at the sound of my keyboard from morning to evening or the next day, studying the Word and typing these lines, following and documenting what was happening around the world, which I have enjoyed doing ever since I volunteered to work as a weekend newscaster for the international news department of an evangelical radio station when I was in my twenties. After almost two years during which God has given me most of the visions mentioned here, I returned from seclusion to the city where I lived with my wife. I had to recover from a lack of verbal communication; a new job was instrumental in regaining my lost fluency in my own tongues and those I had acquired as a child.

I am no friend of religion, which is man speaking of

God while trying to make Him unreachable to others, placing themselves between them and Him. Many are well-learned demagogues, philosophers, and ideologues who make themselves monarchs of Christendom but are not really feeding the sheep. I am one of these unfed and forgotten ones, abandoned to die in ignorance of the Word, inviting you to venture into it with an infallible and faithful guide, the Lord's Holy Spirit, in search of the truth, which sets people free. John wrote, "So Jesus said to the Jews who had believed in him, "If you abide in my word, you are truly my disciples, and you will know the truth, and the truth will set you free" (John 8:31-32).

I was a teen when the Lord showed me, in a dream, a conic mountain with a narrow road spiraling up and told me that I had to fulfill a mission at the very top. When I mentioned to Him that I was a child, He handed me a staff saying, "With this you will accomplish your mission." I knew that one day He would use me for something important to Him. He spoke to me a second time, right before I left for other shores. One evening before I went to bed, I kneeled down and asked Him to deliver me from sin, and in a dream that night He appeared to me as a sphinx. He had the head of an eagle and it was of gold, and the body of a lion and it was of brass. And when I looked into his eyes, I felt a love that I had never experienced before and cried out "Jesus!" And as I was weeping under the weight of my sins, He extended His hand and pulled my head against His chest and said to me, "Do not cry. You are forgiven." He then took me in spirit between earth and heaven; He showed me riches where most everything was of gold and said to me, "All this belongs to you." He then took me to another location and asked me to look up, and when I did I saw a message written in Hebrew and the letters were of gold. And He said to me, "When you see this sign, you shall know that my coming is near."

For a very long time, I could not figure out why He appeared to me as an eagle and a lion, but later on, I stumbled onto the following verses that John wrote: "And before the throne there was as it were a sea of glass, like crystal. And around the throne, on each side of the throne, are four living creatures, full of eyes in front and behind: the first living creature like a lion, the second living creature like an ox, the third living creature with the face of a man, and the fourth living creature like an eagle in flight" (Revelation 4:6-7).

I realized then that He appeared to me among the cherubs tending his throne, as seen by the prophet Ezekiel when he saw the Glory of God. Angels described in Ezekiel who had their facial features quite similar to these four beings are the ones assigned to the throne of God. They are always

in His presence. This is how he saw them by the Chebar
River: "As for the likeness of their faces, each had a human
face. The four had the face of a lion on the right side, the
four had the face of an ox on the left side, and the four had
the face of an eagle" (Ezekiel 1:10). But when he saw them
at the temple in Jerusalem, transporting the Glory of God,
he described them differently, substituting the face of an ox
by that of a cherub, "And every one had four faces: the first
face was the face of the cherub, and the second face was a
human face, and the third the face of a lion, and the fourth
the face of an eagle" (Ezekiel 10:14). We can conclude that
the cherub face was that of an ox, since he later wrote,
"And as for the likeness of their faces, they were the same
faces whose appearance I had seen by the Chebar canal.
Each one of them went straight forward" (Ezekiel 10:22).

As we approached the end of the millennium, Satan had
a plan. Seeing the great multitude being saved through the
Gospel, which was reaching them via new technologies,
mainly satellites and the Internet, he wanted to cause a
world conflict and the annihilation of Israel, which would
cause millions to die without knowing Jesus Christ and His
promise of salvation through His death on the cross and the
shedding of His blood for humanity. But the Almighty
God, who loves so much the world that He has given His
only begotten Son so that whoever believes in Him may not

perish but inherit eternal life, would not give free rein to Satan.

Around January 1998, Saddam Hussein was taunting the U.S. into attacking Iraq, I was entering my fifty-third year, and I was following with interest the unfolding of these events. During the first days of February, as President Bill Clinton was building up his armada in the Persian Gulf, ready to order an attack, the Lord opened up my eyes and I could see everything concerning the conflict, and He uploaded knowledge into my brain in millions of terabytes per second. My perceptive faculties were enhanced thousands of times. I became cognitive of secrets and thoughts of Saddam and knew then that my mission was to prevent a catastrophic event from taking place; millions were about to die in a nuclear conflict. This agent of Satan had a stockpile of weapons of mass destruction, biological and chemical, intending to use them against Israel at the first waves of attacks by the U.S. I could see Israel, as well as the U.S., responding with nuclear weapons and the allies on all sides getting involved.

I felt the urgency to warn the president. After a couple of days of hesitation, I finally emailed the message upon the Lord's insistence, and a few hours later the attack was aborted. Along with a series of emailed messages that same year, I revealed to President Clinton, after the Lord had shown me a map, the exact location of the stockpile of chemical and biological weapons that Saddam wanted to use if the president had ordered the attack then; the weapons cache was later destroyed. I also warned the president of Saddam's evil plan to support international terrorists in a plot to carry out kamikaze attacks against government buildings using small planes loaded with explosives, as the Lord had informed me. Since then, many more messages have followed.

Without revealing to you the content of subsequent warnings and intelligence material from the Lord that I forwarded to President Clinton, I am willing to share with you that since those days, in the spirit I have been conveyed to different locations around the world to witness specific events, during which I was taken to Saddam's hiding place before he was eventually caught. I saw him disheveled, with a long unkempt beard, the same way he was eventually caught, walking past a small cinder-block hut, going downhill as toward a river after he had emerged from a hole carved in a rock in the background. He looked like someone who had just woken early in the morning and was in a hurry to go wash. I could clearly see that his dirty white shirt, loose over his pants, was attached by only two buttons below his sternum.

One morning, I witnessed ahead of time the aftermath

of his arrest as the media was commenting on the circumstances leading to it and about his lifestyle as a fugitive, which I thought was news. But at no moment then did I realize that I was watching the news in a remote future, until the real event took place and I knew that I was re-watching it in real time.

Many years earlier in 1991, in a dream I was shown Saddam falling down backward with a pistol in his right hand as he was reaching the top of a mountain facing Israel. On March 20, 2003, from an elevation where the Lord wanted me to be, I knew then that his downfall was at hand when I saw a crimson moon rising as the military operation in Iraq began. He was finally captured by U.S. forces, and after a long trial, he was handed over to Iraqi executioners. Hundreds, mostly among the Shiites, danced in the streets of Baghdad to celebrate the hanging of this brutal dictator who had ordered the torture and killing of many of their family members and friends. Before U.S. troops entered Baghdad, in a day vision, I was shown a convoy crossing Iraq's northern border into Syria.

As 2000 was ending, the Lord in my spirit let me know that I needed to receive my father's blessings. (When his mother was pregnant with him, in a dream an angel told her she was going to have a boy and should name him John the Baptist, but because she wanted to name him after his paternal grandfather and was not much convinced, he was born with his name printed on his shoulder. When he was a baby, an angel appeared to his mother after he had fallen into a deep ravine as she was riding a horse and went down to fetch him and returned him to her unhurt. My father was in his seventies when an assassin's bullet went through his body, yet even his shirt was not damaged). I said, "Lord I do not have the necessary money to travel." In miraculous ways, my trip was taken care of, and I went to visit my parents. As I was leaving, my father stood up and, for the first time, blessed me. That moment, I received a double portion of anointing. Since my earthly father is a representation of the one who had preceded the Messiah, his anointing was transferred to me to officiate as a voice that would prepare the way for Jesus' glorious coming as the King of kings, to reign on all nations with an iron scepter.

When I returned home, I became convinced that the Lord was preparing me for something important. In my spirit, I heard more than once that He was replacing my attire with a new one. Before long, He let me know that I should give away everything I had but the essentials and go to visit my sister's family in another city. I did and was invited to stay; my sister is a fervent servant of the Lord. There I remained for a few months after I found work.

One morning in February 2001, around six o'clock, in

my spirit I was told to step outside and look up, just as when I was witness to the Hebrew message being written by skywriters on June 4, 1998. I did and saw a brilliant burning fire falling from the sky. I thought to myself, isn't Satan being hurled down to earth?

One night in a dream, angels showed me my new attire, and one of them even modeled it, as he was on a staircase walking up to heaven into a cloud. There was an embroidery at the bottom of the vest and at the hem of the pants, similar to the one at the bottom of a robe I saw myself wearing many times in a recurring dream in which I saw myself crossing a village of red huts where, looking down at my sandals, I noticed that the soil was red sand. I would go to a water hole in the rocks nearby where I would sit alone.

Around May 2001, The Lord revealed to me that the terrorists were about to launch new attacks and the numerous targets whose destruction was intended to affect our economy, and I passed that information on right away. Around July of that year in a day vision, I was shown a jumbo jet flying toward the World Trade Center towers, and I scrambled to borrow a computer since I had given mine away. I was fearful of the risk that someone could accidentally have knowledge of it if I used a library computer as I had for the previous message. But I ran out of time; the attack occurred when I was a few days away from having Internet access. Later I realized that God did not allow me to warn the president of the pending attack because it would be futile, since He had shown me an event that He was going to allow to occur. When I asked Him why He did not let me warn the nation, He made it clear to me that He wanted it to be a strong warning to a people walking away from Him. During the first week of September, I went to visit my sister, who told me she'd had a dream that morning where she saw the number 999. She was shown the encoded date of the event but I did not tell her anything about it. I understood it was a message for me. As the nations of the world were reeling from the shock of September 11, hardly able to comprehend what had occurred, the Lord gave me a message concerning what He was expecting of Church leaders. After that fatidic day, intelligence from the Lord remained a daily occurrence for about a year and became less frequent as the years went by until visions and dreams for the writing of this book took precedence.

Brothers! Do not let fear paralyze you. The angels of the Lord can guard you against all enemies and dangers. They have never failed me; it would take hundreds of pages to tell all. Once I was detained, forced to sleep almost naked in a cold cell, accused of plotting against a foreign government and was to be executed. As I was surrounded by soldiers ready to kill me if I tried to escape, my Lord gave me authority over them, and I calmly left. Even though they knew where to find me, they did not come for me. That night I prayed to my Lord asking Him to save me as He had saved Daniel from the lions in the pit. When I was eighteen, an inner city gang armed to the teeth surrounded me, but my Lord did not allow them to touch even one hair of my head. I looked around, and they stood as if frozen and then left. I know now what happened then. I simply was made invisible by the Lord; and since in the angelic realm every being moves at a speed at least one thousand times the speed of light, my enemies appeared motionless. They have stayed away from me since. From my childhood to adulthood, Satan's agents have tried to destroy me. Poison in many forms has been used unsuccessfully; I always put myself in the hands of my Lord, knowing He would never fail to protect me.

In Gethsemane, Jesus cried, "Saying, 'Father, if you are willing, remove this cup from me. Nevertheless, not my will, but yours, be done'" (Luke 22:42). Through Him flowed all our suffering: pain, anguish, fear, despair, and guilt. The weight of our sins became heavier and heavier until He felt crushed, overburdened, but He did not give up. He carried through till the cross and death, shedding the last drop of blood and then water for our justification. The

Church as the body of Christ must act as such and stand up as one in faith to oppose the forces of evil in prayer and fasting. Let the Church be sensitive to its surroundings and vibrate in unison.

As the enemy is launching assault after assault to destabilize the Church foundation, let the whole body stand up and pray. As his agents prepare pestilence and massive destruction, as they plan to create havoc in our midst, cover yourself with the armor of God.

Twice, I witnessed destructive winds flying in their course toward two cities; my intercession spared them. If one member has such authority, how much more can the whole body? I was writing this book when hurricane Katrina hit the Gulf Coast states and left indescribable destruction in its wake. It could have been worse if it hadn't been for persistent intercession by others and myself to change its course and to slow it down, to allow the great majority to get out of harm's way and to weaken it, even though the conditions were right to maintain it a Category 5 at peak intensity, sparing New Orleans its full fury. Just imagine the flooding without any home standing to protect those who stayed behind. Let us thank the Lord for his mercy. In the face of tragedy, there was an enormous outpouring of love and help from the Church.

Many false prophets, to mislead the faithful, have

clamored that we are being told wrongly that God uses earthquakes, hurricanes, tornadoes, and the like against us to punish us or to send us strong warnings, but the word of God dispels their outcries. From the Scriptures we read, "He loads the thick cloud with moisture; the clouds scatter his lightning. They turn around and around by his guidance, to accomplish all that he commands them on the face of the habitable world. Whether for correction or for his land or for love, he causes it to happen" (Job 37:11-13).

VISIONS OF THE DEAD BIRD AND THE SERPENT

On the morning of the fourteenth day of the third month of 2005, in a dream as I was observing the sea from what seems to be a sturdy, covered wooden structure, a man who was standing next to me pointed out a large bird's remains decaying in a body of water, and the dream ended. Then, as a continuum, I was shown the Old Serpent of the sea. The waters were murky from the trashing of its tail. I was in there at a distance and I swam to the safety of the wooden structure where I had previously been. As I came out of the dream, in a vision someone standing by my bed asked me, "What day is it?" and I answered, "Monday," and became perplexed.

The first part of the dream was to direct my attention to a specific event. The large decaying bird in the waters foreshadowed the late pontiff's death that came about on Saturday, April 02, 2005. And he was down from his high position into the grave, just like the end of a bird that had fallen from the sky.

The second part was to establish how Satan, the Old Serpent, through the late pontiff's personality and work had caused millions of all tongues, nations, and creeds, especially Christians, to worship him. In the dream, the Old Serpent's posture was that of authority and pride. It was holding its head under water motionless and upright, with a great part of its body erect from the bottom to near the surface, while its huge tail moved violently across the waters, disturbing them greatly. That vision showed how Satan was conquering and subduing with authority and assertiveness the great multitude represented by the waters, stirring up emotions and beliefs that he had been insidiously depositing as sediments in their hearts, year after year, and that surfaced at John Paul II's funeral. The part of the waters above its head represented that very small percentage of a multitude it had no control over. My head was far above water, watching the event unfolding.

On the morning of the seventh day of the fourth month of the year 2005, after I had made known to the Cardinals who were to elect a new pontiff what the Lord had placed in my heart, I found myself in the spirit wandering inside St. Peter's Basilica where John Paul II lay in state. I heard the corpse sneeze, and a wind blew droplets into my nostrils. As the vision ended, I felt my lungs contracting and felt death had come to take me away, but I refused to surrender and fought back in faith, calling upon my Lord, and was delivered. That day as I was watching the events, anxious to verify what had occurred in the vision, knowing that the Lord would certainly confirm it with a visible sign, I saw what I expected in the natural. In a close-up shot, it became obvious that the corpse's head had moved at an angle toward the right shoulder. The burning sensation in my lungs was less severe seven days later when, as I changed the TV channel, a man of God, through word of knowledge, said something to the effect of "Lungs are being healed." I had stepped into Satan's den.

VISIONS OF THE LIONS

On April 8, I had two other visions. In the first one, a proud lion appeared with the Vatican seal over its head. In the second one, I saw myself in bed and there came another lion, leaner than the first one. It jumped on the opposite side, stood there a few seconds but did not attack me, and lay there for a moment as if exhausted. It jumped back down and went around the other side as though it wanted to approach me but could not. It remained there for a brief moment but left running, desperately roaming the streets looking for food and speaking as a man, saying, "I am hungry." The prophet Daniel describing a strange animal he saw in a vision wrote, "The first was like a lion and had eagles' wings. Then as I looked its wings were plucked off, and it was lifted up from the ground and made to stand on two feet like a man, and the mind of a man was given to it" (Daniel 7:4).

Peter, in a letter to several churches, recommended, "Be sober-minded; be watchful. Your adversary the devil prowls around like a roaring lion, seeking someone to devour" (1 Peter 5:8).

Paul, recounting the hardship of his ministry to Timothy, who was like a son to him, wrote, "But the Lord stood by me and strengthened me, so that through me the message might be fully proclaimed and all the Gentiles might hear it. So I was rescued from the lion's mouth" (2 Timothy 4:17).

SECOND VISION OF THE SERPENT

On the morning of the fifteenth day of the fourth month of the year 2005, in another dream after the pontiff had passed away, I saw myself standing by the waters at the same wooden structure that sat on solid ground. By my side the same man was standing, and as I observed the waters at low tide, there was the Old Serpent lying immobile in the marsh as though it was stalking its prey; as soon as I pointed it out, it silently and swiftly retreated and disappeared among the vegetation. Jesus was the man who stood by me.

Beware! Satan is adopting a more subtle attitude, moving more stealthily in the Church and rallying many as he is weakening faith, spreading sexual immorality, idolatry, the occult, false practices, and sedition.

Between the two dreams, the first one dated March 14, 2005—which was to foreshadow the Saturday, April 02, 2005, death of the late pontiff, whom many were already calling "John Paul the Great," and the unprecedented event that followed when millions from all over the world came to mourn and pray over his tomb—and the last one on April 15, 2005, which was to conclude the former, lie three horrific visions I had on April 7 and April 8, 2005, to warn of Satan's multiple and relentless attacks against the believers using the Vatican as his headquarters.

I was still a child when God pointed out to me all the false teachings from Rome. He raised me up for a time such as this, when the Old Serpent would come with words of deceit to cause many to worship it. Now that it is operating inside the Church, many do not recognize it. Instead they praise it because of false teachings. Millions from the four corners of the world—kings, heads of state and other government officials, theologians, ministers and prophets, believers and non-believers, young and old, small and great, rich and poor, friends and foes, people of all tongues, races, and creeds—have traveled to exalt it. Israeli president Moshe Katsav shook hands and chatted with the leaders of Israel's archenemies, Syria and Iran, during John Paul II's funeral.

BEWARE THE DECEIVER!

The robber has come into the fold, and many of the flock that did not know the shepherd's voice are being taken away. If they had ears to hear and eyes to see, they would not have been misled by the counterfeit. They were warned, and still when it came, they did not recognize it. The Bible says, "So I gave them over to their stubborn hearts, to follow their own counsels" (Psalms 81:12). Thus said the Lord to the prophet Jeremiah concerning the stubbornness of the people of Israel, "This evil people, who refuse to hear my words, who stubbornly follow their own heart and have gone after other gods to serve them and worship them, shall be like this loincloth, which is good for nothing" (Jeremiah 13:10). Speaking of the Pharisees and the Scribes, Jesus, quoting the prophet Isaiah, said, "This people honors me with their lips, but their heart is far from me" (Matthew 15:8).

Many have abandoned their flock into the hands of the deceiver because they have not been faithful to the Lord. They wake up in the morning with a scheme in their hypocritical hearts, elevating some and demeaning others according to their endeavors. They quote the Lord when He has not spoken to them; they boast of their holiness when their mouths are full of lies beguiling broken and desperate souls into believing that everything that comes from them is holy and can transfer healing, wealth, or protection, creating confusion and causing them to become the judge of others whether they are holy or not, Satanist or not. Jesus said, "Judge not, that you be not judged" (Matthew 7:1).

These are marketing ploys that are causing people to abandon their intimacy with God and to get involved in animism. The following from an Associated Press article dated May 23, 2005, and quoted by permission is proof that some churches are covertly Satanic:

Ponchatoula, La. Authorities gathered new evidence from the home of a former pastor accused of leading a church group in "cult-like" rituals involving the sexual abuse of children and animals. Tangipahoa Parish Sheriff Daniel Edwards said members of a Ponchatoula church carried out the practices for years as part of a devil-worshipping ritual involving cat blood. "This is hard to talk about and harder to believe, but some of the suspects have told us their intention in all of this was devil worshipping," Edwards said.

SHOULD WE KNOW WHAT SATAN IS CAPABLE OF?

Those in authority have removed from our schools prayer and anything making reference to our Lord. The Internet has all kinds of harmful information on witchcraft and satanic rituals, and our libraries have thousands of satanic and magic books on their shelves to which our children have free access, while we worry much about the fantasy series Harry Potter's abracadabra, which is to today's generation what Ali-Baba's Arabian nights and the like was to ours. We need to restore prayer and the Bible to our schools; we need to return God and the true teaching of His word back to where they were in our lives and those of our children.

We need to be responsible parents and teach them right from wrong by our testimonies and our actions in faith and obedience to Him. We must clean up our act and remove from the body of Christ complacency, false teachings, idolatry, individualism, personality cults, sexual liberalism, and many more that are the work of the spirit of the Antichrist, destroying the Church from within.

It is more harmful not to know God than to know about all the tricks in Satan's bag. Knowledge and obedience of the Word of God is the armor that protects us against Satan's attacks. Satan is an archangel who fell in disgrace after he rebelled against God and was thrown out of God's kingdom along with others who had followed him. He had to accuse Job and ask God permission to destroy his business, to kill all his children, and to afflict him with ulcers all over his body, because he had no authority over him and could not interfere in his life except to the degree that God allowed it and wanted him to test Job. From the Scriptures we read, "Now there was a day when the sons of God came to present themselves before the LORD, and Satan also came among them. The LORD said to Satan, 'From where have you come?' Satan answered the LORD and said, 'From going to and fro on the earth, and from walking up and down on it.' And the LORD said to Satan, 'Have you considered my servant Job, that there is none like him on the earth, a blameless and upright man, who fears God and turns away from evil?' Then Satan answered the LORD and said, 'Does Job fear God for no reason? Have you not put a hedge around him and his house and all that he has, on every side? You have blessed the work of his hands, and his possessions have increased in the land. But stretch out your hand and touch all that he has, and he will curse you to your face.' And the LORD said to Satan, 'Behold, all that he has is in your hand. Only against him do not stretch out your hand.' So Satan went out from the presence of the LORD" (Job 1:6-12).

Satan's demons stay away from believers because they always have angels guarding them unless they open themselves to these evil entities through unfaithfulness to God or unless He allows Satan to test them as he did Job.

After Job received news, from four servants who were spared, that he had lost all the animals he owned, a last one arrived with news that most of us could hardly survive. The Scriptures say, "While he was yet speaking, there came another and said, 'Your sons and daughters were eating and drinking wine in their oldest brother's house, and behold, a great wind came across the wilderness and struck the four corners of the house, and it fell upon the young people, and they are dead, and I alone have escaped to tell you.' Then Job arose and tore his robe and shaved his head and fell on the ground and worshiped" (Job 1:18-20).

But the evil one is quick at claiming those who are willing to follow him. He even claimed that Moses belonged to him and wanted to take him into the prisons of Hell, probably because he had killed an Egyptian who was beating a Hebrew or because he hit the rock where water was to flow from instead of extending his staff over it as God had commanded because the Israelites needed badly to quench their thirst. He was just overzealous. God is the only one with complete authority over everyone and everything. Satan is just a servant doing the Lord's bidding, sometimes against those who are disobedient. An anointed servant made it evident to us this way: "But when the archangel Michael, contending with the devil, was disputing about the body of Moses, he did not presume to pronounce a blasphemous judgment, but said, 'The Lord rebuke you'" (Jude 1:9).

Satan drags to hell those who serve him as soon as they get their last breath, after he has tricked them into believing there is happiness in rebellion, which is false since all their torments — abortion, alcoholism, juvenile delinquency, crime, divorce, drug dependency, jealousy, suicide, etc.— are direct consequences of his lies. No book has described Satan and what he is capable of better than the Bible. When my eldest son argued with me that there were no demons, I referred him to the Bible.

WHAT IS SATAN UP TO?

In the seventh chapter of the book of Daniel, four beasts are shown in succession, but one appears in John's vision as a composite of three of them, a hideous beast, which denotes simultaneity. Describing what he saw, Daniel wrote, "And I saw a beast rising out of the sea, with ten horns and seven heads, with ten diadems on its horns and blasphemous names on its heads. And the beast that I saw was like a leopard; its feet were like a bear's, and its mouth was like a lion's mouth. And to it the dragon gave his power and his throne and great authority" (Revelation 13:1-2). These are Satan's three different spheres of action as he is waging war against the faithful in their place of worship like a lion on the prowl, while like the bear he is creating worldwide carnage, terrorizing, pursuing the believers, and destroying their churches, killing them as well as their children. Like the agile leopard, Satan is reaching higher and higher on the ladder of political and secular arena, agitating them to oppose the free expression of Christian faith, in incessant attacks to remove the name of their God everywhere, even from the mouths of their children. He wants to replace God by many other ones. Jesus warned of how many Christians would react in this difficult time, for many would quickly surrender to Satan, "And these are the ones sown on rocky ground: the ones who, when they hear the word, immediately receive it with joy. And they have no root in themselves, but endure for a while; then, when tribulation or persecution arises on account of the word, immediately they fall away" (Mark 4:16-17).

IS JERUSALEM BABYLON THE GREAT?

This is what was revealed to the apostle John after the seventh bowl containing God's wrath was poured out and He remembered the sins of the city He calls Babylon the great, the mother of harlots: "Then one of the seven angels who had the seven bowls came and said to me, 'Come, I will show you the judgment of the great prostitute who is seated on many waters, with whom the kings of the earth have committed sexual immorality, and with the wine of whose sexual immorality the dwellers on earth have become drunk.' And he carried me away in the Spirit into a wilderness, and I saw a woman sitting on a scarlet beast that was full of blasphemous names, and it had seven heads and ten horns. The woman was arrayed in purple and scarlet, and adorned with gold and jewels and pearls, holding in her hand a golden cup full of abominations and the impurities of her sexual immorality. And on her forehead was written a name of mystery: 'Babylon the great, mother of prostitutes and of earth's abominations' " (Revelation 17:1-5).

And that angel further identified it as a city that sits on seven mountains. "This calls for a mind with wisdom: the seven heads are seven mountains on which the woman is seated" (Revelation 17:9).

Evidently it is not Jerusalem, the Holy City, also symbolically called Sodom and Egypt in the following verse: "And their dead bodies will lie in the street of the great city that symbolically is called Sodom and Egypt, where their Lord was crucified" (Revelation 11:8).

The following verses exclude the great city Jerusalem as being Babylon the Great, leaving Rome as the only other city mentioned in the Bible which was built on seven hills: "The seventh angel poured out his bowl into the air, and a loud voice came out of the temple, from the throne, saying, 'It is done!' And there were flashes of lightning, rumblings, peals of thunder, and a great earthquake such as there had never been since man was on the earth, so great was that earthquake. The great city was split into three parts, and the cities of the nations fell, and God remembered Babylon the great, to make her drain the cup of the wine of the fury of his wrath'" (Revelation 16:17-19).

Here are the seven hills on which Rome sits, east of the

river Tiber: Palatine, Aventine, Capitoline, Quirinal, Vimi-
nal, Esquiline, and Caelian. Babylon The Great, the Mother
of Harlots is definitely this Italian city. The State of the
Vatican City sits on the eighth, called Vatican Hill, located
west of the Tiber river. Papal authority was once beyond
the actual city limits after the collapse of the Roman Empire, when pontiffs ruled and defended Rome against bar-
baric and Islamic invaders. Leo I (440-461) even rebuilt his
beloved city after the Vandals, led by Gaiseric, ransacked
and destroyed it. The Quirinal Palace on the Quirinal, one
of the seven hills, was the residence of the popes until
1870. The angel making reference to past, present, and future rulers of Rome further explained to John the meaning
of the seven heads of the beast, saying, "They are also
seven kings, five of whom have fallen, one is, the other has
not yet come, and when he does come he must remain only
a little while" (Revelation 17:10).

Popes were also very influential over most western
kingdoms, making alliances with many and enemies with
many more. John further reporting his encounter with the
angel wrote, "And the angel said to me, 'The waters that
you saw, where the prostitute is seated, are peoples and
multitudes and nations and languages. And the ten horns
that you saw, they and the beast will hate the prostitute.
They will make her desolate and naked, and devour her

flesh and burn her up with fire, for God has put it into their hearts to carry out his purpose by being of one mind and handing over their royal power to the beast, until the words of God are fulfilled. And the woman that you saw is the great city that has dominion over the kings of the earth' " (Revelation 17:15-18).

BABYLON'S JUDGMENT

On a Tuesday morning, the third day of the fifth month of 2005, I woke up from an unusual dream. I was in a coastal city, and the inhabitants were horrified and being terrorized by fearsome and hideous demons and beasts out of the Vatican. They had to barricade themselves in their houses and wherever they could find shelter. Even I was pursued by the demons' hired hands—cruel, strong, and cunning men—until I fought back and they retreated. Then I heard a loud voice warning the inhabitants, saying, "An earthquake will occur in one hour," and I saw them scrambling to save their lives, running away from colonnade-supported buildings, which moments earlier had been their safe haven, toward huge rocks bordering the sea. This vision parallels these Revelation verses:

> *After this I saw another angel coming down from heaven, having great authority, and the earth was made*

bright with his glory. And he called out with a mighty voice, "Fallen, fallen is Babylon the great! She has become a dwelling place for demons, a haunt for every unclean spirit, a haunt for every unclean bird, a haunt for every unclean and detestable beast. For all nations have drunk the wine of the passion of her sexual immorality, and the kings of the earth have committed immorality with her, and the merchants of the earth have grown rich from the power of her luxurious living." Then I heard another voice from heaven saying, "Come out of her, my people, lest you take part in her sins, lest you share in her plagues; for her sins are heaped high as heaven, and God has remembered her iniquities. Pay her back as she herself has paid back others, and repay her double for her deeds; mix a double portion for her in the cup she mixed. As she glorified herself and lived in luxury, so give her a like measure of torment and mourning, since in her heart she says, 'I sit as a queen, I am no widow, and mourning I shall never see.' For this reason her plagues will come in a single day, death and mourning and famine, and she will be burned up with fire; for mighty is the Lord God who has judged her." And the kings of the earth, who committed sexual immorality and lived in luxury with her, will weep and wail over her when they see the

smoke of her burning. They will stand far off, in fear of
her torment, and say, "Alas! Alas! You great city, you
mighty city, Babylon! For in a single hour your judg-
ment has come." (Revelation 18:1-10)

In a night vision I had on October 26, 2005, I saw myself a second time at what seemed to be a library or archive
room at the Vatican where I found myself after a previous
attempt. As I started exploring that partially dark room, I
heard steps and dived under a long table behind a chair;
then from my vantage point I could see an old prelate, bent
double, on a late evening round, dragging a little old white
dog with big eyes and short ears. I could clearly see several
wide and open ulcers on the prelate's left leg since he was
wearing a nightgown down to his knees. He passed his
head through that open side of the large double-door, in-
specting the semi-dark room and tugging on the leash of the
little dog that sat reluctantly, refusing to step inside and
holding its head high away from the door. Finally, the old
prelate turned around, but as he was walking away, the lazy
mutt started sniffing near the floor, then stopped and
turned, as if it had picked up my scent, arousing his han-
dler's curiosity. The old prelate looked suspiciously toward
the room where I was, and when fear I would be discovered
gripped my heart, I woke up. It was so clear a vision that I

could see the sparsely spread hairs on this old little dog as though I could count them. This vision is an indication that the papacy is approaching its last days like this bent old prelate, not doing anything to remove idolatry and other sins represented by the multiple ulcers on the man's left leg, which is no other than the corrupt tradition on which it is operating. The lazy little dog represents the long period of inaction and complacency that has settled in, and when it seemed to catch my scent at the last moment, that portrays the Holy See that might never change course or do so too late to shake off tradition and repent, notwithstanding this message and others.

WHEN JESUS OPENS THE SIXTH SEAL

A year after the vision I had in the morning of May 5, 2005, in which an earthquake was announced to occur in one hour, in a day vision on Thursday May 11, 2006, at 8:32 p.m., I heard in the news that a powerful earthquake had shaken the world, and I was shown a map of North America and a fault running across it from California to New York. This earthquake might well be the one that is to occur after Jesus opens the sixth seal; those who were be-headed for his sake are demanding retribution.

In the morning of July 17, 1999, I was on the east coast,

when in a night vision I was shown an earthquake so severe fiery lava was gushing from the ground. Everyone was trying to escape the furor of nature; as I was running among the fleeing crowd, an angel stopped and told me "No need for me to stay with you any longer," and departed. I woke up almost right away. The Bible says, "When he opened the fifth seal, I saw under the altar the souls of those who had been slain for the word of God and for the witness they had borne. They cried out with a loud voice, 'O Sovereign Lord, holy and true, how long before you will judge and avenge our blood on those who dwell on the earth?' Then they were each given a white robe and told to rest a little longer, until the number of their fellow servants and their brothers should be complete, who were to be killed as they themselves had been" (Revelation 6:9-11).

John, a faithful witness of Jesus, reported the first event, preceding the seven plagues that will afflict the earth and its inhabitants, as seen in his visions: "When he opened the sixth seal, I looked, and behold, there was a great earthquake, and the sun became black as sackcloth, the full moon became like blood, and the stars of the sky fell to the earth as the fig tree sheds its winter fruit when shaken by a gale. The sky vanished like a scroll that is being rolled up, and every mountain and island was removed from its place. Then the kings of the earth and the great ones and the generals and the rich and the powerful, and everyone, slave and free, hid themselves in the caves and among the rocks of the mountains, calling to the mountains and rocks, 'Fall on us and hide us from the face of him who is seated on the throne, and from the wrath of the Lamb, for the great day of their wrath has come, and who can stand?" (Revelation 6:12-17).

On June 4, 2006 (the eight anniversary of the fulfill-ment of the vision I had in 1981 when Jesus showed me a Hebrew message in the sky and told me that when I will see it, I shall know that His coming is near), my sister told me she was shown the number 2555 in a dream that morning and, like the 999 number she was shown in a night vision a few days before the 9/11 attack that was connected to that event, I understood that it was connected to the earthquake I was warned about. On the morning of June 6, 2006, two days later (the eighth anniversary of the Lord's first mes-sage sent to Church leaders), I was given knowledge that the number 2555 meant one hour, five minutes, and five seconds past the twenty-fourth hour or 1:05:05 a.m. EST as being the time when the earthquake would occur, consider-ing that I was on the east coast.

Other Revelation verses paint the horrible end of the city called "Babylon the great, mother of prostitutes and of earth's abominations," to take place after Jesus opens the seventh seal. The Bible says, "Then I saw the seven angels who stand before God, and seven trumpets were given to them" (Revelation 8:2), and after the first six angels would have blown their trumpets, at the sound of the last one, as the Bible says, "The seventh angel poured out his bowl into the air, and a loud voice came out of the temple, from the throne, saying, 'It is done!' And there were flashes of lightning, rumblings, peals of thunder, and a great earthquake such as there had never been since man was on the earth, so great was that earthquake. The great city was split into three parts, and the cities of the nations fell, and God remembered Babylon the great, to make her drain the cup of the wine of the fury of his wrath" (Revelation 16:17-19).

Many would ask what had become of the previous four seals. When Jesus opened the first one, the Word of God came out riding to take over the world and the Gospel was being preached. The Bible says, "And I looked, and behold, a white horse! And its rider had a bow, and a crown was given to him, and he came out conquering, and to conquer" (Revelation 6:2).

When He opened the second one, those who were the first to preach the Gospel were to be persecuted, given in pasture to wild animals, crucified and beheaded, and millions more were to suffer and die from persecution and other atrocities till this day. The Bible says, "When he opened the second seal, I heard the second living creature say, 'Come!' And out came another horse, bright red. Its rider was permitted to take peace from the earth, so that men should slay one another, and he was given a great sword" (Revelation 6:3-4).

When He opened the third one, millions were to die of starvation death from previous centuries to our time in Africa, China, Russia, Ukraine, and other parts of the globe. The Bible says, "When he opened the third seal, I heard the third living creature say, 'Come!' And I looked, and behold, a black horse! And its rider had a pair of scales in his hand. And I heard what seemed to be a voice in the midst of the four living creatures, saying, 'A quart of wheat for a denarius, and three quarts of barley for a denarius, and do not harm the oil and wine!'" (Revelation 6:5-6).

When He opened the forth one, millions more were to die, first by pestilences such as the Plagues of Justinian, the Black Death, the Third Pandemic, the Spanish flu, and AIDS; second by chemical agents that were to be used to kill many, such as the ones used during WWI and WWII, the Vietnam war, by Saddam on his own people, and during the Iraq and Iran war; and third by conditions created because of wars and terrorism, natural and man-made disasters, and destruction of wildlife habitat. The Bible says, "When he opened the fourth seal, I heard the voice of the fourth living creature say, 'Come!' And I looked, and behold, a pale horse! And its rider's name was Death, and Hades followed him. And they were given authority over a fourth of the earth, to kill with sword and with famine and with pestilence and by wild beasts of the earth" (Revelation 6:7-8).

The next plagues will begin only after Jesus opens the seventh seal and after God will allow a period of time to elapse between the previous ones (from the first to the fourth seal) that were to affect humanity, those that would have finished their course up to the sixth seal, when Satan and the fallen angels are thrown down to the earth. The Bible says, "When the Lamb opened the seventh seal, there was silence in heaven for about half an hour" (Revelation 8:1).

SEEKER OF THE TRUTH

One night I confessed to my Lord how bad I felt that, being alone in my house, I was spending all hours of the day receiving scores of women, and that I needed Him to help me stop, even though I believed at that time that my sin was not in the act but in the high number of females visitors I was entertaining. He came to me that very same night and forgave me my sins in a vision mentioned in the previous chapter, and I knew then that He wanted me to travel to new shores, but I did not know it would be for a very long time.

My religious background was from my Baptist grandmother and mother who warned me, when I was eleven, that sex was dangerous and addictive and that I should wait for the right time, which explains why I waited until I met my wife, and from the Catholic school that I had attended.

The absence of the right teaching and the lives of Abraham, David, Salomon, and other great men of the Old Testament—the book which had been the strong foundation of my faith—and of their many concubines, led me to believe that it was not only okay but a duty and not a sin for men, single or married, to have many women, and that wives were to be found culpable of adultery if they were to violate their marriage vows.

I had never heard any sermon that would suggest the contrary. No one when I was growing up was preaching against fornication. Priests and ministers were well known for having many affairs and out-of-wedlock children. I was taught who Jesus was, of His infinite love for us, and how He had died on the cross and had shed His blood for our salvation, but not His teachings. I was as much a sinner as thieves, killers, and liars, because by being guilty of one sin, I was guilty of them all: "For whosoever shall keep the whole law, and yet offend in one point, he is guilty of all" (James 2:10 KJV). And I had no excuses, even though a missal was used instead of the Bible by the Catholic Church. It was my responsibility to look deeper for the truth, which I found after many years of earnestly digging for it through reading, meditating on, and studying the word of God with the help of his Holy Spirit.

WHERE DID GOD PLANT THE GARDEN OF EDEN?

Many still debate the physical location of Paradise, this beautiful garden called Eden. Some say they believe God placed this garden that He Himself prepared for Adam and Eve somewhere in Ethiopia, Africa; others believe that it sat between the Tigris and Euphrates rivers in Northeast Iraq. A small minority among scientists and science-fiction aficionados have proposed other planets as the possible site where it existed and from where Adam and Eve were transported to an unknown location on our planet. But God speaking to Ezekiel concerning the fate of the king of Tyre, a cherub, who was the angel in charge of Eden, said, "You were in Eden, the garden of God; every precious stone was your covering, sardius, topaz, and diamond, beryl, onyx, and jasper, sapphire, emerald, and carbuncle; and crafted in gold were your settings and your engravings. On the day that you were created they were prepared. You were an anointed guardian cherub. *I placed you; you were on the holy mountain of God*; in the midst of the stones of fire you walked" (Ezekiel 28:13-14).

The holy mountain of God is Mount Zion, Jerusalem. God speaking to Isaiah concerning the Jews scattered among all the nations of the world and whom He will bring back to Jerusalem said, "And they shall bring all your brothers from all the nations as an offering to the LORD, on horses and in chariots and in litters and on mules and on dromedaries, *to my holy mountain Jerusalem,* says the LORD, just as the Israelites bring their grain offering in a clean vessel to the house of the LORD" (Isaiah 66:20).

God's holy mountain Jerusalem, Mount Zion was in the midst of the Garden of Eden, which was in the center of the earth. God asked Ezekiel to prophesy against Gog from the land of Magog, who will come against Jerusalem at the end of the millennium reign of Christ, "To seize spoil and carry off plunder, to turn your hand against the waste places that are now inhabited, and the people who were gathered from the nations, who have acquired livestock and goods, *who dwell at the center of the earth*" (Ezekiel 38:12).

Is it possible that the "tree of knowledge of good and evil" was planted in the Garden of Eden on the exact location where Jesus was crucified? To the Romans Paul wrote, "Therefore, as one trespass led to condemnation for all men, so one act of righteousness leads to justification and life for all men." (Romans 5:18)

ARE WE EVOLVED APES?

Many are still upholding Charles Darwin's theory of evolution in clear opposition to the revelation of creation by God the creator. From the Scriptures we read, "In the beginning God created the heaven and the earth" (Genesis 1:1 KJV). "Then God said, 'Let us make man in our image, after our likeness. And let them have dominion over the fish of the sea and over the birds of the heavens and over the livestock and over all the earth and over every creeping thing that creeps on the earth' " (Genesis 1:26). And to Job He asked, "Where were you when I laid the foundation of the earth? Tell me, if you have understanding. Who determined its measurements—surely you know! Or who stretched the line upon it? On what were its bases sunk, or who laid its cornerstone, when the morning stars sang together and all the sons of God shouted for joy?" (Job 38:4-7).

The apostle Paul wrote, "For by him all things were created, in heaven and on earth, visible and invisible, whether thrones or dominions or rulers or authorities—all things were created through him and for him" (Colossians 1:16).

To those who support Darwin's theory of evolution we can wish farewell, because if they claimed that their distant ancestors were apes, their progeny and they should expect to return to that primordial state, since everything in nature is cyclical, like the seasons, the global climate, or the appearance of comets.

IS HELL PURGATORY?

The teaching of hell as being a purgatory where we go to expiate our sins and then make the trip to heaven is another of the Vatican's misrepresentations of biblical truth; speaking to scribes and Pharisees, Jesus warned, "You serpents, you brood of vipers, how are you to escape being sentenced to hell?" (Matthew 23:33).

Jesus illustrated life in hell in the following story: "And at his gate was laid a poor man named Lazarus, covered with sores, who desired to be fed with what fell from the rich man's table. Moreover, even the dogs came and licked his sores. The poor man died and was carried by the angels to Abraham's side. The rich man also died and was buried, and in Hades, being in torment, he lifted up his eyes and saw Abraham far off and Lazarus at his side. And he called out, 'Father Abraham, have mercy on me, and send Lazarus to dip the end of his finger in water and cool my tongue, for I am in anguish in this flame.' But Abraham said, 'Child, remember that you in your lifetime received your good things, and Lazarus in like manner bad things; but now he is comforted here, and you are in anguish. And besides all this, between us and you a great chasm has been fixed, in order that those who would pass from here to you may not be able, and none may cross from there to us' "(Luke 16:20-26).

Hell is a place where God sends those who are disobedient. Simon Peter in a letter to the faithful wrote, "For if God spared not the angels that sinned, but cast them down to hell, and delivered them into chains of darkness, to be reserved unto judgment" (2 Peter 2:4 KJV). The Bible says, "Then the Lord knows how to rescue the godly from trials, and to keep the unrighteous under punishment until the day of judgment, and especially those who indulge in the lust of defiling passion and despise authority. Bold and willful, they do not tremble as they blaspheme the glorious ones" (2 Peter 2:9-10).

A lake of fire is another place even more terrible and the next step after hell, where God will throw them after the last judgment. John wrote, "And the sea gave up the dead who were in it, Death and Hades gave up the dead who were in them, and they were judged, each one of them, according to what they had done. Then Death and Hades were thrown into the lake of fire. This is the second death, the lake of fire. And if anyone's name was not found written in the book of life, he was thrown into the lake of fire" (Revelation 20:13-15).

Some are sent back from hell and experience what is known as near-death, to warn others of the terrible torments there, like the atheist who denied the existence of God and who died, but after he had experienced the horror of hell, he lived to tell his story, vowing not to ever return there, and became a believer. Elihu filled of the Holy Spirit said to his friend Job, "Behold, God does all these things, twice, three times, with a man, to bring back his soul from the pit, that he may be lighted with the light of life" (Job 33:29-30).

IS THE FLAMING DRAGON JUST A MYTHICAL CREATURE?

This great sea monster so common to many cultures is not a crocodile, which has very little in common with this terrible and marvelous creature God has described to Job, God said, "Can you draw out Leviathan with a fishhook or press down his tongue with a cord?" (Job 41:1), and further added, "His sneezings flash forth light, and his eyes are like the eyelids of the dawn. Out of his mouth go flaming torches; sparks of fire leap forth. Out of his nostrils comes forth smoke, as from a boiling pot and burning rushes. His breath kindles coals, and a flame comes forth from his mouth" (Job 41:18-21). But to Isaiah He said, "In that day the LORD with his hard and great and strong sword will punish Leviathan the fleeing serpent, Leviathan the twisting serpent, and he will slay the dragon that is in the sea" (Isaiah 27:1). At Armageddon, an angel will come down with the key to hell and a great chain to pursue and destroy Leviathan. The Bible says, "And he seized the dragon, that ancient serpent, who is the devil and Satan, and bound him for a thousand years, and threw him into the pit, and shut it and sealed it over him, so that he might not deceive the nations any longer, until the thousand years were ended. After that he must be released for a little while" (Revelation 20:2-3).

SHOULD WE GIVE TO PLEASE MAN AND NOT GOD?

On the matter of the financial needs of the Church, God has given instructions on the why and how it should be carried out, with no mention of a specific amount but of a specific share so that no one would be overburdened. The Bible says, "Will man rob God? Yet you are robbing me. But you say, 'How have we robbed you?' In your tithes and contributions. You are cursed with a curse, for you are robbing me, the whole nation of you. Bring the full tithes into the storehouse, that there may be food in my house. And thereby put me to the test, says the LORD of hosts, if I will not open the windows of heaven for you and pour down for you a blessing until there is no more need" (Malachi 3:8-10).

Many Church leaders are overburdening the "sheep," the congregants, with their jaw at their jugular; they are the hungry prowling lion, Satan's church servants, destroying it from inside and misleading them like the one wearing the Vatican's seal representing his destructive power from

Rome. The Bible says, "Shepherd the flock of God that is among you, exercising oversight, not under compulsion, but willingly, as God would have you; not for shameful gains, but eagerly" (1 Peter 5:2).

Furthermore Jesus taught that giving to please God is in how much we sacrifice, not in how much we give. Many are encouraged to borrow to give, with the assumption that the larger the offering, the greater the blessing. Many borrow many times their weekly wage, responding to increased pressure from their church because they expect greater and quicker material blessings but end up in deeper financial trouble, which translates into despair, anger, distrust of Church leaders, loss of faith, defection, divorce and all its consequences, and worst of all, a more sinful life dominated by sexual immorality, unwanted pregnancy, and abortions. "Jesus looked up and saw the rich putting their gifts into the offering box, and he saw a poor widow put in two small copper coins. And he said, 'Truly, I tell you, this poor widow has put in more than all of them. For they all contributed out of their abundance, but she out of her poverty put in all she had to live on'" (Luke 21:1-4).

God wants us to be generous and joyful givers; Paul in a letter to the church of Corinth wrote, "The point is this: whoever sows sparingly will also reap sparingly, and whoever sows bountifully will also reap bountifully. Each one must give as he has made up his mind, not reluctantly or under compulsion, for God loves a cheerful giver. And *God is able to make all grace abound to you*, so that having all sufficiency in all things at all times, you may abound in every good work. As it is written, "He has distributed freely, he has given to the poor; his righteousness endures forever" (2 Corinthians 9:6-9).

We receive even more blessings as we support his work, as Paul further wrote, "He who supplies seed to the sower and bread for food will supply and multiply your seed for sowing and increase the harvest of your righteousness. You will be enriched in every way for all your generosity, which through us will produce thanksgiving to God" (2 Corinthians 9:10-11).

To those who tithe and make offerings, He said this, "I will rebuke the devourer for you, so that it will not destroy the fruits of your soil, and your vine in the field shall not fail to bear, says the LORD of hosts. Then all nations will call you blessed, for you will be a land of delight, says the LORD of hosts" (Malachi 3:11-12).

The assumption during these present days that Christians must pursue wealth to be able to fund the high cost of preaching the Gospel all over the world is erroneous because the wealth of this country, the richest, has always been in the hands of Christians. Those who arrived in this part of the world centuries ago sought the kingdom first, tithed faithfully, made offerings as they could, and were blessed. We are End-Time generations; we are reaping what we have not sown; we are at the receiving end of an immense wealth and cutting-edge technologies, which are allowing us to reach millions at the speed of light as proof that God has already taken care of everything and that all He expects of us is obedience, obedience, and obedience, that we ought to be preaching instead of acting like the Israelites who were asking for meat when they had manna and kindled God's anger. There is more than enough wealth in the Church to fulfill the great commission of taking the Gospel to all men. We must stop wasting the precious time left until the coming of the Lord; let us feed the sheep well: "But seek first the kingdom of God and his righteousness, and all these things will be added to you" (Matthew 6:33).

God wants us to deserve His blessings. The Bible says, "And if you faithfully obey the voice of the LORD your God, being careful to do all his commandments that I command you today, the LORD your God will set you high above all the nations of the earth. And all these blessings shall come upon you and overtake you, if you obey the voice of the LORD your God. Blessed shall you be in the city, and blessed shall you be in the field. Blessed shall be the fruit of your womb and the fruit of your ground and the fruit of your cattle, the increase of your herds and the young of your flock. Blessed shall be your basket and your kneading bowl. Blessed shall you be when you come in, and blessed shall you be when you go out. 'The LORD will cause your enemies who rise against you to be defeated before you. They shall come out against you one way and flee before you seven ways. The LORD will command the blessing on you in your barns and in all that you undertake. And he will bless you in the land that the LORD your God is giving you' " (Deuteronomy 28:1-8). He wants us to enjoy life in this world and the other. Talking to His disciples and other Jews, Jesus said, "The thief comes only to steal and kill and destroy. I came that they may have life and have it abundantly" (John 10:10).

IS THERE FOOD WE SHOULD NOT EAT?

Some even pass judgment on others concerning the food they eat, or what they drink, and on the observance of the Sabbath. The apostle Paul advised the Romans to abstain from judging others, "One person believes he may eat anything, while the weak person eats only vegetables. Let not the one who eats despise the one who abstains, and let not the one who abstains pass judgment on the one who eats, for God has welcomed him. Who are you to pass judgment on the servant of another? It is before his own master that he stands or falls. And he will be upheld, for the Lord is able to make him stand. One person esteems one day as better than another, while another esteems all days alike. Each one should be fully convinced in his own mind. The one who observes the day, observes it in honor of the Lord. The one who eats, eats in honor of the Lord, since he gives thanks to God, while the one who abstains, abstains in honor of the Lord and gives thanks to God. For none of us lives to himself, and none of us dies to himself. If we live, we live to the Lord, and if we die, we die to the Lord. So then, whether we live or whether we die, we are the Lord's. For to this end Christ died and lived again, that he might be Lord both of the dead and of the living" (Romans 14:2-9).

No food is unclean. Eat anything you like. Some are still observing ordinances Moses wrote for the people of Israel as they wandered forty years in the desert; people today still worry whether this food or that is allowed. As far as the uncleanness of a certain food, Paul in a letter to the Romans wrote, "I know and am persuaded in the Lord Jesus that nothing is unclean in itself, but it is unclean for anyone who thinks it unclean" (Romans 14:14).

To the Christians of Colossae in Asia Minor, Paul sent words of exhortation reminding them they should stand high in faith and not let others' judgments concerning what they eat and drink, or whether they attend service on Saturday or Sunday or any other day of the week, be a distraction to them. He wrote, "And you, who were dead in your trespasses and the uncircumcision of your flesh, God made alive together with him, having forgiven us all our trespasses, by canceling the record of debt that stood against us with its legal demands. This he set aside, nailing it to the cross. He disarmed the rulers and authorities and put them to open shame, by triumphing over them in him. Therefore let no one pass judgment on you in questions of food and drink, or with regard to a festival or a new moon or a Sabbath. These are a shadow of the things to come, but the substance belongs to Christ" (Colossians 2:13-17).

Do not share with others food they consider unclean, as Paul commanded, "Do not, for the sake of food, destroy the work of God. Everything is indeed clean, but it is wrong for anyone to make another stumble by what he eats. It is good not to eat meat or drink wine or do anything that causes your brother to stumble. The faith that you have, keep between yourself and God. Blessed is the one who has no reason to pass judgment on himself for what he approves. But whoever has doubts is condemned if he eats, because the eating is not from faith. For whatever does not proceed from faith is sin" (Romans 14:20-23).

The Pharisees criticized that Jesus' disciples were eating without washing their hands, "And he said to them, 'You have a fine way of rejecting the commandment of God in order to establish your tradition!' " (Mark 7:9). And He further declared, "There is nothing outside a person that by going into him can defile him, but the things that come out of a person are what defile him" (Mark 7:15).

WHY AM I POOR? WHY AM I RICH?

Poverty and wealth are inseparable, as the small and the great, as valleys and mountains, as darkness and light, as offense and forgiveness, as life and death, as bitter and sweet, and as hatred and love—since the notion of either one is impossible in the absence of its opposite; no one would speak of daylight if we lived in a world without night. Karl Marx was a philosopher who wrote *The Communist Manifesto* in 1848 and *Das Kapital* after 1866, with the help of Friedrich Engels. It is evident that the German economist and revolutionary Marx did not know of the wisdom of our God, who has chosen of whom and in which economic environment each one of us would be born. He has also given free will and different gifts to each one of us so that some would live in abject poverty and others would be very wealthy, in a manner that the ones who make an expensive pair of shoes are not the same who can afford them, and vice versa. The Bible says, "Oh, the depth of the riches and wisdom and knowledge of God! How unsearchable are his judgments and how inscrutable his ways!" (Romans 11:33).

The first great truth God revealed to me when I was just nine years old was that those who were in need and panhandling by the main entrance of my church were not only closer to Him but were greater than many because of their greater humility and were also His representatives on earth, ones we should learn from, love, serve, and be good to. Along the years He has taught me they are a reason for blessings, a means to gauge and prove our love for Him, which is important in our relationship with Him. Jesus, talking of the ephemeral nature of His ministry, let His disciples know also the perennial need for them, saying, "The poor you always have with you, but you do not always have me" (John 12:8).

Those of us who are poor must understand that our poverty is not the result of a lack of blessing, because we are greater sinners, more disobedient than those who have more material possession than we, or because we have not made very large offerings as greedy and power-hungry Church leaders are insinuating. The Bible says, "And he lifted up his eyes on his disciples, and said: 'Blessed are you who are poor, for yours is the kingdom of God' " (Luke 6:20). God is using us just the same way He has used the Jewish people in an actual setting, amid trials, to depict and fulfill his promise of salvation for us as the apostle Paul wrote: "For if their casting away means reconciliation for the world, what will their acceptance be, if not life from the dead?" (Romans 11:15 EMTV).

We are hungry and homeless because we are underpaid by those for which we work, and victimized by financial institutions eager to plunder the little we have by charging excessive fees and interests, and by service providers who overcharge us and steal from us when we can hardly make ends meet and cannot feed our kids who go often to bed with empty bellies. He has chosen us to be living sacrifices so all can have the opportunity to be obedient and please Him through us. To this effect Jesus said, "Listen, my beloved brothers, has not God chosen those who are poor in the world to be rich in faith and heirs of the kingdom, which he has promised to those who love him?" (James 2:5).

Those of us who are born of wealthy parents were not asked whom we wanted them to be. God made that choice for us, and we cannot claim any credit for starting out in life better off than many. Wealth is a symbol of power and abundance, but without poverty, which is a symbol of humility and penury, we cannot prove to God that we love Him. Jesus explained it to us, "He said also to the man who had invited him, 'When you give a dinner or a banquet, do not invite your friends or your brothers or your relatives or rich neighbors, lest they also invite you in return and you be repaid. But when you give a feast, invite the poor, the crippled, the lame, the blind, and you will be blessed, because they cannot repay you. You will be repaid at the resurrection of the just' " (Luke 14:12-14).

In our abundance we are a symbol of the reward He promised. If we do not faithfully play our part, which is to treat our poor brethren with compassion and justice, as they are playing theirs in humility, what can we expect from Him? He described what will be His retribution if we fail to perform as He expects of us. From the New Testament we read, "Come now, you rich, weep and howl for the miseries that are coming upon you. Your riches have rotted and your garments are moth-eaten. Your gold and silver have corroded, and their corrosion will be evidence against you and will eat your flesh like fire. You have laid up treasure in the last days. Behold, the wages of the laborers who mowed your fields, which you kept back by fraud, are crying out against you, and the cries of the harvesters have reached the ears of the Lord of hosts. You have lived on the earth in luxury and in self-indulgence. You have fattened your hearts in a day of slaughter. You have condemned; you have murdered the righteous person. He does not resist you" (James 5:1-6).

CAN HELPING OTHERS BE A LIFESTYLE?

Many boast of their success, and of the value of their material possessions, but homelessness and hunger are becoming a serious problem in the richest country where the majority calls itself followers of Jesus; this is not a problem because of a lack of dedication at helping our fellow man but because of division in the body of Christ. If the Church remains satisfied with the status quo, what could be the chances for Christians to become a more coherent body under the Antichrist's rule? Almost none. To the contrary, it may slide into further disintegration, every one for himself. Christians must stop the fragmentation of the body of Christ and consolidate their resources before it is too late! Jesus has a reward for those who help the least of us. He will separate those who have demonstrated compassion for their fellow man and place them on His right, apart from those who have not. "Then he will say to those on his left, 'Depart from me, you cursed, into the eternal fire prepared for the devil and his angels. For I was hungry and you gave me no food, I was thirsty and you gave me no drink, I was a stranger and you did not welcome me, naked and you did not clothe me, sick and in prison and you did not visit me.' Then they also will answer, saying, 'Lord, when did we see you hungry or thirsty or a stranger or naked or sick or in prison, and did not minister to you?' Then he will answer them, saying, 'Truly, I say to you, as you did not do it to one of the least of these, you did not do it to me.' And these will go away into eternal punishment, but the righteous into eternal life" (Matthew 25:41-46).

DO WE SIN WHEN WE LIE?

We all have at least once in our lifetimes used excuses to escape punishment from our parents or a teacher, or reprisal from an unjust instructor or a boss, mostly because we believe that we are not obligated to compromise our privacy. From the Scriptures we read, "What is desired in a man is steadfast love, and a poor man is better than a liar" (Proverbs 19:22).

We do not become liars just because our perception or recollection of an event differs from someone else's. But when we do present facts to mislead others, we are liars. Whatever our reason, it is wrong even when it is to make people see us in a better light, as in the case of a young man who inflates his income to impress a lender or a girlfriend, or as in the case of a girl who tells several of her boyfriends that he is the only one she is seeing. From the Scriptures we read, "You shall not steal; you shall not deal falsely; you shall not lie to one another" (Leviticus 19:11). Paul, to the faithful of Colossi, commands; "Do not lie to one another, seeing that you have put off the old self with its practices" (Colossians 3:9).

But when the intention behind a lie is to put someone else in a disadvantageous position, or to outright destroy the reputation of someone else, whether it is we want someone else to bear the blame of our own failures or mistakes, or to deprive others of what belongs to them, we are guilty of a crime against them. The Bible says, "You are of your father the devil, and your will is to do your father's desires. He was a murderer from the beginning, and has nothing to do with the truth, because there is no truth in him. When he lies, he speaks out of his own character, for he is a liar and the father of lies" (John 8:44).

God considers a lie that causes harm equal to committing murder and other sins that are punishable by the hell of fire and eternal damnation in the lake of fire. From the Scriptures we read, "You shall not spread a false report. You shall not join hands with a wicked man to be a malicious witness. You shall not fall in with the many to do evil, nor shall you bear witness in a lawsuit, siding with the many, so as to pervert justice" (Exodus 23:1-2). The Bible says, "And a ruler asked him, 'Good Teacher, what must I do to inherit eternal life?' And Jesus said to him, "Why do you call me good? No one is good except God alone. You know the commandments: 'Do not commit adultery, Do not murder, Do not steal, Do not bear false witness, Honor your father and mother' " (Luke 18:18-20).

If a lie is directed at ones parents, it also carries a life-time curse sentence until repentance changes the outcome. From the Scriptures we read, "Cursed be anyone who dis-honors his father or his mother.' And all the people shall say, 'Amen' "(Deuteronomy 27:16). To Pharisees and scribes Jesus said, "For God commanded, 'Honor your father and your mother,' and, 'Whoever reviles father or mother must surely die' " (Matthew 15:4).

WHAT IS SEXUAL IMMORALITY?

Some of us are not really sure whether fornication and other sexual acts are sins capable of causing us to be re-jected by God and thrown into the lake of fire. Our lack of knowledge about it is the result of the complaisance that has settled along the years in the Church, paired with com-placency and the depravation of some of our leaders who have not been willing to preach against what they themselves have been practicing. Let us find out the truth for our sake.

The Vatican promotes the annulment of marriage, which is only plausible according to man's law when it is recorded but not according to the scriptures. In the eyes of God it is equivalent to shredding a marriage certificate, since He only allows a couple to divorce because of adultery. If you should face the situation where your spouse annuls the marriage and remarries or is in another relationship, it should then be considered as having committed adultery, and you could give him or her a simple letter of divorce, handwritten or typed, which would be acceptable to God, since your separation would have been already finalized by a judge.

Pharisees asked Jesus if, according to the Law of Moses, a man could divorce his wife, "And Jesus said to them, 'Because of your hardness of heart he wrote you this commandment. But from the beginning of creation, 'God made them male and female.' 'Therefore a man shall leave his father and mother and hold fast to his wife, and they shall become one flesh.' So they are no longer two but one flesh. What therefore God has joined together, let not man separate" (Mark 10:5-9).

Whether in marriage or another situation, if at least one

of the parties involved uses subterfuge and lies, the fraudulent agreement between them is not binding in the eyes of God, but the union of a man and a woman recorded in heaven cannot be voided because even divorce is condemned by God except for adultery. Jesus further said to his disciples, "But I say to you that everyone who divorces his wife, except on the ground of sexual immorality, makes her commit adultery. And whoever marries a divorced woman commits adultery" (Matthew 5:32). But is it the whole law? The following verse answers the question for us: "And he said to them, 'Whoever divorces his wife and marries another commits adultery against her, and if she divorces her husband and marries another, she commits adultery' " (Mark 10:11-12).

What about fornication, which is sexual intercourse between people who are not married? Many who are still cohabiting do not know they are living in sin. They assume that because they have good intentions God may accept them just as though they were married. Jesus dispelled such a belief in a conversation He had with a Samaritan woman, whom He asked for a drink at a Jacob's well. "Jesus said to her, 'Go, call your husband, and come here.' The woman answered him, 'I have no husband.' Jesus said to her, 'You are right in saying, 'I have no husband'; for you have had five husbands, and the one you now have is not your husband. What you have said is true.' The woman said to him, 'Sir, I perceive that you are a prophet'" (John 4:16-19). The Bible says many Israelites perished in the desert when they committed such an act: "We must not indulge in sexual immorality as some of them did, and twenty-three thousand fell in a single day" (1 Corinthians 10:8).

A great number of young and older Christian singles are cohabiting before they get married, thence living in a sinful relationship, either with the intention to know each other better for fear of a failed marriage, or because they feel they are not financially ready. Concerning this nefarious trend, the Lord gave me a word, which will allow them to be delivered from this bondage where Satan is holding them. Its pervasiveness is alarming; because of it, there is less and less commitment in marriage, which translates into a higher divorce rate in the Church.

To his disciples Jesus said, "Again I say to you, if two of you agree on earth about anything they ask, it will be done for them by my Father in heaven." (Matthew 18:19). Then if a man and a woman stand before God and declare that they take the other as their spouse, they are considered married in the eyes of God and it is better that they live this way together until they can afford to proceed with civil and religious matters, instead of a lifestyle in sin, which can cause them to die unrepentant.

Lust, which is an intense sexual desire, is the least preached about, as though it were not a sin capable of opening wide the gates of hell to accept us. Jesus warned us not to fall into its trap. "You have heard that it was said, 'You shall not commit adultery.' But I say to you that everyone who looks at a woman with lustful intent has already committed adultery with her in his heart" (Matthew 5:27-28).

 Looking at scantily clad people at the beach is not a sin until we look at a particular individual, fantasizing over certain areas of the body with the intention of experiencing some type of sexual satisfaction or contemplating engaging in a sexual act with that person. Even long after we have had them in our sight, if we do replay those images with the same intention, we are still guilty according to what Jesus said in the above-mentioned passage. Idolatry, the worship of a false god, also applies to the excessive adulation of another person or object, with of without sexual overtones.

A female minister who has been living with another woman and a gay Bishop were protesting the position taken by other Church members who asked for their dismissal from the pulpit. Were they wrong even though they had many supporters? The following verses show clearly that God sentences to eternal death those He finds guilty of such acts unless they repent. The Lord spoke to Moses saying, "If a man lies with a male as with a woman, both of them have committed an abomination; they shall surely be put to death; their blood is upon them" (Leviticus 20:13). The Bible says, "Just as Sodom and Gomorrah and the surrounding cities, which likewise indulged in sexual immorality and pursued unnatural desire, serve as an example by undergoing a punishment of eternal fire" (Jude 1:7).

This is what Jesus said of eternal punishment, "If your right eye causes you to sin, tear it out and throw it away. For it is better that you lose one of your members than that your whole body be thrown into hell. And if your right hand causes you to sin, cut it off and throw it away. For it is better that you lose one of your members than that your whole body go into hell" (Matthew 5:29-30). He was obviously referring to the soul when it is thrown in hell.

Sodom and Gomorrah were destroyed by God because men young and old, even boys, in those cities were all sexually perverted long before Lot, Abraham's nephew, and his family went to live among them. They slept with each other and gang-raped any male stranger who would venture there. Three angels sent to convince Lot and his family to leave Sodom before they had poured God's wrath over these cities were hounded by a throng that wanted to rape them. "And they struck with blindness the men who were at the entrance of the house, both small and great, so that they wore themselves out groping for the door. Then the men said to Lot, 'Have you anyone else here? Sons-in-law, sons, daughters, or anyone you have in the city, bring them out of the place. For we are about to destroy this place, because the outcry against its people has become great before the LORD, and the LORD has sent us to destroy it.' So Lot went out and said to his sons-in-law, who were to marry his daughters, 'Up! Get out of this place, for the LORD is about to destroy the city.' But he seemed to his sons-in-law to be jesting. As morning dawned, the angels urged Lot, saying, 'Up! Take your wife and your two daughters who are here, lest you be swept away in the punishment of the city.' But he lingered. So the men seized him and his wife and his two daughters by the hand, the LORD being merciful to him, and they brought him out and set him outside the city. And as they brought them out, one said, 'Escape for your life. Do not look back or stop anywhere in the valley. Escape to the hills, lest you be swept away'" (Genesis 19:11-17). They did flee to a nearby city, and their lives were spared. But those who remained in the city of Sodom perished. Lot's wife disobeyed, looked back, and turned into a pillar of salt. The Bible says, "Then the LORD rained on Sodom and Gomorrah sulfur and fire from the LORD out of heaven. And he overthrew those cities, and all the valley, and all the inhabitants of the cities, and what grew on the ground. (Genesis 19:24-25).

WHAT DOES THE BIBLE SAY OF
BIRTH CONTROL?

Many churches with extreme views on procreation are teaching that it is a sin to use any form of birth control or even to discharge sperm outside the female, knowing full well that even abortion is found nowhere, in specific terms, in the Bible. Meanwhile their congregants, in great number, are having out-of-wedlock children, and some of their ministers are romantically involved with members of their flock at an alarming level. God created Adam and Eve, "And God blessed them. And God said to them, 'Be fruitful and multiply and fill the earth and subdue it and have dominion over the fish of the sea and over the birds of the heavens and over every living thing that moves on the earth' " (Genesis 1:28). Some would argue that God took the life of Onan the son of Judah because he spilled his sperm to the ground. To the contrary, Onan was punished because he disobeyed his father, refusing to impregnate his sister-in-law, whom he had married as per Judah's request. According to their custom he was to give offspring to his brother Er, the firstborn who was wicked and was killed by God. From the Scriptures we read, "But Onan knew that the offspring would not be his. So whenever he went in to his brother's wife, he would waste the semen on the ground, so as not to give offspring to his brother. And what he did was wicked in the sight of the LORD, and he put him to death also" (Genesis 38:9-10).

We can conclude that God gave to mankind total authority over all aspects of procreation and that children are born of the will of their parents, versus the angels who were born of the will of God, as evidenced in the following verse, "But to all who did receive him, who believed in his name, he gave the right to become children of God, who were born, not of blood nor of the will of the flesh nor of the will of man, but of God" (John 1:12-13).

Many would argue otherwise, but the biblical writer meant to say that the angels were made by the will of God versus children who are born by the procreative action of their parents. To Sadducees who wanted to know who of seven brothers would have for his wife a certain woman in the resurrection if all of them were to marry her, Jesus declared, "For in the resurrection they neither marry nor are given in marriage, but are like angels in heaven" (Matthew 22:30), who are called "Sons of God."

Today's medical applications allow doctors to start the process of procreation in their labs. Some parents are already able to choose the gender of their children, and others hope that one day doctors will be able to prevent harmful genes to be passed on to their progeny thanks to advanced genomic discoveries and existing technologies such as one called inheritable genetic modification (IGM). Probably in the future God will allow man to discover how to simplify the process even further, considering that wisdom and understanding are given by God to man as well as to a creature as small as an ant. Science is a gift from God, and man cannot know more than He allows and has planned for him. To Moses God said, "See, I have called by name Bezalel the son of Uri, son of Hur, of the tribe of Judah, and I have filled him with the Spirit of God, with ability and intelligence, with knowledge and all craftsmanship, to devise artistic designs, to work in gold, silver, and bronze, in cutting stones for setting, and in carving wood, to work in every craft." (Exodus 31:2-5). He further said to Job concerning the ostrich, that "She deals cruelly with her young, as if they were not hers; though her labor be in vain, yet she has no fear, because God has made her forget wisdom and given her no share in understanding" (Job 39:16-17).

Many Christians are falsely taught that it is sin to use any form of birth control even when they are in a sinful relationship. Many men and women, married or not, decide sometimes to engage in sexual intercourse without second thought of accidental pregnancy as one of the consequences of their action. Very often it occurs between two people who are dating or between two total strangers who have no intention of seeing each other ever again; and the woman gets pregnant either for not having any form of birth control at her disposal and the fact that the one-night stand or steady partner does not care of what might happen to her, or sometimes because one of the partners or both do not want to practice birth control. When reality hits home, they cannot think of anything but to abort the pregnancy.

What does the Bible say about abortion? There is no mention of it in either the Old or New Testament. Why did not Jesus speak against a practice that was common during his time, nor the apostles? Is it because it has no bearing on our salvation? Yes and no! If we can discern the signs that tell us that we are close to exceeding the reasonable level acceptable to God and exert restraint, we will do well. But if we do not recognize the gray area where we will soon step into the forbidden zone that makes us sinners, we will suffer the consequences of our negligence.

The Bible has some gray areas where knowledge of the Word and wisdom come in handy as far as making a conscious decision of how far one can go in a manner not to commit sin. After the original sin, God forbade Adam and Eve to ever eat from the Garden of Eden but had compassion for them because food was essential to their survival. "And to Adam He said, 'Because you have listened to the voice of your wife and have eaten of the tree of which I commanded you, 'You shall not eat of it,' cursed is the ground because of you; in pain you shall eat of it all the days of your life'" (Genesis 3:17). Nevertheless God condemned excessive eating but left it to us to know when it is considered excessive, since He has never recommended how much food we must eat and when we should eat. Paul warning the faithful declared, "Envies, murders, *drinking bouts, revelries*, and the like; which I tell you beforehand, just as I also told you in time past, that those who practice such things will not inherit the kingdom of God" (Galatians 5:21 EMTV).

While He encourages us to enjoy eating and drinking moderately, a preacher wrote the following biblical passage, "Go, eat your bread in joy, and drink your wine with a merry heart, for God has already approved what you do" (Ecclesiastes 9:7).

Rest assured that everyone will be born as God planned it. David wrote, "I have relied on you from the day I was born. You brought me safely through birth, and I always praise you" (Psalms 71:6 CEV).

To Jeremiah God said, "Before I formed you in the womb I knew you, and before you were born I consecrated you; I appointed you a prophet to the nations" (Jeremiah 1:5).

From the following story: "And Isaac prayed to the

LORD for his wife, because she was barren. And the LORD granted his prayer, and Rebekah his wife conceived" (Genesis 25:21); and from the story of two cousins, Mary and Elizabeth, which is also the story of the miraculous conception of Jesus, our Savior and Lord, and his forerunner John The Baptist, we have extracted these verses that are uplifting. The Bible says, "And when Elizabeth heard the greeting of Mary, the baby leaped in her womb. And Elizabeth was filled with the Holy Spirit, and she exclaimed with a loud cry, 'Blessed are you among women, and blessed is the fruit of your womb! And why is this granted to me that the mother of my Lord should come to me? For behold, when the sound of your greeting came to my ears, the baby in my womb leaped for joy'" (Luke 1:41-44).

The psalmist Solomon wrote, "Behold, children are a heritage from the LORD, the fruit of the womb a reward" (Psalms 127:3). At Mount Sinai, God speaking to Moses and the people of Israel said, "Thou shalt not kill" (Exodus 20:13 KJV). The preceding verses are a reminder on the one hand that a child is a gift of God and on the other that one must be careful in not overstepping the boundary where one can become a murderer as easy as one can become a glutton and a drunkard, both deserving punishment in hell according to the word of God.

WHO CAN FORGIVE TRESPASSES?

The Catholic Church teaches that one cannot confess sins but to a priest to receive forgiveness because Jesus when establishing His church, said to Peter, "I will give you the keys of the kingdom of heaven, and whatever you bind on earth shall be bound in heaven, and whatever you loose on earth shall be loosed in heaven" (Matthew 16:19).

But Jesus gave that authority to everyone who believes in Him and reiterated it to the twelve disciples, "Truly, I say to you, whatever you bind on earth shall be bound in heaven, and whatever you loose on earth shall be loosed in heaven" (Matthew 18:18).

That authority is also extended to civil authorities since they too are also his servants in the exercise of their duty (a clerk that performs the wedding of a man and a woman or a judge that sentences a criminal). The Bible says, "Be subject for the Lord's sake to every human institution, whether it be to the emperor as supreme, or to governors as sent by him to punish those who do evil and to praise those who do good. For this is the will of God, that by doing good you should put to silence the ignorance of foolish people" (1 Peter 2:13-15).

The authority to forgive is not only given to everyone, God requires it of everyone. Jesus, surrounded by His disciples, was addressing large crowds that were following Him, and He taught them saying, "For if you forgive others their trespasses, your heavenly Father will also forgive you, but if you do not forgive others their trespasses, neither will your Father forgive your trespasses" (Matthew 6:14-15).

Jesus was alone with his disciples and "Then Peter came up and said to Him, 'Lord, how often will my brother sin against me, and I forgive him? As many as seven times?' Jesus said to him, 'I do not say to you seven times, but seventy times seven'" (Matthew 18:21-22).

SHOULD THE VATICAN PREVENT PRIESTS FROM MARRYING?

Sexual immorality has been one of the many negative influences of the Catholic Church on Christianity. Others are the selling of spiritual blessings, despotism, political plots and schemes, and internal strife that has led to assassination and poisoning, among other murders. Siricius (384-399), who was the first to assume the title of Pope, was also the first to prescribe celibacy for priests. Nevertheless, John XII (955-964), among others, led an openly licentious life and was reputed to have died of a stroke while in bed with a married woman. Alexander VI (1492-1503), who had four illegitimate children in a relationship with Vannozza

Cattanei, a Roman woman, and five others by other women, ordered the Dominican monk Girolamo Savonarola, who preached against the corruption of Alexander's papacy, burned alive. His successor, Julius II (1503-1513), fathered three children before he became Pope.

Many young men entered seminary with practically no understanding of what living single and celibate entails. Many priests feel the need to get married, but the Vatican always denies their request and has no God-given authority to prevent them from doing so.

Jesus, speaking to his disciples who apparently felt that no man should marry according to what He has commended concerning marriage and divorce, explained, "For there are eunuchs who have been so from birth, and there are eunuchs who have been made eunuchs by men, and there are eunuchs who have made themselves eunuchs for the sake of the kingdom of heaven. Let the one who is able to receive this receive it" (Matthew 19:12).

The apostle Paul wrote the following concerning the personal decision of remaining single or being married: "Now concerning the matters about which you wrote: 'It is good for a man not to have sexual relations with a woman.' But because of the temptation to sexual immorality, each man should have his own wife and each woman her own husband" (1 Corinthians 7:1-2). And he further said, "I wish that all were as I myself am. But each has his own gift from God, one of one kind and one of another. To the unmarried and the widows I say that it is good for them to remain single as I am. But if they cannot exercise self-control, they should marry. For it is better to marry than to be aflame with passion" (1 Corinthians 7:7-9).

The Vatican prevents priests from marrying when they feel the need to do so, just so as not to incur the cost of having to increase their stipend to allow them to care for a family. In this way it is imposing a sinful life on them, being an unjust leader and employer in contradiction of the Word of God. The Bible says, "Shepherd the flock of God that is among you, exercising oversight, not under compulsion, but willingly, as God would have you; not for shameful gain, but eagerly" (1 Peter 5:2). The Vatican should reconsider and pay priests what they deserve and stop threatening them with excommunication, which has no biblical truth, since nothing can separate man from his maker but sin: "For the Scripture says, 'You shall not muzzle an ox when it treads out the grain,' and, 'The laborer deserves his wages' " (1 Timothy 5:18).

God does not recognize religion, which is of man, since He is no respecter of person. The Bible says, "So Peter opened his mouth and said: 'Truly I understand that God shows no partiality, but in every nation anyone who fears him and does what is right is acceptable to him' " (Acts 10:34-35).

Those who feel the need to marry should do so and should sever their ties with the Vatican if need be. They should continue to preach the word of God, who is their only Master, as many others before them have done and have departed from a corrupt and despotic institution whose lavishness they are supporting and whose sins and judgment are recorded in heaven. Jude warned the faithful concerning those in the Church who because of their position are imposing their own views on others, perverting the word and trying to take the place of our Lord. He wrote, "For certain people have crept in unnoticed who long ago were designated for this condemnation, ungodly people, who pervert the grace of our God into sensuality and deny our only Master and Lord, Jesus Christ" (Jude 1:4).

SHOULD WOMEN BE CONSECRATED PRIEST OR PASTOR?

In today's Church, women are consecrated as pastors, and many are in doubt whether it is of Jesus' teachings. According to the scriptures, God has never called a woman to be priest. He ordered Moses to consecrate his brother Aaron and his sons priests over Israel, saying, "Then bring near to you Aaron your brother, and his sons with him, from among the people of Israel, to serve me as priests— Aaron and Aaron's sons, Nadab and Abihu, Eleazar and Ithamar" (Exodus 28:1).

Miriam the prophetess, Moses' sister, spoke evil of him to Aaron his brother. "And the LORD came down in a pillar of cloud and stood at the entrance of the tent and called Aaron and Miriam, and they both came forward. And he said, 'Hear my words: If there is a prophet among you, I the LORD make myself known to him in a vision; I speak with him in a dream. Not so with my servant Moses. He is faithful in all my house. With him I speak mouth to mouth, clearly, and not in riddles, and he beholds the form of the LORD. Why then were you not afraid to speak against my servant Moses?' And the anger of the LORD was kindled against them, and he departed. When the cloud removed from over the tent, behold, Miriam was leprous, like snow. And Aaron turned toward Miriam, and behold, she was leprous" (Numbers 12:5-10).

Jesus established the foundation of His Church on Simon his apostle; speaking to him He said, "And I tell you, you are Peter, and on this rock I will build my church, and the gates of hell shall not prevail against it" (Matthew 16:18).

Then came the time for Jesus to send his apostles away

to proclaim repentance, to cast out demons, and to heal the sick. "And he called the twelve and began to send them out two by two, and gave them authority over the unclean spirits. He charged them to take nothing for their journey except a staff—no bread, no bag, no money in their belts—but to wear sandals and not put on two tunics" (Mark 6:7-9).

But to provide for His apostles and Himself, He used the help of his mother. "And also some women who had been healed of evil spirits and infirmities: Mary, called Magdalene, from whom seven demons had gone out, and Joanna, the wife of Chuza, Herod's household manager, and Susanna, and many others, who provided for them out of their means" (Luke 8:2-3).

However, willing to show that women were also bound as children of the promise to work for the good of the kingdom and spread the good news of His death and resurrection, through His word and testimony, He chose Mary Magdalene to witness His crucifixion, to be the first to see Him alive near the tomb where they laid Him, and to be the first to receive and pass on the message of His resurrection. "Jesus said to her, 'Do not cling to me, for I have not yet ascended to the Father; but go to my brothers and say to them, 'I am ascending to my Father and your Father, to my God and your God' "(John 20:17).

After Jesus was lifted up to heaven, His mother, and the other women continued to be helpful around the apostles. "All these with one accord were devoting themselves to prayer, together with the women and Mary the mother of Jesus, and his brothers" (Acts 1:14).

FALSE TEACHINGS AND PRACTICES

Today's Pharisees would oppose Jesus because of their prejudices and would not have checked his genealogy, which would indicate that His lineage was that of King David, and that He was the Messiah announced by the prophets, and that He was the Son of God, creator of Earth and Heaven and everything therein, and that He was the Word made flesh. Because He would have again selected His disciples among the poorest and would hang out with drug addicts, strange people with braided and colored hair, tattoos and pierced noses; because He would be seen often at their backyard barbecues, birthday parties and weddings, eating and drinking, as food, cheap wine and beer would abound; because they would form, around Him, a crowd that many would consider ill-mannered, loud, and rowdy, wherever He would be preaching, these pharisees would accuse Him of disturbing their peace and would limit His meetings to, according to them, where He would belong—

inner-city slums. They would again reject His teachings, would falsely accuse Him of heresy and crimes He would not have committed and would try to silence Him. Jesus said, "Blessed are those who are persecuted for righteousness' sake, for theirs is the kingdom of heaven. Blessed are you when others revile you and persecute you and utter all kinds of evil against you falsely on my account. Rejoice and be glad, for your reward is great in heaven, for so they persecuted the prophets who were before you'" (Matthew 5:10-12).

Modern day religious hypocrites proudly announce often that "We love sinners," as though they themselves aren't; the apostle Paul to the Romans wrote, "For all have sinned and fall short of the glory of God" (Romans 3:23).

As Jesus was addressing a crowd and was talking of John the Baptist, who was in prison and had sent some of his disciples to ask Him if He were really the Messiah, He said this, "From the days of John the Baptist until now the kingdom of heaven has suffered violence, and the violent take it by force. For all the Prophets and the Law prophesied until John" (Matthew 11:12-13).

We have become a people drowning more and more in dogmatic magma of condemnation of those who do not belong to a religious mutant called Christendom, and less and less are we disciples of Christ. It is time that we point the finger at our puffed-up selves to examine how far we have strayed from the Master's teachings instead of pointing it at everyone else with the assumption that if we can cry havoc of others' shortcomings, ours will look less offensive to God, forgetting that we will face Him alone to be judged according to His Word, not by others' sins. We are not judged by how many good things we do, minus our sins evaluated against those of others; our sins are judged according to God's Word, not in comparison to sins committed by our neighbors, friends, or someone behind bars. To a crowd Jesus declared, "The one who rejects me and does not receive my words has a judge; the word that I have spoken will judge him on the last day" (John 12:48).

Without a revolution in the body of Christ, as Satan is relentlessly trying to tear it apart, many will fall prey to the beast, the Outlaw. Many have been so entangled in vain philosophies and their own deceits instead of applying the Word of God that they are incapable of distinguishing the thief from the shepherd who said, "Truly, truly, I say to you, he who does not enter the sheepfold by the door but climbs in by another way, that man is a thief and a robber. But he who enters by the door is the shepherd of the sheep. To him the gatekeeper opens. The sheep hear his voice, and he calls his own sheep by name and leads them out. When he has brought out all his own, he goes before them, and the sheep follow him, for they know his voice" (John 10:1-4).

Today's Church teachings are based more on modernism than on biblical principles; Christians rely more on their psychologists and less on the Word to solve interpersonal problems, causing more of them to choose divorce and its consequences. There are more books and sermons written by Christians on wealth building than on the sins of fornication and adultery with all their woes, including abortion, which is a symptom of sexual immorality that we need to combat to eradicate it. Jesus said, "But it is easier for heaven and earth to pass away than for one dot of the Law to become void" (Luke 16:17). Talking to a certain ruler, He reminded him of the commandments saying, "You know the commandments: 'Do not commit adultery, Do not murder, Do not steal, Do not bear false witness, Honor your father and mother'" (Luke 18:20). Paul to the Corinthians wrote, "We must not indulge in sexual immorality as some of them did, and twenty-three thousand fell in a single day" (1 Corinthians 10:8). Jude, a disciple and brother of James, exhorting the faithful to stay away from fornication and sexual immorality, wrote, "Just as Sodom and Gomorrah and the surrounding cities, which likewise indulged in sexual immorality and pursued unnatural desire, serve as an example by undergoing a punishment of eternal fire" (Jude

1:7). The Bible says, "But put on the Lord Jesus Christ, and make no provision for the flesh, to gratify its desires" (Romans 13:14).

IS THERE HEALING POWER IN RAGS?

Why didn't Jesus instruct his apostles to cut into small pieces and share among themselves and their followers his coat, robe, undergarment, the very large piece of fabric used to wrap his body, the one that has covered his face, the bed sheets He slept on, or the fabric of the seats He sat on? Why didn't He ask them to keep a collection of utensils He used, of dirt, sand, shell, pebble, or rock from everywhere He walked? He said, "So everyone who acknowledges me before men, I also will acknowledge before my Father who is in heaven" (Matthew 10:32), indicating clearly that we need to have our eyes focused solely on Him to be acknowledged by His Father; if we allowed ourselves to be distracted by those things, we would fall into idolatry, worshipping them instead, with terrible consequences. He continued saying, "But whoever denies me before men, I also will deny before my Father who is in heaven" (Matthew 10:33).

Why not limit Church practices to true Biblical teachings? "Is anyone among you sick? Let him call for the elders of the church, and let them pray over him, anointing him with oil in the name of the Lord" (James 5:14).

If some believe that they have certain gifts, it is better for them to let God use them as He chooses, as when He did extraordinary miracles by the hands of Paul instead of causing others to stumble. Miracles are neither commodities nor products to be packaged and delivered from the assembly line into the consumer's hand; they are the expression of the will of God. The Bible says, "This continued for two years, so that all the residents of Asia heard the word of the Lord, both Jews and Greeks. *And God was doing extraordinary miracles by the hands of Paul,* so that even handkerchiefs or aprons that had touched his skin were carried away to the sick, and their diseases left them and the evil spirits came out of them. Then some of the itinerant Jewish exorcists undertook to invoke the name of the Lord Jesus over those who had evil spirits, saying, 'I adjure you by the Jesus, whom Paul proclaims.' Seven sons of a Jewish high priest named Sceva were doing this. But the evil spirit answered them, 'Jesus I know, and Paul I recognize, but who are you?' " (Acts 19:10-15).

Once God was doing extraordinary miracles through His servant, such as even a cloudless sky turned dark with great winds in a few seconds on a dry, sunny, and windless day, and many who have witnessed them or have probably heard of them, were willing to touch him to be healed, but even though he knew well that it was possible, nothing being impossible to God, he discouraged them from attempting that because it would lead to idolatry in the form of a personality cult, and he did not want to take his focus away from his mission, since the healing ministry was not his calling then. He told them that if they had faith in the Lord they would be healed. When he gets sick, the Lord heals him. Once his wife was to have a fibrosis removed, but because they had decided to move to another state where the climate was more clement, she had to postpone the operation. As she had to go ahead of him, since he could not immediately quit his hospital job, in his heart he prophesied total healing, as she was about to board the plane. A few months later another X-ray revealed nothing abnormal. The Bible says, "God himself showed that his message was true by working all kinds of powerful miracles and wonders. He also gave his Holy Spirit to anyone he chose to" (Hebrews 2:4 CEV).

ARE THE LORD'S GIFTS EXCHANGEABLE?

Let us work with all the gifts He has given us in truthfulness in the manner prescribed by Him. The Bible says,

"Every good gift and every perfect gift is from above, coming down from the Father of lights with whom there is no
variation or shadow due to change" (James 1:17). The
apostle Peter, reminding to the faithful to put to good use
the gifts they have received from the Holy Spirit, wrote,
"As each has received a gift, use it to serve one another, as
good stewards of God's varied grace" (1 Peter 4:10).

If a child were to be born with an arm and an eye in
each other's spot, and if it were so for a leg and the nose
and as well for an ear and the mouth, you know well that it
would not survive long after birth. If the body of Christ
were born in that manner, the Gospel would not have
reached us. Today's Church is losing its identity and is dying because too many of its members do not use their God-
given gifts and pretend to work with gifts they do not have,
being motivated only by worldly pursuits: glamour, fame,
and filthy lucre. They want to try their hand at all the gifts.
We should stop this foolishness before it is too late. Paul,
explaining how Church members should behave concerning
their unique calling, said, "So we, though many, are one
body in Christ, and individually members one of another.
Having gifts that differ according to the grace given to us,
let us use them: if prophecy, in proportion to our faith; if
service, in our serving; the one who teaches, in his teaching; the one who exhorts, in his exhortation; the one who

contributes, in generosity; the one who leads, with zeal; the one who does acts of mercy, with cheerfulness" (Romans 12:5-8).

SHOULD WE BE PARTAKERS OF EVIL SCHEMES?

Do not support those who are liars, using the name of the Lord in vain, saying He has spoken to them when they quote Him from the Old Testament or have plagiarized. Do not support those who are idolaters, making use of numerology, asking offerings of a certain amount, according to their church address or biblical numbers or any other, which non-believers call "lucky numbers." At telethons it is common to hear requests for different amounts to be sent as offerings, from participating preachers purporting they are from God, unless they mean from various gods, because if they were from the Holy Spirit, it would be one message, one amount. Being caught up in the marketing process, they get into the habit of using the name of God in vain, hoping that if they are raising money for His work, He might sweep those lies under the rug. Our God, who said to Job, "Where were you when I laid the foundation of the earth? Tell me, if you have understanding" (Job 38:4), uses numbers to allow us to connect different events and understand them, and to encode messages to be revealed; those who are attributing any spiritual quality to them are committing idolatry, just like those who believe in numerology. The apostle Paul wrote, "But now I am writing to you not to associate with anyone who bears the name of brother if he is guilty of sexual immorality or greed, or is an idolater, reviler, drunkard, or swindler—not even to eat with such a one. For what have I to do with judging outsiders? Is it not those inside the church whom you are to judge? God judges those outside. 'Purge the evil person from among you'" (1 Corinthians 5:11-13).

Do not support those who are head-hunters instead of sheep-herders, more interested in how many will occupy their seats, which does not please God, taking pride in the size of their congregation instead of leading it in wisdom and truth. Seventy thousand Israelites perished because David had them numbered. The Bible says, "So the LORD sent a pestilence on Israel, and 70,000 men of Israel fell" (1 Chronicles 21:14). They are not feeding the sheep; they are only eating their fat. From the Scriptures we read, "Thus saith the Lord GOD; Behold, I am against the shepherds; and I will require my flock at their hand, and cause them to cease from feeding the flock; neither shall the shepherds feed themselves any more; for I will deliver my flock from their mouth, that they may not be meat for them" (Ezekiel

34:10 KJV).

Remember that no servant is greater than his master and whatever gift we have received, we haven't done anything to deserve it. *God uses gifts for His sake and will keep performing miracles through us for the sake of those who are receiving His Gospel,* regardless how badly we behave, until He decides on either our reward or our demise. "For the gifts and the calling of God are irrevocable" (Romans 11:29).

Those who persist in those lies, surely God will come against them. Jesus is clear about the reception they deserve: "On that day many will say to me, 'Lord, Lord, did we not prophesy in your name, and cast out demons in your name, and do many mighty works in your name?' And then will I declare to them, 'I never knew you; depart from me, you workers of lawlessness' " (Matthew 7:22-23). And to many He might say, "You were good fundraisers, but I never knew you liars! You have worked to satisfy your ego, and polish your image, not for my glory."

WHO IS THE END-TIME JEZEBEL?

Jezebel—teacher of idolatry and false practices—is like a lamb and speaks like a dragon and is causing many to practice idolatry, which I have been warning against as the Lord put it in my heart; she is motivated by greed and power and she is seducing many. Because of her popularity, a great number of the faithful are being misled. Her repentance is never genuine. Warning! Do not sit at her table. Paul to the faithful of Colossae wrote, "You cannot drink the cup of the Lord and the cup of demons. You cannot partake of the table of the Lord and the table of demons" (1 Corinthians 10:21).

John, reporting what the Spirit says to the Church, the one who has eyes like a flame of fire and whose feet are like burnished bronze, wrote, "But I have this against you, that you tolerate that woman Jezebel, who calls herself a prophetess and is teaching and seducing my servants to practice sexual immorality and to eat food sacrificed to idols" (Revelation 2:20).

Because of these misleading practices that are neither of our Lord Jesus Christ's teachings nor of the Holy Spirit, but are of Satan, churches are full of liars, idolaters, fornicators, adulterers, and criminals who are making the headlines more often than ever before. Few are preaching against those things; instead many are getting entangled in them. These are just Satan's schemes to take many to perdition. The Bible says, "Now the Spirit expressly says that in later times some will depart from the faith by devoting themselves to deceitful spirits and teachings of demons" (1

Timothy 4:1).

IS IDOLATRY IN THE CHURCH NEVER TO GO AWAY?

Idolatry is the great chasm that separates us from God; consequently, how many might lose their souls because of it? Depart from those who are idolaters lest you are among them when destruction comes their way. The Vatican preaches the worship of the dead and their image, especially Mary, the mother of Jesus. They deify her as a "Queen of Heaven," called also "Lady of Fatima," whom the late pontiff credited with saving his life when he was shot. He placed the bullet that struck him on top of one of the statues erected to honor her in Fatima, Portugal. According to the Vatican's Catechism, Jesus was Mary's only begotten son and she was free of all stain of original sin. She was taken up body and soul into heaven, and was exalted by the Lord as Queen over all things. In his apostolic letter titled "Rosarium Virginis Mariae," Pope John Paul II wrote how he would prostrate himself in spirit before the image of Mary. He was often photographed praying fervently before an artistic work made either of wood, clay, or plastic, shaped to resemble a woman. God commanded the people of Israel saying, "You shall not make for yourself a carved image, or any likeness of anything that is in heaven above, or that is in the earth beneath, or that is in the water under the earth. You shall not bow down to them or serve them, for I the LORD your God am a jealous God, visiting the iniquity of the fathers on the children to the third and the fourth generation of those who hate me" (Exodus 20:4-5).

Where is the wisdom of those who are bowing and praying to statues and images not to understand that these are lifeless and are made of the same clay or plastic used to make the utensils in their kitchen, of the same wood they burn in their chimney, of the same stones they build it with? Of them God said, "No one considers, nor is there knowledge or discernment to say, 'Half of it I burned in the fire; I also baked bread on its coals; I roasted meat and have eaten. And shall I make the rest of it an abomination? Shall I fall down before a block of wood?' " (Isaiah 44:19). He again spoke to declare, "Woe to him who says to a wooden thing, Awake; to a silent stone, Arise! Can this teach? Behold, it is overlaid with gold and silver, and there is no breath at all in it" (Habakkuk 2:19).

They roll the beads of the rosary between their fingers, reciting a prayer over and over to Mary, who cannot hear them since she is dead. Why are they persisting in this false practice and teaching? Jesus is clear about whom we must pray to: "But when you pray, go into your room and shut the door and pray to your Father who is in secret. And your Father who sees in secret will reward you. 'And when you pray, do not heap up empty phrases as the Gentiles do, for they think that they will be heard for their many words. Do not be like them, for your Father knows what you need before you ask him' " (Matthew 6:6-8). He further said, "If you then, who are evil, know how to give good gifts to your children, how much more will your Father who is in heaven give good things to those who ask him!" (Matthew 7:11).

And since His Father and He are one, He emphasized, saying, "So also you have sorrow now, but I will see you again and your hearts will rejoice, and no one will take your joy from you. In that day you will ask nothing of me. Truly, truly, I say to you, whatever you ask of the Father in my name, he will give it to you" (John 16:22-23).

They are kindling God's anger with their preaching of idol worship. He warned ancient Babylon saying, "Declare among the nations and proclaim, set up a banner and proclaim, conceal it not, and say: 'Babylon is taken, Bel is put to shame, Merodach is dismayed. Her images are put to shame, her idols are dismayed' " (Jeremiah 50:2).

They have canonized and are worshipping the same entities adored by voodoo or Santeria priests and other Satanists under the same names and many others. They pray to

the dead and offer libations in which God takes no pleasure. Paul referring to Jesus declared, "Consequently, when
Christ came into the world, he said, 'Sacrifices and offerings you have not desired, but a body have you prepared for
me; in burnt offerings and sin offerings you have taken no
pleasure' " (Hebrews 10:5-6).

IS MARY THE MOTHER OF JESUS A QUEEN IN HEAVEN?

Mary's "ascension to heaven" dogma established by Pope
Pius XII and perpetuated by his successors, and her title
"Queen of Heaven," purportedly given by Jesus, is pure
fabrication. We can read the whole New Testament, and we
will not find any account that Jesus gave his mother this
title. After the death, resurrection, and ascension of Jesus
into Heaven, Mary did not travel with the disciples; however, they were welcomed at the house that the apostle John
shared with her. No further information exists of her last
days and death. The only Queen of Heaven mentioned in
the Bible is a Persian and Assyrian deity worshipped by
apostate Israelites of whom God said, "Do you not see what
they are doing in the cities of Judah and in the streets of
Jerusalem? The children gather wood, the fathers kindle
fire, and the women knead dough, to make cakes for the

queen of heaven. And they pour out drink offerings to other gods, to provoke me to anger" (Jeremiah 7:17-18).

In heaven the angels are called sons of God, as He referred to them when He spoke to Job. "Where were you when I laid the foundation of the earth? Tell me, if you have understanding. Who determined its measurements— surely you know! Or who stretched the line upon it? On what were its bases sunk, or who laid its cornerstone, when the morning stars sang together *and all the sons of God shouted for joy?*" (Job 38:4-7).

It is obvious that there is no woman in heaven and there will not be any. We all, male and female, will be like angels, proof that there is no queen in heaven and that there never will be one. A crown is reserved in the kingdom of God for those who remain faithful to Him, and if Mary did so, she also was entitled to hers as the King of Kings announced it to John: "I am coming soon. Hold fast what you have, so that no one may seize your crown" (Revelation 3:11).

There have been many reports of statues of Mary shedding tears or changing posture. We must regard these as the work of Satan, the devil, whom God has given the power to deceive even the faithful before the Lord's coming. God will allow Satan to share the power He gave him with a man, an "antichrist," called "the beast," "the man of sin," "the son of perdition," or "the man of lawlessness." Satan will also share his power with this man's spokesperson, a false prophet who will perform signs and wonders, as John put it: "It performs great signs, even making fire come down from heaven to earth in front of people, and by the signs that it is allowed to work in the presence of the beast it deceives those who dwell on earth, telling them to make an image for the beast that was wounded by the sword and yet lived. And it was allowed to give breath to the image of the beast, so that the image of the beast might even speak and might cause those who would not worship the image of the beast to be slain" (Revelation 13:13-15).

Jesus established clearly that even though Mary was chosen to be His earthly mother, she was a servant like anyone else and was to do the will of God to be acknowledged by Him. "And a crowd was sitting around him, and they said to him, 'Your mother and your brothers are outside, seeking you.' And he answered them, 'Who are my mother and my brothers?' And looking about at those who sat around him, he said, 'Here are my mother and my brothers! Whoever does the will of God, he is my brother and sister and mother' " (Mark 3:32-35).

After He had cast out a demon that had caused a man to be mute, allowing him to speak, a woman who was in the crowd blessed the woman who gave birth to Him, but He rebuked her. The Bible says, "As he said these things, a woman in the crowd raised her voice and said to him, 'Blessed is the womb that bore you, and the breasts at which you nursed!' But he said, 'Blessed rather are those who hear the word of God and keep it!' " (Luke 11:27-28).

Mary had several other children. When Jesus went to his hometown synagogue, his old neighbors felt offended that this man who was the little boy next door was claiming that He was the one referred to in the Scriptures as being the promised Messiah, and they said, "Is not this the carpenter's son? Is not his mother called Mary? And are not his brothers James and Joseph and Simon and Judas? And are not all his sisters with us? Where then did this man get all these things?" (Matthew 13:55-56).

On the cross, "When Jesus saw his mother and the disciple whom he loved standing nearby, he said to his mother, 'Woman, behold, your son!' Then he said to the disciple, 'Behold, your mother!' And from that hour the disciple took her to his own home" (John 19:26-27). Jesus was expressing his concern for the physical well being of Mary, who was then a middle-aged widow and John the youngest of his disciples, but was not making her the mother of all humanity as the Catholic Church claims.

Whoever accepts those false teachings and are found guilty of idolatry, bowing and praying to statues and to the dead, will not enter into the Kingdom of God. They will be thrown in the lake of fire where they will join Satan, his angels, the beast, and his false prophet, and where they will remain for eternity. The apostle Paul in a letter to the Galatians wrote, "Idolatry, sorcery, enmity, strife, jealousy, fits of anger, rivalries, dissensions, divisions, envy, drunkenness, orgies, and things like these. I warn you, as I warned you before, that those who do such things will not inherit the kingdom of God" (Galatians 5:20-21).

A magnitude 8.0 quake followed by strong after-shocks hit the hardest Ica and Pisco, two cities of Peru's southern desert at 6:40 p.m. on Wednesday, August 15, 2007. Churches there and in other cities were destroyed, resulting in the deaths of many parishioners while they were celebrating the Virgin Mary's rise into heaven.

The apostle John reporting his visions of those thrown in the lake of fire wrote, "And the beast was captured, and with it the false prophet who in its presence had done the signs by which he deceived those who had received the mark of the beast and those who worshiped its image. These two were thrown alive into the lake of fire that burns with sulfur" (Revelation 19:20). He further described the fate of Satan, the deceiver of the world, "And the devil who had deceived them was thrown into the lake of fire and sulfur where the beast and the false prophet were, and they will be tormented day and night forever and ever" (Revelation 20:10), as well as the destruction of the angel of death, of his abode, and of those who did not accept Christ as their personal Savior and never repented of their sins. "Then Death and Hades were thrown into the lake of fire. This is the second death, the lake of fire. And if anyone's name was not found written in the book of life, he was thrown into the lake of fire" (Revelation 20:14-15).

Many, after reading John's account, "And a great sign appeared in heaven: A woman clothed with the sun, with the moon under her feet, and on her head a crown of twelve stars" (Revelation 12:1), in error refer to Mary as being that woman in his vision, but when we read the whole chapter we understand that she symbolizes Israel instead, as confirmed by the following verse: "But the earth came to the help of the woman, and the earth opened its mouth and swallowed the river that the dragon had poured from his mouth" (Revelation 12:16), which is a prophesy of how a remnant of Israel (the woman) will be saved through a valley created by a great earthquake when Jesus sets foot on Mount of Olives, consequently destroying a great number of troops from the beast's army (the river), which will come against them.

For a period of three years and a half or 1,260 days, Jerusalem will be under siege by the beast's army that will finally conquer part of it. John, after his encounter with a mighty angel and after the Seven Thunders (the voices of the Seven Spirits of God) had spoken, reported what the angel told him, and he wrote, "Then I was given a measuring rod like a staff, and I was told, 'Rise and measure the temple of God and the altar and those who worship there, but do not measure the court outside the temple; leave that out, for it is given over to the nations, and they will trample the holy city for forty-two months' " (Revelation 11:1-2).

God will rescue a remnant of Israel, and they will flee to a secure place as described here, and for three years and a half, God will provide for their needs. The Bible says, "But the woman was given the two wings of the great eagle so that she might fly from the serpent into the wilderness, to the place where she is to be nourished for a time, and times, and half a time" (Revelation 12:14).

They will escape from their enemies as prophesied here by the prophet Zechariah, the son of Berechiah, son of Iddo. "For I will gather all the nations against Jerusalem to battle, and the city shall be taken and the houses plundered and the women raped. Half of the city shall go out into exile, but the rest of the people shall not be cut off from the city. Then the LORD will go out and fight against those nations as when he fights on a day of battle. On that day his feet shall stand on the Mount of Olives that lies before Jerusalem on the east, and the Mount of Olives shall be split in two from east to west by a very wide valley, so that one half of the Mount shall move northward, and the other half southward. And you shall flee to the valley of my mountains, for the valley of the mountains shall reach to Azal. And you shall flee as you fled from the earthquake in the days of Uzziah king of Judah. Then the LORD my God will come, and all the holy ones with him" (Zechariah 14:2-5).

SHOULD CROSSES BE OBJECTS OF WORSHIP?

At the cross, as our Passover lamb, Jesus Christ willingly gave His life to redeem us: "Just as the Father knows me and I know the Father; and I lay down my life for the sheep. And I have other sheep that are not of this fold. I must bring them also, and they will listen to my voice. So there will be one flock, one shepherd. For this reason the Father loves me, because I lay down my life that I may take it up again" (John 10:15-17). But crosses have become objects of worship instead of being for all an instrument of torture, used to cause His slow and agonizing death that lasted six hours from the third till the ninth hour when He died. One of His apostles described it this way: "Now it was the third hour, and they crucified Him. And there was the inscription of His charge having been inscribed: THE KING OF THE JEWS. And together with Him they crucified two bandits, one on His right side and the one on His left. So the Scripture was fulfilled which says, 'And He was numbered with the transgressors.' And those passing by were blaspheming Him, shaking their heads and saying, 'Aha! You who destroy the temple and build it in three days, save Yourself, and come down from the cross!' Likewise the chief priests also, mocking Him to each other with the scribes said, 'He saved others; Himself He is not able to save. Let the Christ, the King of Israel, come down now from the cross, so that we may see and believe Him.' Even those who were crucified with Him were reviling Him. Now when the sixth hour had come, darkness came upon the whole land until the ninth hour. And at the ninth hour Jesus cried out with a loud voice, saying, 'Eloi, Eloi, lima sabachthani?' which is translated, 'My God, My God, why have You forsaken Me?' Some of those standing by when they heard, said, 'Look, He is calling Elijah.' And one, running and having filled a sponge with vinegar, and having put it around a reed, was giving a drink to Him, saying, 'Leave Him alone; let us see if Elijah is coming to take Him down.' And Jesus, uttering a loud cry, expired" (Mark 15:25-37 EMTV).

Some even speak wrongly of the front and the back of the cross as the sources of salvation and healing, giving credit to the tree where He was nailed and shed his precious blood to the last drop for our redemption. Paul in a letter to the Ephesians wrote, "In him we have redemption through his blood, the forgiveness of our trespasses, according to the riches of his grace" (Ephesians 1:7).

According to the following verse, we know the truth is that the back of the cross has nothing to do with our healing: "But he was wounded for our transgressions; he was crushed for our iniquities; upon him was the chastisement that brought us peace, and with his stripes we are healed" (Isaiah 53:5). It is misleading to speak of the front and back of the cross instead of our Savior's agony and blood shed at the cross. Those who did would argue that they spoke figuratively.

When the Israelites were in the desert, they were dying from the bite of serpents because they had sinned. "And the LORD said to Moses, 'Make a fiery serpent and set it on a pole, and everyone who is bitten, when he sees it, shall live.' So Moses made a bronze serpent and set it on a pole. And if a serpent bit anyone, he would look at the bronze serpent and live" (Numbers 21:8-9). This event was to foreshadow Christ Jesus nailed on a tree, the cross, and it is clear that their healing came from looking at the serpent that symbolized Jesus made sin and not at the pole that symbolized the cross. Who would embrace, kiss, and worship a tree where a loved one was hanged by evil men? Twice Jesus asked us to take our cross before He was crucified, saying, "And whoever does not take his cross and follow me is not worthy of me" (Matthew 10:38). He spoke figuratively to refer to the plight of those condemned to crucifixion and had to carry the cross they would be nailed upon, meaning that we must accept the burden He would lay on our shoulders.

Whenever his apostles made mention of the cross, it was either to tell the story of His death on the cross or to refer to the meaning of His suffering and His blood shed at the cross where He set us free, canceling our debt. The cross must be only a reminder of His six-hour agony and the horrific death He accepted for our salvation.

CAN MAN WORSHIP THE HOLY ANGELS?

Beware of those who are practicing the worship of angels. The apostle John quoted one of the seven angels who had the seven bowls after he was shown the Holy City, New Jerusalem, coming down from heaven, "And he said to me, 'These words are trustworthy and true. And the Lord, the

God of the spirits of the prophets, has sent his angel to show his servants what must soon take place.' 'And behold, I am coming soon. Blessed is the one who keeps the words of the prophecy of this book.' I, John, am the one who heard and saw these things. And when I heard and saw them, I fell down to worship at the feet of the angel who showed them to me, but he said to me, 'You must not do that! I am a fellow servant with you and your brothers the prophets, and with those who keep the words of this book. Worship God' " (Revelation 22:6-9).

Jesus is the only intermediary between God and us. Speaking to Simon Peter, Jesus said, "I am the way, and the truth, and the life. No one comes to the Father except through me" (John 14:6).

Jesus never mentioned at any moment that we ought to question angels. To the contrary, when we have need of anything, we must pray to His Father or to Him. He said, "If you ask me anything in my name, I will do it" (John 14:14), and later declared, "In that day you will ask nothing of me. Truly, truly, I say to you, whatever you ask of the Father in my name, he will give it to you" (John 16:23).

He even told the disciples of the only helper and teacher God will give them after He is gone: "But the Helper, the Holy Spirit, whom the Father will send in my name, he will teach you all things and bring to your remembrance all that

I have said to you" (John 14:26).

Some, trying to retell the story of creation and write their own version of the true Bible by mixing some truth from it with their own concepts, have spoken to fallen angels, Satan and his demons, believing that they have spoken to the holy angels, who would never disobey God to respond to their enquiries. God forbids such actions. From the Scriptures we read, "When you come into the land that the LORD your God is giving you, you shall not learn to follow the abominable practices of those nations. There shall not be found among you anyone who burns his son or his daughter as an offering, anyone who practices divination or tells fortunes or interprets omens, or a sorcerer or a charmer or a medium or a wizard or a necromancer, for whoever does these things is an abomination to the LORD. And because of these abominations the LORD your God is driving them out before you" (Deuteronomy 18:9-12).

The assertion that the Great Pyramid is a memorial to God is purely false, since man did not have then the vast knowledge of astronomy and stellar phenomena incorporated in its design and construction, which were only the purview of the fallen angels who where on earth and had taken the daughters of man for wife as mentioned in this biblical passage: "There were giants in the earth in those days; and also after that, when the sons of God came in unto the daughters of men, and they bare children to them, the same became mighty men which were of old, men of renown" (Genesis 6:4 KJV).

The word of God came to Ezekiel the priest and son of Buzi concerning the city of Tyre, which could be Plato's lost city of Atlantis off the coast of Crete in the Mediterranean Sea and whose fate He described, saying, "But now Tyre is in ruins, and the people on the coast stare at it in horror and tremble in fear. I, the LORD God, will turn you into a ghost-town. The ocean depths will rise over you and carry you down to the world of the dead, where you will join people of ancient times and towns ruined long ago. You will stay there and never again be a city filled with people. You will die a horrible death! People will come looking for your city, but it will never be found. I, the LORD, have spoken" (Ezekiel 26:18-21 CEV).

A powerful volcanic eruption destroyed the city, and the Lord has given a clue to such an end in the following passage: "Everything on board was lost—your valuable cargo, your sailors and carpenters, merchants and soldiers. The shouts of your drowning crew were heard on the shore. Every ship is deserted; rowers and sailors and captains all stand on shore, mourning for you. They show their sorrow by putting dust on their heads and rolling in ashes" (Ezekiel 27:27-30 CEV).

Archeologists have also found in Knossos, Crete, vestiges of multi-story palaces and mansions with sophisticated piping and drainage systems, as well as bathrooms with amenities similar to those found in today's homes, which attest of a people with knowledge way ahead of their time; this we can attribute to fallen angels since their king was one of them. And the Lord's word came again to the prophet concerning a fallen angel who became a prince of the city of Tyre and whose palace was built on the island about which the Lord had proclaimed a dreadful end. "The word of the LORD came to me: 'Son of man, say to the prince of Tyre, Thus says the Lord GOD: "Because your heart is proud, and you have said, 'I am a god, I sit in the seat of the gods, in the heart of the seas,' yet you are but a man, and no god, though you make your heart like the heart of a god—you are indeed wiser than Daniel; no secret is hidden from you; by your wisdom and your understanding you have made wealth for yourself, and have gathered gold and silver into your treasuries; by your great wisdom in your trade you have increased your wealth, and your heart has become proud in your wealth—therefore thus says the Lord GOD: Because you make your heart like the heart of a god, therefore, behold, I will bring foreigners upon you, the most ruthless of the nations; and they shall draw their swords against the beauty of your wisdom and defile your splendor. They shall thrust you down into the pit, and you shall die the death of the slain in the heart of the seas. Will you still say, 'I am a god,' in the presence of those who kill you, though you are but a man, and no god, in the hands of those who slay you? You shall die the death of the uncircumcised by the hand of foreigners; for I have spoken, declares the Lord GOD." (Ezekiel 28:1-10)

The fate of the Prince of Tyre was no different than that awaiting Lucifer, the ancient leader of all the angels who also became blinded by his pride and thought that he could be like God and was thrown out of heaven. He will soon look to be worshiped through a man called the Son of Perdition, whom he will give his power and authority. But his demise will be swift. According to Isaiah's prophecy, "Sheol beneath is stirred up to meet you when you come; it rouses the shades to greet you, all who were leaders of the earth; it raises from their thrones all who were kings of the nations. All of them will answer and say to you: 'You too have become as weak as we! You have become like us!' Your pomp is brought down to Sheol, the sound of your harps; maggots are laid as a bed beneath you, and worms are your covers. "How you are fallen from heaven, O Day Star, son of Dawn! How you are cut down to the ground, you who laid the nations low! You said in your heart, 'I will ascend to heaven; above the stars of God I will set my throne on high; I will sit on the mount of assembly in the far reaches of the north; I will ascend above the heights of the clouds; I will make myself like the Most High.' But you are brought down to Sheol, to the far reaches of the pit. Those who see you will stare at you and ponder over you: 'Is this the man who made the earth tremble, who shook kingdoms, who made the world like a desert and overthrew its cities, who did not let his prisoners go home?' " (Isaiah 14:9-17).

Spontaneous combustion was the sentence God pronounced concerning the King of Tyre, a cherub who had lost his holy position as the principal guardian of the Garden of Eden and probably had corrupted by his actions other angels who became princes under his command, in the management of his earthly kingdom after they were thrown out of the garden and were condemned to become mere mortals. The Lord spoke to Ezekiel and said, "Son of man, raise a lamentation over the king of Tyre, and say to him, Thus says the Lord GOD: 'You were the signet of perfection, full of wisdom and perfect in beauty. You were in Eden, the garden of God; every precious stone was your covering, sardius, topaz, and diamond, beryl, onyx, and jasper, sapphire, emerald, and carbuncle; and crafted in gold were your settings and your engravings. On the day that you were created they were prepared. You were an anointed guardian cherub. I placed you; you were on the holy mountain of God; in the midst of the stones of fire you walked. You were blameless in your ways from the day you were created, till unrighteousness was found in you. In the abundance of your trade you were filled with violence in your midst, and you sinned; so I cast you as a profane thing from the mountain of God, and I destroyed you, O guardian cherub, from the midst of the stones of fire. Your heart was proud because of your beauty; you corrupted your wisdom for the sake of your splendor. I cast you to the ground; I exposed you before kings, to feast their eyes on you. By the multitude of your iniquities, in the unrighteousness of your trade you profaned your sanctuaries; so I brought fire out from your midst; it consumed you, and I turned you to ashes on the earth in the sight of all who saw you. All who know you among the peoples are appalled at you; you have come to a dreadful end and shall be no more forever' " (Ezekiel 28:12-19).

To assert, as some did, that we are all the fallen angels waiting to return to our previous glorious state is not a biblical truth, even though Jesus said that those who believe in Him and are saved will be like angels. To Sadducees who asked which of seven brothers who would marry the same woman would have her for wife in the resurrection, Jesus responded, "For in the resurrection they neither marry nor are given in marriage, but are like angels in heaven. (Matthew 22:30).

Isn't it true that in the Scriptures there is an account of the sons of God who took the daughters of man for wives as mentioned above? "When man began to multiply on the face of the land and daughters were born to them, the sons of God saw that the daughters of man were attractive. And they took as their wives any they chose" (Genesis 6:1-2).

But those angels were also punished and thrown in the bottomless pit for their actions because it was forbidden of them to interact in such manners with the human race. In his letter to fellow Christians, Jude wrote, "And the angels who did not stay within their own position of authority, but left their proper dwelling, he has kept in eternal chains under gloomy darkness until the judgment of the great day" (Jude 1:6).

The angels who were thrown out of the Kingdom of Heaven because of rebellion were allowed to inhabit the galaxies away from the face of God and were not allowed to return there. But some of them were punished and sent to Hell for coming to inhabit planet Earth and start a superhuman race. Only Satan was permitted to petition on their behalf and for himself. From the Scriptures we read, "Now there was a day when the sons of God came to present themselves before the LORD, and Satan also came among them" (Job 1:6).

They are today's fallen angels, also called demons, some of those whose evil spirit Jesus cast out of many men and women as a token that we are definitely not them, as these lost souls, willing to create a new theology, would want us to believe. The aberrant assertion that we are those fallen angels is pure fantasy, a product of their wild imagination. Luke, an eyewitness of Jesus' casting thousands of demons out of a man, reported the event and wrote, "When Jesus had stepped out on land, there met him a man from the city who had demons. For a long time he had worn no clothes, and he had not lived in a house but among the tombs. When he saw Jesus, he cried out and fell down before him and said with a loud voice, 'What have you to do with me, Jesus, Son of the Most High God? I beg you, do not torment me.' For he had commanded the unclean spirit to come out of the man. (For many a time it had seized him. He was kept under guard and bound with chains and shackles, but he would break the bonds and be driven by the demon into the desert.) Jesus then asked him, 'What is your name?' And he said, 'Legion,' for many demons had entered him. And they begged him not to command them to depart into the abyss. Now a large herd of pigs was feeding there on the hillside, and they begged him to let them enter these. So he gave them permission" (Luke 8:27-32).

The Lord warned us of such deception; Paul to his friend Timothy wrote, "Now the Spirit expressly says that in later times some will depart from the faith by devoting themselves to deceitful spirits and teachings of demons, through the insincerity of liars whose consciences are seared" (1 Timothy 4:1-2) .

The perfect and pure form of God's authority is conic in essence and his Glory floats at the very tip, where He allows only His son, the visible I AM, the Alpha and the Omega, to sit on His throne in Heaven and to permeate everything flawlessly and evenly downward. The first time He came to me He showed me the tip of a conic mountain, which symbolizes kingship.

Consequently, the Great Pyramid of Egypt is neither a memorial to God nor built by Enoch with the help of the holy angels, as those promoting a new cult are purporting it to be, but was built with Satan's help and the fallen angels he commanded, to establish the headquarters of his own religion in Egypt, which represents imperfection and original sin as opposed to the Holiness of God and his redemptive power. They have gone all over the planet as far as the deep forests of Mexico, Guatemala, and Belize to build other pyramids and to teach to the Maya the rituals of worshiping them. Neither the Egyptians nor the Indians knew the God of Abraham but delved in animism and the worship of fallen angels who came to them during those days.

The angels, also called sons of God, were all created holy, one by one, to enjoy God's kingdom in heaven.

One day Lucifer, an archangel, who is Satan, the prince of demons, also called Leviathan the twisting serpent, decided to campaign against God and war broke in heaven after he had convinced one third of the angels to side and be doomed with him. The holy angels won and drove them out of the kingdom of God, and they were allowed to occupy the galaxies where they have developed sophisticated flying machines with technologies surpassing ours. They invade our airspace via galactic portals. UFOs are seen by many all over the world.

Long before He had created them, God knew of their rebellion and had a plan to replenish heaven. He is about to replace his lost sons by the dust of stones (mud) through procreation started by the first man and woman. The Bible says, "And some of the Pharisees in the crowd said to him, 'Teacher, rebuke your disciples.' He answered, 'I tell you, if these were silent, the very stones would cry out' " (Luke 19:39-40).

The mud that He had formed and that He called, Adam, passed down his mud characteristics to his progeny developed in the womb of Eve the first woman formed from his bones' DNA.

Jesus, by His shed blood, at the cross, bought the right to transform man made of dirt into Sons of God. To some Sadducees who did not believe in the resurrection of the dead, Jesus explained, "But those who are considered worthy to attain to that age and to the resurrection from the dead neither marry nor are given in marriage, for they cannot die anymore, because they are equal to angels and are sons of God, being sons of the resurrection" (Luke 20:35-36).

May the Word of our faithful and just God sink deep into our heart and mind, lest these aberrant assertions destroy our faith. Many are coming with words of deceit, creating new concepts of God. They talk of a connected and higher consciousness as though we were all together creation and creator, notwithstanding the omnipotent, omniscient, and omnipresent God of Abraham. They mix some pseudo-scientific knowledge with animism and use some biblical passages as a sweet topping on a bad cake recipe to allow its deglutition. They usually promote their literary materials mainly via syndicated nightly radio shows and are only after financial gains and fame. Reject any alteration of biblical terminologies by the addition of scientific terms, which is the work of the devil.

Let us sing Moses' song that he spoke in the ears of the people of Israel, saying, "Give ear, O heavens, and I will speak, and let the earth hear the words of my mouth. May my teaching drop as the rain, my speech distill as the dew, like gentle rain upon the tender grass, and like showers upon the herb. For I will proclaim the name of the LORD; ascribe greatness to our God! 'The Rock, his work is perfect, for all his ways are justice. A God of faithfulness and without iniquity, just and upright is he'" (Deuteronomy 32:1-4).

ARE WE SAVED BY GOOD DEEDS OR GOD'S MERCY?

We are all sinners, but God loves us and has compassion on us no matter the sins we have committed. The Bible says, "For whoever keeps the whole law but fails in one point has become accountable for all of it" (James 2:10).

We still can receive His forgiveness and be saved if we ask for it and repent, recognizing that we were redeemed for a price: The shed blood of His son, Jesus, who was nailed to the cross. Jesus speaking to a crowd of followers who wanted to know if a group of people who became victims of a certain accident where paying for their sins explained, "Or those eighteen on whom the tower in Siloam fell and killed them: do you think that they were worse offenders than all the others who lived in Jerusalem? No, I

tell you; but unless you repent, you will all likewise perish"
(Luke 13:4-5).

By our good deeds can we repay God who has created
everything and to whom everything belongs? To the faithful Paul wrote, "God doesn't accept people simply because
they obey the Law. No, indeed! All the Law does is to point
out our sin. Now we see how God does make us acceptable
to him. The Law and the Prophets tell how we become acceptable, and it isn't by obeying the Law of Moses. God
treats everyone alike. He accepts people only because they
have faith in Jesus Christ. All of us have sinned and fallen
short of God's glory" (Romans 3:20-23 CEV).

Then how does His righteousness become manifest?
From Paul's epistles we read, "There is therefore now no
condemnation for those who are in Christ Jesus. For the
law of the Spirit of life has set you free in Christ Jesus from
the law of sin and death. For God has done what the law,
weakened by the flesh, could not do. By sending his own
Son in the likeness of sinful flesh and for sin, he condemned sin in the flesh, in order that the righteous require-
ment of the law might be fulfilled in us, who walk not according to the flesh but according to the Spirit" (Romans
8:1-4).

He further explained, "For God has consigned all to
disobedience, that he may have mercy on all. Oh, the depth

of the riches and wisdom and knowledge of God! How unsearchable are his judgments and how inscrutable his ways! 'For who has known the mind of the Lord, or who has been his counselor?' 'Or who has given a gift to him that he might be repaid?' For from him and through him and to him are all things. To him be glory forever. Amen' " (Romans 11:32-36).

Repentance is a personal act, and the Church, our pastor, our parents, our siblings, and our friends cannot do it for us. It is the firm resolution not to ever commit the same sin again. Jesus had healed a man, and "Afterward Jesus found him in the temple and said to him, 'See, you are well! Sin no more, that nothing worse may happen to you' " (John 5:14).

But those who repent will be saved if by faith they accept Jesus as their personal Savior. Paul explained how one can acquire faith; he wrote to the Romans, "So then faith comes by hearing, and hearing by the word of God" (Romans 10:17 EMTV).

Faith is essential in our relationship with God. The Bible says, "And without faith it is impossible to please him, for whoever would draw near to God must believe that he exists and that he rewards those who seek him" (Hebrews 11:6). But what is it without works? James the brother of John exhorting the Jews scattered abroad warned them,

"Do you want to be shown, you foolish person, that faith apart from works is useless? Was not Abraham our father justified by works when he offered up his son Isaac on the altar? You see that faith was active along with his works, and faith was completed by his works; and the Scripture was fulfilled that says, 'Abraham believed God, and it was counted to him as righteousness'—and he was called a friend of God. You see that a person is justified by works and not by faith alone. And in the same way was not also Rahab the prostitute justified by works when she received the messengers and sent them out by another way? For as the body apart from the spirit is dead, so also faith apart from works is dead" (James 2:20-26).

IS GOING TO CHURCH THE FIRST STEP TO SALVATION?

Some establish a clear path to heaven, starting with church attendance as the first step, and finishing with the Bible as the last. Shouldn't it be the other way around? First we start with the word of God that we hear, either in church, from the mouth of an evangelist, a friend, a family member, or that we read ourselves. Second, after we understand the concept of salvation, as the Bible says, "In him we have redemption through his blood, the forgiveness of our trespasses, according to the riches of his grace" (Ephesians 1:7), we accept Jesus Christ as our personal Savior and repent, asking for forgiveness, the Bible says, "Then he opened their minds to understand the Scriptures, and said to them, 'Thus it is written, that the Christ should suffer and on the third day rise from the dead, and that repentance and forgiveness of sins should be proclaimed in his name to all nations, beginning from Jerusalem' " (Luke 24:45-47).

Third, after we have accepted the free gift of salvation and have repented with the firm decision that we will not let sins cause us to go to hell (a burning and nightmarish place where demons and remorse will torment us day in, day out) and then to the Lake of Fire (where we will be seared and charred in an eternal fire, along with hideous demons, with no chance of parole), *we make up our mind to* stop seeing the friends we do those bad things with, promising that we will tell them that we will no more do drugs, get drunk, or steal. We will tell our lovers that we said no to fornication between the same gender and no to sex outside of marriage because we have said no to pleasing anyone willing to drag us into the horror of hell and the eternal fire. Fourth, we surround ourselves with people who have made the same choice, whom we can learn from, whom we can pray and worship with, *whether it is at church, at the park, or in a home.* Jesus said, "For where two or three are gathered in my name, there am I among them" (Matthew 18:20).

We then receive water baptism and afterward, because we understand that it is to get rid of our old nature, we draw a line to remind us to never return to our past mistakes.

Then, we take communion, which means we come together, as a couple, as a small or large group to partake of the bread and of the wine in remembrance of the Lord's sacrifice at the cross, as often as possible, even daily, and as He commanded before He laid down His life for our salvation. The Bible says, "Now as they were eating, Jesus took bread, and after blessing it broke it and gave it to the disciples, and said, 'Take, eat; this is my body.' And he took a cup, and when he had given thanks he gave it to them, saying, 'Drink of it, all of you, for this is my blood of the covenant, which is poured out for many for the forgiveness of sins'" (Matthew 26:26-28). Jesus has fed a large crowd with five barley breads and two fish one day, and they expected Him to repeat the same miracle and feed them again. "So Jesus said to them, 'Truly, truly, I say to you, unless you eat the flesh of the Son of Man and drink his blood, you have no life in you. Whoever feeds on my flesh and drinks my blood has eternal life, and I will raise him up on the last day. For my flesh is true food, and my blood is true drink. Whoever feeds on my flesh and drinks my blood abides in me, and I in him. As the living Father sent me, and I live because of the Father, so whoever feeds on me, he also will live because of me. This is the bread that came down from heaven, not as the fathers ate and died. Whoever feeds on this bread will live forever' " (John 6:53-58).

And we keep reading the Word. Jesus went to Mount of Olives and went to teach in the temple where the Pharisees and the scribes had brought a woman they accused of having committed adultery. After He bent down and wrote in the dust all the sins they had committed, they left one after the other. He continued preaching to other Jews who had come to listen to Him, stressing the importance of learning from his Word, "So Jesus said to the Jews who had believed in him, 'If you abide in my word, you are truly my disciples, and you will know the truth, and the truth will set you free'" (John 8:31-32).

We invite the Holy Spirit to come and remain in our heart as our guide, our helper, and best friend. Surrounded by His apostles after He had the Passover dinner with them, Jesus was teaching them saying, "If you love me, you will keep my commandments. And I will ask the Father, and he will give you another Helper, to be with you forever, even the Spirit of truth, whom the world cannot receive, because it neither sees him nor knows him. You know him, for he dwells with you and will be in you. 'I will not leave you as orphans; I will come to you' " (John 14:15-18).

And we faithfully pay our tithes periodically. This means that we must give the ten percent of our gross income to the church we attend or to more than one ministry including our church, every time we get paid or every time we pay ourselves if we are self-employed. We must also make offerings, which are money we can give in excess of our tithes. Who commanded these, God or Church leaders? The Lord himself did. From the Scriptures we read, "You people are robbing me, your God. And, here you are, asking, " Will man rob God? Yet you are robbing me. But you say, 'How have we robbed you?' In your tithes and contributions. You are cursed with a curse, for you are robbing me, the whole nation of you. Bring the full tithes into the storehouse, that there may be food in my house. And thereby put me to the test, says the LORD of hosts, if I will not open the windows of heaven for you and pour down for you a blessing until there is no more need. I will rebuke the devourer for you, so that it will not destroy the fruits of your soil, and your vine in the field shall not fail to bear, says the LORD of hosts. Then all nations will call you blessed, for you will be a land of delight, says the LORD of hosts" (Malachi 3:8-12). Myself have experienced great losses when I did not pay my tithes; Satan was given so much power over what I was earning that right before my eyes, a one hundred dollar bill changed into a twenty, when the Lord allowed me to see how my money was always less after I would have cashed my check and verified that the bank clerk did not make any mistake.

If we are still struggling with weaknesses such as pride, anger, infidelity, lust, alcoholism, drug addiction, and others, we will confess them one to another that we may overcome them. James, a faithful servant of the Lord trying to reach scattered Jews in countries too far for him to go visit them, wrote them these encouraging words, "Therefore, confess your sins to one another and pray for one another, that you may be healed. The prayer of a righteous person has great power as it is working" (James 5:16).

John sharing with the faithful messages that the Holy Spirit had given him penned these words, "If we say we have no sin, we deceive ourselves, and the truth is not in us. If we confess our sins, he is faithful and just to forgive us our sins and to cleanse us from all unrighteousness. If we say we have not sinned, we make him a liar, and his word is not in us" (1 John 1:8-10). We must guard ourselves against disclosing someone else's sin while confessing ours to each other or to a multitude. If we mention someone else's name, or in a manner such that others would know whom we are talking about, as being co-author in a sin we are confessing, we are judging and pronouncing condemnation against this person, and our Lord will not forgive us. The Bible says, "Therefore you have no excuse, O man, every one of you who judges. For in passing judgment on another you condemn yourself, because you, the judge, practice the very same things. We know that the judgment of God rightly falls on those who do such things (Romans 2:1-2).

And last, when we commit sins, we must repent, which means that we take the firm resolution not to continue committing them after asking God for forgiveness. If sin becomes a lifestyle fixture it may cause us to die unrepentant. Jesus was addressing a crowd that was asking Him if certain people that were killed by Pilate died because of their sins. "And he answered them, 'Do you think that these Galileans were worse sinners than all the other Galileans, because they suffered in this way? No, I tell you; but unless you repent, you will all likewise perish" (Luke 13:2-3). To John who received the revelation of Jesus Christ, He declared, "Those whom I love, I reprove and discipline, so be zealous and repent" (Revelation 3:19). The Bible says, "Now after John was arrested, Jesus came into Galilee, proclaiming the gospel of God, and saying, "The time is fulfilled, and the kingdom of God is at hand; repent and believe in the gospel" (Mark 1:14-15).

DO WE NEED TO RECEIVE WATER BAPTISM?

We often hear Christians express doubt concerning water baptism. Nicodemus, a ruler of the Jews, a Pharisee who visited Jesus by night, not willing to be seen with Him during the day, asked Him how it could be possible for a man to be borne again, and "Jesus answered him, 'Truly, truly, I say to you, unless one is born again he cannot see the kingdom of God.' Nicodemus said to him, 'How can a man be born when he is old? Can he enter a second time into his mother's womb and be born?' Jesus answered, 'Truly, truly, I say to you, unless one is born of water and the Spirit, he cannot enter the kingdom of God' " (John 3:3-5). After Jesus has resurrected He commanded his eleven disciples: "Go therefore and make disciples of all nations, baptizing them in the name of the Father and of the Son and of the Holy Spirit, teaching them to observe all that I have commanded you. And behold, I am with you always, to the end of the age" (Matthew 28:19-20). Peter preaching to Cornelius, a centurion who sent for him, and other Gentiles after the Holy Spirit fell on them all, said, "Can anyone withhold water for baptizing these people, who have received the Holy Spirit just as we have?" (Acts10:47). The Bible says, "And he commanded them to be baptized in the name of Jesus Christ. Then they asked him to remain for some days" (Acts 10:48).

WHAT ABOUT HOLINESS?

Some say no to it, but the word of God says otherwise. "But as he who called you is holy, you also be holy in all your conduct, since it is written, 'You shall be holy, for I am holy'" (1 Peter 1:15-16), which is impossible without his grace, "for all have sinned and fall short of the glory of God" (Romans 3:23).

We must accept Jesus as our personal Savior and remain faithful to Him to become holy as He is holy. He said, "Yet a little while and the world will see me no more, but you will see me. Because I live, you also will live. In that day you will know that I am in my Father, and you in me, and I in you" (John 14:19-20). He further added, "Abide in me, and I in you. As the branch cannot bear fruit by itself, unless it abides in the vine, neither can you, unless you abide in me. I am the vine; you are the branches. Whoever abides in me and I in him, he it is that bears much fruit, for apart from me you can do nothing. If anyone does not abide in me he is thrown away like a branch and withers; and the branches are gathered, thrown into the fire, and burned" (John 15:4-6).

Paul to the faithful wrote, "If the dough offered as firstfruits is holy, so is the whole lump, and if the root is holy, so are the branches" (Romans 11:16).

HOW IMPORTANT IS THE LORD'S PRAYER?

Some ministers are preaching that the Lord's Prayer is passé and that it is no more necessary to use it, but are they right? This is how Jesus taught his disciples, telling them, "Pray then like this: 'Our Father in heaven, hallowed be your name'" (Matthew 6:9). Don't we still need to glorify the name of God?

When He said, "Your kingdom come, your will be done, on earth as it is in heaven." (Matthew 6:10), wasn't Jesus referring to his Father's kingdom, which is still in heaven and to whom He has to deliver those of us who have remained faithful to Him to be His subjects? After His resurrection, His disciples convened often, and "To them he presented himself alive after his suffering by many proofs, appearing to them during forty days and speaking about the kingdom of God" (Acts 1:3), and "So when they had come together, they asked him, 'Lord, will you at this time restore the kingdom to Israel?' He said to them, 'It is not for you to know times or seasons that the Father has fixed by his own authority' " (Acts 1:6-7).

Paul, in a letter to the church of Corinth, wrote, "For as in Adam all die, so also in Christ shall all be made alive. But each in his own order: Christ the firstfruits, *then at his coming those who belong to Christ. Then comes the end*, when he delivers the kingdom to God the Father after destroying every rule and every authority and power. For he must reign until he has put all his enemies under his feet" (1 Corinthians 15:22-25).

Jesus continued saying, "Give us this day our daily bread, (Matthew 6:11). Don't we still need rain to grow food?

"And forgive us our debts, as we also have forgiven our debtors" (Matthew 6:12). Don't we still have to ask for forgiveness?

"And lead us not into temptation, but deliver us from evil" (Matthew 6:13). Don't we still need His protection against temptation and deliverance from Satan, since all of us can be deceived by him? Only Jesus could not sin even though He was tempted.

We must pray to our Father in heaven with the same simplicity as when we speak to our earthly one. A short prayer gets a quick answer, and when we are troubled or in danger or when we petition Him on behalf of someone, we simply ask Him for His help without saying much, since He knows everything about us and all our problems before we were born and till we die.

WHO ELSE DO WE NEED BESIDES JESUS?

Those who have received His calling must be truthful in their dealing with His children. Intimacy with God is a right that Jesus has won and granted to each one of us to express directly to our Lord in praise, thanksgiving, and love and to make a petition for ourselves or a particular person, a group, our country, or the whole world through prayers. Jesus said, "Whatever you ask in my name, this I will do, that the Father may be glorified in the Son. If you ask me anything in my name, I will do it" (John 14:13-14).

He clearly stated that He would send us another Comforter: "And I will ask the Father, and he will give you another Helper, to be with you forever, even the Spirit of truth, whom the world cannot receive, because it neither sees him nor knows him. You know him, for he dwells with you and will be in you. 'I will not leave you as orphans; I will come to you' " (John 14:16-18).

Simon Magus, a sorcerer, tried to buy spiritual power from Peter. "But Peter said to him, 'May your silver perish with you, because you thought you could obtain the gift of

God with money!'" (Acts 8:20). Peter further said to him, "You have neither part nor lot in this matter, for your heart is not right before God. Repent, therefore, of this wickedness of yours, and pray to the Lord that, if possible, the intent of your heart may be forgiven you. For I see that you are in the gall of bitterness and in the bond of iniquity" (Acts 8:21-23).

We know that Pope Leo X and his assistants have misled many by causing them to believe they could buy God's forgiveness, and these Peter would have rebuked in the same manner. We see something similar happening today; to entice many to contribute to their ministry, many Church leaders are offering false hope by promising their intercession on prayer requests sent to them that they will never be able to read because of the large number of letters they receive. Is that the teaching of our Lord Jesus Christ? Is it why He died on the cross for us? When we send them offerings, do we need to send them a prayer for them to pray over? I can tell you emphatically that it is false teaching and the work of the spirit of the Antichrist, the devil, although they are at liberty to thank God in secret, in the assembly, via electronic media to the whole world, with songs, music, dance, colorful festivals, or in any other manner they choose to please Him, and ask Him to bless you or even prophesy blessings for your pledges, tithes, offerings, or whatever else you may decide to send them.

Since Jesus said, "But when you give to the needy, do not let your left hand know what your right hand is doing, so that your giving may be in secret. And your Father who sees in secret will reward you" (Matthew 6:3-4), and He further added, "But when you pray, go into your room and shut the door and pray to your Father who is in secret. And your Father who sees in secret will reward you" (Matthew 6:6). Isn't it clear that whatever we give in tithes or offerings to whomever—an individual, an organization, or our church—our Father in heaven needs neither a brother, a prophet, a minister, nor anyone else to pray over it for Him to see it and reward us? Can't we conclude that anyone who would tell us otherwise is contradicting Jesus, is a liar, and acts on Satan's behalf?

The apostle Paul wrote, "Or do you not know that your body is a temple of the Holy Spirit within you, whom you have from God? You are not your own, for you were bought with a price. So glorify God in your body" (1 Corinthians 6:19-20). We can conclude that when we are honoring God by our giving and are petitioning Him, it can be in the secret of our heart, since our body is the temple of the Living God and the altar cannot be anywhere other than in this very temple on Earth or the one in heaven until the word is fulfilled and Jesus returns. Then those who say to you that they need to place your prayers on their altar are telling a lie and are not truthful to the word of God. They are trying to make you believe that you have no access to God but through them. Those who come to you with tales of direct communication with certain angels, which can only be the fallen ones, are false prophets. There is even the teaching of venerating wooden copies of the ark of the covenant of the Lord, and there are also claims that the Holy Spirit dwells in and around them, which is idolatry and another stage set by the spirit of the Antichrist, which is Satan who transforms himself sometimes into an angel of light; those promoting it are of the false teachers and the end time Jezebel that Jesus warned us about. Furthermore, Jesus said, "For where two or three are gathered in my name, there am I among them" (Matthew 18:20), and nowhere did He ever say that we need to have a wooden box resembling the Ark of the Covenant for Him to be among us. God and Jesus Christ will be our temple in the Holy City, called New Jerusalem, that we will see coming down from heaven. John, reporting his visions, wrote, "And I saw no temple in the city, for its temple is the Lord God the Almighty and the Lamb. And the city has no need of sun or moon to shine on it, for the glory of God gives it light, and its lamp is the Lamb" (Revelation 21:22-23).

THE BEAST—THE NEXT WORLD CONFLICT

Reading and understanding the last book of the Bible was a challenge to me, but I applied myself to reading it, often trying to decipher certain of its mysteries, convinced that without the help of the Holy Spirit it would be an impossible task. I was well aware of the many interpretations, and I agreed with some of them because I felt that they were correct as far as the logical story development, but I never accepted that the number of the beast, 666, was to be taken literally and would be what we would see on people's forehead and in their hands. In early 2005, I decided to take a different look at the 666 mystery, as the Holy Spirit had inspired me to do.

The Tower of Babel was a turning point in the history of humanity, when man thought of a society whose members would unite toward one goal: The building of a city where they would all reside and a tower that would be high enough to reach God's abode. From the Scriptures we read, "Now the whole earth had one language and the same words. And as people migrated from the east, they found a plain in the land of Shinar and settled there. And they said to one another, 'Come, let us make bricks, and burn them thoroughly.' And they had brick for stone, and bitumen for mortar. Then they said, 'Come, let us build ourselves a city and a tower with its top in the heavens, and let us make a name for ourselves, lest we be dispersed over the face of the whole earth.' And the LORD came down to see the city and the tower, which the children of man had built. And the LORD said, 'Behold, they are one people, and they have all one language, and this is only the beginning of what they will do. And nothing that they propose to do will now be impossible for them. Come, let us go down and there confuse their language, so that they may not understand one another's speech.' So the LORD dispersed them from there over the face of all the earth, and they left off building the city. Therefore its name was called Babel, because there the LORD confused the language of all the earth. And from there the LORD dispersed them over the face of all the earth" (Genesis 11:1-9).

But Satan kept trying through the ages and has agitated the heart of many. As new Babel-type confederations are being built, God strikes them down; such will be the fate of the last ones.

The number 999 was revealed to me through my sister,

our Lord's servant, during the first week of September 2001. I understood that it meant September 11, after the last two digits were replaced by binary digits 0 and 1, when expressed as 9/99. In 1998, our Lord had me relate to the leadership of this country, in great detail, the ill plan that would culminate in the total destruction of the twin towers of the World Trade Center. Around May of 2001, our Lord warned them of a new plan of attack at work by the enemy, but even though in early August 2001 I was shown in a day vision the first plane flying into the towers, I was not allowed to send a third message because that event was to be a warning to a people walking away from God. He gave Israel into the hand of King Nebuchadnezzar of Assyria because it has rebelled against Him. Let us embark, with the help of the Holy Spirit, on the road to understanding the 666 mystery. John describing his visions of the beast, wrote, "This calls for wisdom: let the one who has understanding calculate the number of the beast, for it is the number of a man, and his number is 666" (Revelation 13:18).

WHAT ABOUT THE MAN WHOSE NUMBER IS 666?

One day I opened my Bible, and the Lord took me to these

verses where in his anger He had pronounced an irreversible judgment and sentence against Judah and its king Jeconiah because of their rebellious attitude towards him, and I read, "As I live, declares the LORD, though Coniah the son of Jehoiakim, king of Judah, were the signet ring on my right hand, yet I would tear you off and give you into the hand of those who seek your life, into the hand of those of whom you are afraid, even into the hand of Nebuchadnezzar king of Babylon and into the hand of the Chaldeans" (Jeremiah 22:24-25). Right away I was given knowledge that there was a link between the 9/11 event encoded as 999 and the coming of destructive entities represented by the mystery number 666.

Is the man responsible for the 9/11 attack the beast whose number is 666? Our human mind cannot understand God's mysteries unless He reveals them to us, so let the Holy Spirit help us understand and decipher the mystery behind that number.

Let us examine the following end-time prophecy, which gives us a clue of the post-Antichrist era and what the people of Israel will reminisce of him. It says, "Your eyes will behold the king in his beauty; they will see a land that stretches afar. Your heart will muse on the terror: 'Where is he who counted, where is he who weighed the tribute? Where is he who counted the towers?' " (Isaiah 33:17-18).

"Where is he who counted?" Where is the scribe? Where is the one taking the census or the one keeping records of your possessions? Babylonians kept records of the Jews they took into captivity, and upon their returning to Judah, a count of people and animals was also done.

These two verses connected with the post-captivity period illustrate it well: "Now these were the people of the province who came up out of the captivity of those exiles whom Nebuchadnezzar the king of Babylon had carried captive to Babylonia. They returned to Jerusalem and Judah, each to his own town. They came with Zerubbabel, Jeshua, Nehemiah, Seraiah, Reelaiah, Mordecai, Bilshan, Mispar, Bigvai, Rehum, and Baanah. The number of the men of the people of Israel. "(Ezra 2:1-2), and upon reading down the list of the families that had returned from captivity, we stumble onto the following: "The sons of Adonikam, 666" (Ezra 2:13).

Those of Adonikam's clan where numbered among others, as well as their possessions, and we read "Besides their male and female servants, of whom there were 7,337, and they had 200 male and female singers. Their horses were 736, their mules were 245, their camels were 435, and their donkeys were 6,720" (Ezra 2:65-67).

One of the previous verses (Ezra 2:13) is a riddle and might contain another clue into revealing the identity of the

Antichrist and the mystery behind his number, which is 666. We read again, "The sons of Adonikam, 666" (Ezra 2:13), where "Adonikam" means "My Lord has risen," and the number of his sons, which is "666," parallels Revelation 13:18 above mentioned.

In light of Isaiah 33:17-18 Ezra 2:1-2, Ezra 2:13 and John's Revelation, let us examine the nature and modus operandi of this man whose number is 666 and also called the beast, the son of destruction, or the man of lawlessness. Paul wrote, "Not to be quickly shaken in mind or alarmed, either by a spirit or a spoken word, or a letter seeming to be from us, to the effect that the day of the Lord has come. Let no one deceive you in any way. For that day will not come, unless the rebellion comes first, and the man of lawlessness is revealed, the son of destruction" (2 Thessalonians 2:2-3).

Will this man whose number is 666 come back to life to imitate Christ? Yes, many will believe that he had died and had come back to life. Let us consider this partial account of John's visions: "One of its heads seemed to have a mortal wound, but its mortal wound was healed, and the whole earth marveled as they followed the beast" (Revelation 13:3).

He is coming from the bottomless pit, which means that he is to come back to life as John reported. "The beast that you saw was, and is not, and is about to rise from the bottomless pit and go to destruction. And the dwellers on earth whose names have not been written in the book of life from the foundation of the world will marvel to see the beast, because it was and is not and is to come" (Revelation 17:8).

He is Judas, the twelfth apostle, whom Jesus called "Son of perdition or son of destruction," talking to his Father who is in heaven. He said, "While I was with them, I kept them in your name, which you have given me. I have guarded them, and not one of them has been lost except *the son of destruction,* that the Scripture might be fulfilled" (John 17:12).

In Isaiah he is referred to as the destroyer and betrayer: "Ah, you destroyer, who yourself have not been destroyed, you traitor, whom none has betrayed! When you have ceased to destroy, you will be destroyed; and when you have finished betraying, they will betray you" (Isaiah 33:1).

He is a usurper, the antitype of Antiochus Epiphanes, who became the eighth king of the Seleucid dynasty of Syria, one of four dynasties that inherited Alexander the Great's empire and of whom the angel Gabriel revealed to Daniel, "By his cunning he shall make deceit prosper under his hand, and in his own mind he shall become great. Without warning he shall destroy many. And he shall even rise up against the Prince of princes, and he shall be broken—

but by no human hand" (Daniel 8:25).

Will he revive an old system of government, under false pretenses? No, it shall be different from all previous ones, as per the angel who interpreted Daniel's visions and told him of a global system of government in the latter days, which is our era. "Thus he said, The fourth beast shall be the fourth kingdom upon earth, which shall be diverse from all kingdoms, and shall devour the whole earth, and shall tread it down, and break it in pieces" (Daniel 7:23 KJV).

It is the fourth kingdom represented by the legs of iron of an image that king Nebuchadnezzar saw in his night vision as interpreted by the prophet Daniel to whom God had revealed the meaning of the king's dream. "And there shall be a fourth kingdom, strong as iron, because iron breaks to pieces and shatters all things. And like iron that crushes, it shall break and crush all these. And as you saw the feet and toes, partly of potter's clay and partly of iron, it shall be a divided kingdom, but some of the firmness of iron shall be in it, just as you saw iron mixed with the soft clay" (Daniel 2:40-41).

WHAT ABOUT DANIEL'S BEASTS VS JOHN'S?

They came up out of the sea, which means from among the

people: "Daniel declared, 'I saw in my vision by night, and behold, the four winds of heaven were stirring up the great sea. And four great beasts came up out of the sea, different from one another' " (Daniel 7:2-3). The Bible says, "And the angel said to me, "The waters that you saw, where the prostitute is seated, are peoples and multitudes and nations and languages" (Revelation 17:15).

They were a lion, a bear, a leopard, and a fourth with ten horns and a little horn, the eleventh one. "The fourth beast was stronger and more terrifying than the others. Its huge teeth were made of iron, and what it didn't grind with its teeth, it smashed with its feet. It was different from the others, and it had horns on its head—ten of them. Just as I was thinking about these horns, a smaller horn appeared, and three of the other horns were pulled up by the roots to make room for it. This horn had the eyes of a human and a mouth that spoke with great pride" (Daniel 7:7-8 CEV).

It shall make war to the saints and exercise authority for three years and a half. From the Scriptures we read, "All ten of those horns are kings who will come from this kingdom, and one more will follow. This horn will be different from the others, and it will conquer three other kings. 'This king will speak evil of God Most High, and he will be cruel to God's chosen ones. He will try to change God's Law and the sacred seasons. And he will be able to do this for a time, two times, and half a time' " (Daniel 7:24-25 CEV).

The first beast of Revelation 13 looks like the first three beasts of Daniel 7, and it behaves like the fourth one that came out of the sea.

It came up out of the sea and has ten horns and seven heads. John wrote, "And I saw a beast rising out of the sea, with ten horns and seven heads, with ten diadems on its horns and blasphemous names on its heads" (Revelation 13:1). And he continues, "And the beast which I saw was like unto a leopard, and his feet were as the feet of a bear, and his mouth as the mouth of a lion: and the dragon gave him his power, and his seat, and great authority" (Revelation 13:2).

The world will adhere to it, as John wrote, "One of its heads seemed to have a mortal wound, but its mortal wound was healed, and the whole earth marveled as they followed the beast. And they worshiped the dragon, for he had given his authority to the beast, and they worshiped the beast, saying, 'Who is like the beast, and who can fight against it?'" (Revelation 13:3-4).

It will speak great things and will exercise authority for three years and a half, as the apostle describes here, "And the beast was given a mouth uttering haughty and blasphemous words, and it was allowed to exercise authority for forty-two months" (Revelation 13:5).

It will persecute Jews and Christians, but those in the "book of life" will not worship it. The Bible says, "Also it was allowed to make war on the saints and to conquer them. And authority was given it over every tribe and people and language and nation, and all who dwell on earth will worship it, everyone whose name has not been written before the foundation of the world in the book of life of the Lamb that was slain" (Revelation 13:7-8).

The beast of Revelation 17 looks like the one of Revelation 13 and has seven heads and ten horns. John describes what one of the angels with the seven bowls showed him: "And he carried me away in the Spirit into a wilderness, and I saw a woman sitting on a scarlet beast that was full of blasphemous names, and it had seven heads and ten horns" (Revelation 17:3).

It was a man, it will rise again, and the world will worship it, but not those found in the book of life. The angel explains, "The beast that you saw was, and is not, and is about to rise from the bottomless pit and go to destruction. And the dwellers on earth whose names have not been written in the book of life from the foundation of the world will marvel to see the beast, because it was and is not and is to come" (Revelation 17:8).

The beast, which is the outlaw, is the eleventh horn, the

little one of Daniel's vision, and he wrote, "I considered the horns, and behold, there came up among them another horn, a little one, before which three of the first horns were plucked up by the roots. And behold, in this horn were eyes like the eyes of a man, and a mouth speaking great things" (Daniel 7:8).

It is the one of the thirteenth chapter of John's Revelation, and we read, "It opened its mouth to utter blasphemies against God, blaspheming his name and his dwelling, that is, those who dwell in heaven" (Revelation 13:6).

It is also the one of the seventeenth chapter of Revelation. It will receive power from the ten horns, and it will make war on the Church and the saints. The angel went on, saying, "And the ten horns that you saw are ten kings who have not yet received royal power, but they are to receive authority as kings for one hour, together with the beast. These are of one mind and hand over their power and authority to the beast. They will make war on the Lamb, and the Lamb will conquer them, for he is Lord of lords and King of kings, and those with him are called and chosen and faithful" (Revelation 17:12-14).

It shall become the eighth after it takes down three of the ten kings. "As for the beast that was and is not, it is an eighth but it belongs to the seven, and it goes to destruction" (Revelation 17:11).

THE BEAST—THE NEXT WORLD CONFLICT

WILL HE TAX NATIONS?

"Where is the receiver?" "Where is he who weighed the tribute?" Will the man whose number is 666 be at such an economical disadvantage or just so energized by a driving hegemonic ideal that he will feel compelled to control other countries' natural resources, production of goods and their movement, and their banking system? Will he collect tax from all the nations of the world, as Solomon required of all tributary countries? From the Scriptures we read, "Now the weight of gold that came to Solomon in one year was 666 talents of gold, besides that which came from the explorers and from the business of the merchants, and from all the kings of the west and from the governors of the land" (1 Kings 10:14-15).

Will he establish a system to be able to control all monetary transactions? The Bible says, "Also it causes all, both small and great, both rich and poor, both free and slave, to be marked on the right hand or the forehead, so that no one can buy or sell unless he has the mark, that is, the name of the beast or the number of its name" (Revelation 13:16-17).

Will the son of perdition use a peaceful and attractive approach to convince countries to rally under a fraudulent economic system, causing them to become tributary fiefdoms? Yes, he will in the manner Paul wrote to his disciples to warn them of these treacheries: "And with all wicked deception for those who are perishing, because they refused to love the truth and so be saved" (2 Thessalonians 2:10).

WILL HE RESORT TO WAR TO REACH HIS GOAL?

"Where is he who counted the towers?" Will he use military might after gaining the trust of those nations to suddenly turn against them when they expect it the least? John wrote, "Also it was allowed to make war on the saints and to conquer them. And authority was given it over every tribe and people and language and nation" (Revelation 13:7).

In a vision in August of 1998, I saw troops from China walking west across Russia. It parallels John's visions concerning those who will march against Israel in the next world conflict and the order God has given His angels to dry up the Euphrates to allow them to cross it on foot with their war machines. The Bible says, "The sixth angel poured out his bowl on the great river Euphrates, and its water was dried up, to prepare the way for the kings from the east" (Revelation 16:12).

The angel who spoke to John further revealed to him that this global system of government will be the association of ten rulers and an eleventh, the beast, and that they will voluntarily surrender their authority to him. He wrote, "And the ten horns that you saw are ten kings who have not yet received royal power, but they are to receive authority as kings for one hour, together with the beast. These are of one mind and hand over their power and authority to the beast" (Revelation 17:12-13).

It will be a disparate form of government, but a better and eternal one will overthrow it, as the prophet Daniel revealed to king Nebuchadnezzar concerning his night vision: "And as you saw the feet and toes, partly of potter's clay and partly of iron, it shall be a divided kingdom, but some of the firmness of iron shall be in it, just as you saw iron mixed with the soft clay. And as the toes of the feet were partly iron and partly clay, so the kingdom shall be partly strong and partly brittle. As you saw the iron mixed with soft clay, so they will mix with one another in marriage, but they will not hold together, just as iron does not mix with clay. And in the days of those kings the God of heaven will set up a kingdom that shall never be destroyed, nor shall the kingdom be left to another people. It shall break in pieces all these kingdoms and bring them to an end, and it shall stand forever" (Daniel 2:41-44).

Is he a ruler of a nation with a stockpile of nuclear, biological, and chemical weapons, willing to blackmail nations to gain total control over their inhabitants, to take many captive, and to reinstitute forced labor? The Bible says, "If anyone is to be taken captive, to captivity he goes; if anyone is to be slain with the sword, with the sword must he be slain. Here is a call for the endurance and faith of the saints" (Revelation 13:10).

Is he just an outlaw who will insidiously use the power and military might of a coalition of ten nations whose leaders will surrender all authority to him? In such circumstances, which are they, these nations that will hand over power to him willingly: The EU bloc, the U.S. and allies, Iran, Russia and the former Soviet republics, China, North Korea, and others of the Eastern Bloc? From the scripture we read, "As for the ten horns, out of this kingdom ten kings shall arise, and another shall arise after them; he shall be different from the former ones, and shall put down three kings. He shall speak words against the Most High, and shall wear out the saints of the Most High, and shall think to change the times and the law; and they shall be given into his hand for a time, times, and half a time" (Daniel 7:24-25), The Bible says, "These are of one mind and hand over their power and authority to the beast" (Revelation 17:13).

WILL THERE BE A PACT BETWEEN
SATAN AND HIM?

Satan will give him his authority to wage war against the believers, as Paul wrote, "The coming of the lawless one is by the activity of Satan with all power and false signs and wonders, and with all wicked deception for those who are perishing, because they refused to love the truth and so be saved" (2 Thessalonians 2:9-10), and God will grant him temporary victory over them, "Also it was allowed to make war on the saints and to conquer them. And authority was given it over every tribe and people and language and nation" (Revelation 13:7).

Is he among the faithful? If not, what could be the motive of his hatred for Rome, the city that sits on seven mountains? Is it because of past and present enmity? It might well be, as we read, "And the ten horns that you saw, they and the beast will hate the prostitute. They will make her desolate and naked, and devour her flesh and burn her up with fire, for God has put it into their hearts to carry out his purpose by being of one mind and handing over their royal power to the beast, until the words of God are fulfilled. And the woman that you saw is the great city that has dominion over the kings of the earth" (Revelation 17:16-18).

WILL HE PUT AN END TO THE PAPACY OF ROME?

Will he destroy all statues and other objects of worship from the Vatican? Will he remove the pontiff and replace him? Paul in his letter to the faithful of Thessalonica wrote of his demeanor, "Who opposes and exalts himself against every so-called god or object of worship, so that he takes his seat in the temple of God, proclaiming himself to be God" (2 Thessalonians 2:4), and prophesying the destruction of his new abode an angel proclaims, "And he called out with a mighty voice, 'Fallen, fallen is Babylon the great! She has become a dwelling place for demons, a haunt for every unclean spirit, a haunt for every unclean bird, a haunt for every unclean and detestable beast'" (Revelation 18:2).

Will he have a spokesperson, a false prophet, who shall also receive power from Satan, act on his behalf? "Then I saw another beast rising out of the earth. It had two horns like a lamb and it spoke like a dragon. It exercises all the authority of the first beast in its presence, and makes the earth and its inhabitants worship the first beast, whose mortal wound was healed. It performs great signs, even making fire come down from heaven to earth in front of people, and by the signs that it is allowed to work in the presence of the beast it deceives those who dwell on earth, telling them to make an image for the beast that was wounded by the sword and yet lived" (Revelation 13:11-14).

Who will be able to stop the son of destruction on his destructive course and his false prophet whom Satan has given his power and his throne? From the epistle of Paul we read, "And then the lawless one will be revealed, whom the Lord Jesus will kill with the breath of his mouth and bring to nothing by the appearance of his coming" (2 Thessalonians 2:8). The Bible says, "They will make war on the Lamb, and the Lamb will conquer them, for he is Lord of lords and King of kings, and those with him are called and chosen and faithful" (Revelation 17:14).

And what will be their fate? John wrote, "And the beast was captured, and with it the false prophet who in its presence had done the signs by which he deceived those who had received the mark of the beast and those who worshiped its image. These two were thrown alive into the lake of fire that burns with sulfur" (Revelation 19:20).

Those who will pledge allegiance to the son of destruction to escape death or captivity and accept his mark will be sent to the lake of fire, as was revealed to John, who gave us an account of what he saw and heard. "And another angel, a third, followed them, saying with a loud voice, 'If anyone worships the beast and its image and receives a mark on his forehead or on his hand, he also will drink the wine of God's wrath, poured full strength into the cup of his anger, and he will be tormented with fire and sulfur in the presence of the holy angels and in the presence of the Lamb. And the smoke of their torment goes up forever and ever, and they have no rest, day or night, these worshipers of the beast and its image, and whoever receives the mark of its name" (Revelation 14:9-11).

Let the Lord guide us further through other doors to find the hidden truth. The beast's culture and language are described in Isaiah as being that of a people whom the Jews consider arrogant, for obviously having lived in captivity among them, and whose spoken language is hard to understand and is punctuated by involuntary pauses or repetitions. From the Scriptures we read, "You will see no more the insolent people, the people of an obscure speech that you cannot comprehend, stammering in a tongue that you cannot understand" (Isaiah 33:19).

In East Asia, Chinese tongues of the Sino-Tibetan family of languages use pitch to distinguish words opposite to Romance languages, making them strangely stammering to the Romance language and Semitic language speakers. They comprise many regional and often mutually unintelligible variants that are not understood and spoken by most Jews. Besides the U.S., which is presently considered a hyperpower, China is emerging as a superpower. With one-fifth of the world's population, it is capable of mustering the greatest army. It has a large stockpile of nuclear weapons. Its rulers have been harboring hegemonic ideals for quite a while, now more than ever. It has blossomed in the last few years from a period of stagnation and military impotence due to centuries of internal conflicts and Maoist rule that favored forced labor into a hybrid economic entity characterized as state capitalism responsible for today's prosperity.

China does satisfy the language requirements as spelled out in Isaiah 33:19. For having implemented forced labor during the years of Maoist regime, it could reintroduce this form of captivity on a worldwide scale if allowed, and if it finds its place in future events in the context of Revelation13:10.

China is striving to become the next great economy. It is actually engaging in a military buildup that is worrying many nations.

Will China side with Russia, whose national symbol is the bear, in case of an armed conflict with the U.S? Would Russia support China if it declared war on the U.S? Will China's armies, as shown to me, walk across Russia as an ally or as an enemy?

IS THE STAGE SET FOR THE NEXT WORLD CONFLICT?

In June 2002, China and Russia, along with the leaders of Kazakhstan, Kyrgyzstan, Tajikistan, and Uzbekistan, met in St. Petersburg. There, they signed the Shanghai Cooperation Organization (SCO) Charter. SCO was created in Shanghai in 1996 with the signing of the Treaty on Deepening Military Trust in Border Regions. It was originally known as the Shanghai Five and later as the Shanghai Six after Uzbekistan joined the organization in 2001. In 1997, all five original members met in Moscow to sign the Treaty on Reduction of Military Forces in Border Regions. This organization was created to maintain proper border security to protect against terrorism and also to eliminate the United States' increasing influence in central Asia.

On Tuesday, June 30, 2005, Chinese president Hu Jintao, started a four-day meeting with Russian president Vladimir Putin to strengthen post-cold-war ties after both countries had previously signed a strategic accord of cooperation and had resolved border issues. Their support to President Islam Karimov of Uzbekistan, who had allowed a bloody reprisal on the opposition during an uprising, raised the concern of the U.S. and other NATO members. Both leaders reacted to what they perceived as U.S. domination in world affairs and an attempt to expand its influence in Central Asia after 9/11. When the U.S. managed to convince two SCO member states, Uzbekistan and Kyrgyzstan, to install military bases in their territories, Putin and Hu Jintao accused the U.S. of instigating regime change in the former Soviet republics of Georgia, Ukraine, and Kyrgyzstan. They have since expanded the SCO to include joint military exercises. On August 18, 2005, Russian navy ships and strategic and long-range bombers joined Chinese forces on the Shandong peninsula to start war games that were to last until August 25. The purpose of these war games was to display their military might. They also talked of sharing weapons technology and forming a free-trade area. They have pledged to take measures to limit the U.S. influence in Central Asia. Four semi-members sought and were granted observer status: Mongolia in 2004, and Pakistan, India, and Iran at the July 5, 2005 summit in Astana, Kazakhstan. China is in dire need of Russian oil and gas and expressed its desire to be granted priority access over Japan to tap the Siberian oil pipeline.

On January 11, 2007, China warned the U.S. not to meddle in its dealings with Iran. On that same day, China destroyed one of its aging satellites using a ground-based, medium-range ballistic missile The Chinese and their leader Premier Wen Jiabao signaled that they are ready for any type of confrontation with the U.S.

On August 16, 2007, SCO members met at Bishkek, Kyrgyzstan. At the summit, Iranian President Mahmoud Ahmadinejad, whose country enjoys observer status, echoed Putin's protest of the U.S. missile shield in Europe. A day later, Vladimir Putin ordered twenty Soviet-era strategic bombers back on long-range patrol over the Artic, Atlantic, and Pacific oceans, after Hu Jintao, other SCO members, and he had watched a joint military exercise of their troops on Russian soil.

The Assyrian language was strange to the Jews, and when they returned from captivity, they did not have to listen to it anymore. Can we still take into account Iraq, once home to the Assyrian culture, as a country capable of mustering the military might strong enough to rule all the nations of the world, mainly after the capture and execution of former president Saddam Hussein? At the present time, Middle Eastern countries cannot accomplish such a feat without the help of a nation with large stockpiles of weapons (nuclear and others), a well-trained army, and a strong presence on land, in the sea, and in the air.

Russian president Vladimir Putin, through a series of subtle maneuvers, has taken steps that might help these countries in reaching such an objective. He and his successor, Russian President Dmitry Medvedev, might make use of an alliance with them to reestablish Russia's old glory.

Is the USSR really defunct or just wounded, in a lethargic state? On December 21, 1991, the Russian leader and those of Azerbaijan, Armenia, Belarus, Kazakhstan, Kyrgyzstan, Moldova, Tajikistan, Turkmenistan, Ukraine, and Uzbekistan, eleven of the fifteen Soviet Socialist Republics, met in Alma-Ata, Kazakhstan, to sign a charter that stated that all the members were independent states, thereby effectively abolishing the U.S.S.R. and ratifying the initial treaty of the Commonwealth of Independent States or CIS, a confederation that is an instrument that allows Russia to maintain its influence over those states. In December 1993, Georgia became the twelfth CIS member. In 2005, Turkmenistan chose to continue as an associate member.

The Collective Security Treaty Organization's (CSTO) member countries were all members of the CIS. Armenia, Belarus, Kazakhstan, Kyrgyzstan, Russia, Tajikistan, and Uzbekistan had previously signed a Collective Security Treaty (CST), and had all pledged not to use force or the threat thereof, to abstain from becoming members of other military alliances and to consider an attack against any one member as an attack against them all. In spite of that, in early 2006, Russia was engaged in the development of a partnership with NATO, with the cooperation of the U.S.

On September 19, 2003, Russia, Belarus, Kazakhstan and Ukraine signed an agreement on a Common Economic Space (CES) to establish a free-trade zone and economic union between the member states in 2005. It was headed by a representative of Kazakhstan and had its headquarters in Kiev. It was intended to be a regional organization with a single currency, like the Euro, with a supranational commission on trade and tariffs that would accept other countries as members. All these state became members of the Eurasian Economic Community (EurAsEC or EAEC) a successor for the Customs Union of the CIS, except the Ukraine, whose president, Viktor Yushchenko, was more interested in seeking membership in the European Union.

The support given by President Valdimir Putin to the opponent of the Ukrainian president during the presidential election of 2004 has caused his country to lean towards the West. This has exacerbated conflicts of interests in the North-South Transportation Corridor dispute between Russia and GUUAM, a grouping of the Ukraine and five other CIS states, Azerbaijan, Georgia, Moldova, and Uzbekistan, because it invited Steven Mann, the U.S. Department of State special representative for Eurasian conflicts, to attend their summit of April 22, 2005, and not Russia. GUUAM has been renamed GUAM, its original name after Uzbekistan withdrew its membership in May 2005.

Another pressing issue that might have angered Russia was that GUUAM was willing to accept the United States' proposed highway/railway link between Europe and Asia through the Ukraine, the Black Sea, and the Caspian Sea. This was in direct competition with Vladimir Putin's North-South Transportation Corridor that would connect Moscow, Russia's capital to Mumbai, a port city of India, via the Caspian Sea, Tehran, Iran's capital, and Bandar Abbas in the Persian Gulf. In September 2000, these three countries had signed an agreement on the development of the North-South link. Iran was recognized the Depository State in transit affairs by India and Russia, and Iran's Transportation and Terminals Organization reviewed all new applications for membership. The states of Armenia, Azerbaijan, Belarus, India, Iran, Kazakhstan, Kyrgyzstan, Oman, Russia, Syria, Tajikistan, Turkey, and Ukraine became official members of the International North-South Transport Corridor (INSTC), and requests from Armenia, Azerbaijan, Bulgaria, Kyrgyzstan, and Syria were under consideration in 2005. Bulgaria is the only observer member.

Russia and Iran's INSTC would serve well at transporting a large number of troops and weapons quickly between the two countries in the new approaching conflict. Some of these thirteen members of the INSTC may well be part of future Asian nations, China included, that could march against Jerusalem. John was shown a series of events that will lead to this final confrontation between Israel and the rest, and he wrote, "The sixth angel poured out his bowl on the great river Euphrates, and its water was dried up, to prepare the way for the kings from the east" (Revelation 16:12).

In 2005, Russian president Vladimir Putin made a series of visits to Egypt, Jerusalem, and Ramallah. He also arranged a meeting between his ambassador Vladimir Chamov and Shiite cleric al-Sadr, who was strongly opposed to the U.S. presence in Iraq. He promised to sell advanced anti-aircraft systems and other sophisticated weapons to Syria and signed a military cooperation agreement with them, which prompted the U.S. and Israel to address their concerns to his government, fearing that these weapons would fall ultimately into Hezbollah's hands.

Putin concluded and signed a deal on February 27, 2005, to deliver nuclear fuel to Iran. All these meetings and deals indicate that he wanted to establish very strong ties with those countries. On April 29, 2005, he offered helicopters, military equipment and training for Palestinian troops to help Palestinian leader Mahmoud Abbas maintain order and disarm militants just to play a greater role in the Israeli-Palestinian peace process and to initiate a permanent Russian presence in the region.

In 2007 I wrote the following: On today's world scene we have two leaders whose terms in office ought to end a few months apart in 2008. Those leaders are George W. Bush and Vladimir Putin, who have many things in common despite opposing agendas. They are about the same age, both married with two daughters, energetic, dynamic, strong, honest, pragmatic, and sports aficionados. The former promotes peace and democracy; the latter has presented himself as being pro-democracy and also anti-communist. Putin believes in a market economy and has extreme views concerning his country's greatness. Putin, a former KGB officer, as well as others of the same background and many members of Russia's armed forces, would not hesitate, in order to satisfy their patriotic ideals, to sacrifice the basic tenets of human rights and freedoms and reinstate the Gulag. At the end of his two consecutive terms, Putin, in an extraordinary tour de force, might remain in power for many years to come by becoming prime minister and wait to participate in the 2012 presidential election.

These two men are rulers of two lands that seem to extend hands to each other, though these sometimes resemble two beasts about to lock horns across the Bering Strait. On the Russian side, not very far inland, there is a 666-foot high mountain ridge quite similar to one of the same height that exists in China.

The U.S. is still the most powerful nation, even though it has stretched thin its assets to fight the Taliban in Afghanistan and Al-Qaeda, Sunni insurgents, and Shia militias in Iraq. China may represent a serious threat due to its massive acquisition of offensive weaponry and technology from Russia, but they should think twice before they launch a surprise attack against the U.S. This is a nation that knows how to unite in the face of danger even though partisan politics and carelessness of the press are corroding and weakening its foundation at an alarming rate. It has proven time and time again that it will not bend to either terrorism or rogue countries like North Korea and Iran.

The U.S. is a nation capable of defending its vital interests anywhere and whenever necessary but also one with a big heart ready to send its military assets and personnel, sometimes at heavy costs, either to protect other nations against unlawful and unwarranted attacks from their bullying neighbors or to intervene in their internal conflicts, where those who are the most productive and have the highest respect for the law would perish by the hands of unscrupulous leaders and their thugs without its intervention.

This is a country always at the forefront of providing humanitarian help whenever or wherever it is needed around the world, even in dangerous situations where U.S. military personnel, philanthropic organizations, or religious groups are conducting rescue operations and feeding efforts in a hostile environment.

The U.S. must remain a superpower because no other country has as much will and determination to help the weak and defenseless, and to promote peace and cooperation among nations, and because God has chosen it to fulfill His will to be a springboard for the Gospel and to stand by the ultimate victor, Israel. But alas! Many in authority and in our churches will side with the beast. The Lord speaking to Isaiah said, "In that day the root of Jesse, who shall stand as a signal for the peoples—of him shall the nations inquire, and his resting place shall be glorious. In that day the Lord will extend his hand yet a second time to recover the remnant that remains of his people, from Assyria, from Egypt, from Pathros, from Cush, from Elam, from Shinar, from Hamath, and from the coastlands of the sea. He will raise a signal for the nations and will assemble the banished of Israel, and gather the dispersed of Judah from the four corners of the earth. The jealousy of Ephraim shall depart, and those who harass Judah shall be cut off; Ephraim shall not be jealous of Judah, and Judah shall not harass Eph-raim. But they shall swoop down on the shoulder of the Philistines in the west, and together they shall plunder the people of the east. They shall put out their hand against Edom and Moab, and the Ammonites shall obey them" (Isaiah 11:10-14).

BECAUSE OF IRAN, IS THERE REASON FOR CONCERN?

At the conclusion of World War I, Germany, was required to accept full responsibility for the war and to pay war reparations and other humiliating concessions to the victors. Its weak economic condition caused by the very large payments and the German reaction to those led to the rise of Adolph Hitler and eventually to World War II, which ended in the defeat of Germany and the suicide of its Fuehrer.

In 1984, Iraq borrowed heavily from Kuwait, the Saudis, and other Arab countries to finance the eight-year war with Iran. As debt repayments weighed heavily on its economy, Saddam Hussein decided to invade those countries and seize control of their immense oil production operations—a very costly decision that led to the Gulf Wars. Extensive human rights violations in Kuwait by his troops prompted the U.N. Security Council to pass Resolution 666 to address the issue. The occupation of Iraq by U.S.-led coalition forces and finally the capture of its blood-thirsty dictator concluded many years of repeated human rights violation in his own country and ended Saddam's efforts at acquiring nuclear weapons and at rebuilding his stockpile of weapons of mass destruction.

Iran is like a lion crouched in tall grass waiting for the right moment to attack its prey. It lies strategically in the Middle East, between the Arabian Peninsula, Central and Southern Asia. It borders Iraq and the Persian Gulf, an oil-rich region. It has become an object of contention between three powerful nations. Russia and China have joined forces with Iran to form an axis of power to challenge what they consider to be U.S. "hegemony" in international affairs. In 2005, President Vladimir Putin approved a deal to sell nuclear fuel to Iran in spite of protest by the U.S. And China has not only protested the U.S. opposition to Iran's nuclear program and openly vowed to oppose U.S. "unilateralism" but has signed a series of deals with Iran in direct challenge to the Bush administration's economic sanctions on Iran.

In an effort to counter the economic sanction imposed by the U.S., Iran is looking to form a strong alliance with those countries and with Iraq. The new Iraqi government has a Shia-majority that has won more than half of the seats in the first freely elected 275-member National Assembly. On July 7, 2005, during a meeting in Tehran, Iraqi Defense Minister Saadoun al-Duleimi's Iranian counterpart, Ali Shamkhani, promised to help modernize Iraq's army and pushed for the removal of U.S.-led coalition troops from Iraqi soil on the assumption that their reason for being there was to serve Israel's interest as a security presence in the area. Shamkhani is believed to have considered waiving the billion dollars in war reparations for the 1980-88 conflict Iran has demanded as a bargaining chip to bring Iraq to agree to an early departure of foreign troops.

Mahmoud Ahmadinejad, the ex-conservative mayor of Tehran and elected president of Iran, has vowed to proceed with the nuclear program, which is an ominous declaration. The U.S. and its allies will not be able to prevent Iran from producing enriched uranium and from outfitting its missiles with nuclear warheads. Iran will never honor, long-term, any agreement it might enter into now or later with the U.S. and Europe.

Iran, desperate for U.S. trade sanctions to be removed, had offered to send twenty million barrels of crude oil to the U.S. in the wake of the September 2005 Hurricane Katrina, which was responsible for interrupting the production of crude oil. Their offer was not accepted. As their frustration mounted, on October 28, 2005, thousands of Iranians flooded the streets of Tehran, echoing their president Mahmoud Ahmadinejad, who marched with them, calling for the annihilation of Israel and the U.S. His declaration has set the stage for the next world conflict.

The fifteen sailors and Royal marine personnel captured by Iranians on March 21, 2007, publicly maintained that they were in Iraqi waters. Their release after thirteen days in captivity on April 7 indicates how desperately Iran is searching for opportunities, without assessing the risks, to bargain its way out of more recent sanctions without complying with the demand of the international community to stop uranium enrichment. Iran may well become the source of humanity's next woes and share the fate of Germany and Iraq.

IS 666 THE MARK OF THE BEAST?

The beast, known also as the man of lawlessness, son of perdition, or son of destruction, will seek alliance with ten leaders of the world, three of whom he will replace by either peacefully or forcibly removing them from power. It is commonly understood that sanctions, which were the common denominator that caused Germany and Iraq to go to war against their neighbors, will also drive Iran down the same path. Because of the aspirations of China, Iran, and Russia, the voiced sentiments of their leaders concerning the U.S. and Israel, and their motivation at forming a geo-political alliance against the U.S., we could conclude that these three nations are the ones that the man of lawlessness, the beast, may form an alliance with and whose leaders he may get rid of once he takes control of their armies.

To verify this assertion, let us locate China, Iran, and Russia on a world map and join them with straight lines. We then notice the shape of a triangle. Now, because of their possible future association with the beast, who will receive demonic power from Satan; let us place the number "6" at each angle. (The number "6" indicates the imperfect nature of Satan, versus the number "7" that expresses God's infallibility.) As a second step, let us envision or let us cut out of white bond paper a second triangle the size of the first one and let us write successively at each corner "Germany was defeated," "Iraq was defeated," and last, "Iran and allies will be defeated," then let us superimpose them in such a manner as to have the last marked corner opposite the country of Iran on the map and as to obtain a hexagram, the Star of David, the symbol of the state of Is-rael, also used by the Nazis during the Holocaust as a means of identifying Jews.

This hexagram shows that a Satan-led coalition of these

three nations and their allies represented by the number 666 from John's Revelation, will definitely come against the Jewish nation of Israel and allies (the U.S., a handful of other nations, and the Church). It is the history of the past defeat of its enemies as well as the verification of the scripture concerning the near-future conflict, when they will be utterly destroyed by the lion of Judah, Jesus, the King of kings, the Lord of lords, and his armies from the end of the heavens. It will be the battle of Armageddon. John wrote, "And I saw the beast and the kings of the earth with their armies gathered to make war against him who was sitting on the horse and against his army. And the beast was captured, and with it the false prophet who in its presence had done the signs by which he deceived those who had received the mark of the beast and those who worshiped its image. These two were thrown alive into the lake of fire that burns with sulfur. And the rest were slain by the sword that came from the mouth of him who was sitting on the horse, and all the birds were gorged with their flesh" (Revelation 19:19-21).

The beast-led coalition, the new confederation and their troops, will take over control of the world economy, including farming, manufacturing of goods, and their distribution. It will seize control of the earth's natural resources, such as the vast oil reserves of the Middle East, Central Asia, and other countries. It will control their banking systems; and religious, scientific, and learning institutions. It will remove world leaders and replace them with puppet governments, and thus controlling their police, military, paramilitary forces, and intelligence services in every country. It will exert total control on their inhabitants through demonic power and cutting edge technologies capable of recording, around the clock, every aspect of their lives. The Bible says, "Also it causes all, both small and great, both rich and poor, both free and slave, to be marked on the right hand or the forehead, so that no one can buy or sell unless he has the mark, that is, the name of the beast or the number of its name. This calls for wisdom: let the one who has under-standing calculate the number of the beast, for it is the number of a man, and his number is 666" (Revelation 13:16-18).

With the Holy Spirit's help, let us decipher the meaning of the riddle "The mark, that is, the name of the beast or the number of its name" from the above-mentioned verses where "the beast" is also a man, since the number of the beast is the number of a man, and where "the mark" stands for "the name of the beast" as well as for "the number of its name."

The number 666 is also the number of "the beast," which is a man, and his institution or the government that he rules, according to the previous paragraph and from knowledge acquired of the beast with the ten horns and the seven heads from the visions of the prophets Daniel and John.

Since "the beast" stands for the man and the institution he rules, 666 being their number, and since the Bible says that "the mark" stands for "the name of the beast" as well as for "the number of its name," we can conclude that "the mark" can either be "the name of the man and of his institution or government" or a "title" he would have given himself. His institution or government can be a group of rebellious religious militants or a country or countries whose government he has taken over. "The number of its name" must refer to either of two entities, "the man" or "his institution," since the Bible specifically says *Let the one who has understanding calculate the number of the beast.*" We must eliminate "the beast-man" and try to figure out what it is concerning the other entity, because one can obtain a number by arranging digits in a certain order for identification or reference or by counting for calculation purposes. Referring to this beast-institution or government, we may count how many people are devoting their time running it by categories. We know already that "the beast" will have an army to subdue nations, because the Bible says, "Also it was allowed to make war on the saints and to conquer them. And authority was given it over every tribe and people and language and nation" (Revelation 13:7). It is obvious what we ought to know is the size of his army. He will have several allied forces under his control. The Bible says, "And the ten horns that you saw are ten kings who have not yet received royal power, but they are to receive authority as kings for one hour, together with the beast. These are of one mind and hand over their power and authority to the beast. They will make war on the Lamb, and the Lamb will conquer them, for he is Lord of lords and King of kings, and those with him are called and chosen and faithful." (Revelation 17:12-14).

The riddle "The mark, that is, the name of the beast" after the appropriate substitution can be read as follows: 1) The mark, that is, GROG (a fictive name based on the beast's predicted behavior); 2) The mark, that is, Emir of GROG, 3) The mark, that is, GROG'S. "The mark," the name of the beast being his name, e.g. GROG, or his new title, e.g. Emir of GROG, or his institution's name, e.g. GROG'S.

Let us go back to Revelation 13:18, and calculate "the number of the beast." First we must go to the following chapter and verses concerning the beginning of the "Second Woe" when the sixth angel sounded the trumpet. We read, "Then the sixth angel blew his trumpet, and I heard a voice from the four horns of the golden altar before God, saying to the sixth angel who had the trumpet, 'Release the four angels who are bound at the great river Euphrates.' So the four angels, who had been prepared for the hour, the day, the month, and the year, were released to kill a third of mankind. The number of mounted troops was twice ten thousand times ten thousand; I heard their number. And this is how I saw the horses in my vision and those who rode them: they wore breastplates the color of fire and of sapphire and of sulfur, and the heads of the horses were like lions' heads, and fire and smoke and sulfur came out of their mouths. By these three plagues a third of mankind was killed, by the fire and smoke and sulfur coming out of their mouths. For the power of the horses is in their mouths and in their tails, for their tails are like serpents with heads, and by means of them they wound" (Revelation 9:13-19).

We find the answer to the last riddle of Revelation 13 in the 16th verse of Revelation's chapter 9, which reads, "The number of mounted troops was twice ten thousand times ten thousand; I heard their number." When we complete the calculation, we get an astronomical number, 200,000,000 troops, which is the size of the beast's coalition armies, on war machines, tanks and others, firing from all sides. John witnessed in his visions fire, smoke, and red-hot projectiles coming from their canons and other pieces of artillery.

Let us solve the second part of the riddle: "The mark that is . . . the number of his name." After the necessary substitutions, it can be read as follows: "The mark, that is, GROG'S two hundred million warriors." "The mark," the number of its name, is the strength of its coalition armies, e.g. two hundred million strong.

Let us go even further by clarifying the following vision of John, who witnessed the conclusion of the Next World Conflict, and who wrote, "And I saw what appeared to be a sea of glass mingled with fire—*and also those who had conquered the beast and its image and the number of its name*, standing beside the sea of glass with harps of God in their hands" (Revelation 15:2).

By replacing "the number of its name" with the strength of its coalition armies, the verse can read, "And I saw what appeared to be a sea of glass mingled with fire—*and also those who had conquered GROG and its image and GROG'S two hundred million warriors,* standing beside the sea of glass with harps of God in their hands," or as, "And I saw what appeared to be a sea of glass mingled with fire— and also those who had conquered the beast and its image and its 'two hundred million strong' armies standing beside the sea of glass with harps of God in their hands."

WHAT IS THE WHEREABOUTS OF THE ANTICHRIST?

Here is now the last End-Time visions I have had concerning the whereabouts and the identity of the Antichrist, who is "the man of lawlessness, the son of perdition or the son of destruction" as Paul described him in 2 Thessalonians 2:3. On the morning of November 8, 2005, as I was alone in my bedroom, a political world map appeared to me in the color scheme that I was familiar with, and I was shown a country in northern Africa that I believed to be the Republic of the Sudan. Then in a picture-in-picture effect, I was shown the man of lawlessness consulting a sage. A few days later, after I told my Lord that I could not recognize the man in the picture, which was very small, I was shown two larger pictures showing the face and profile of the outlaw standing next to the man he was with in the previous vision. He was none other than the man who is responsible for the 9/11 attacks and other attacks across the world.

Iranian President Mahmoud Ahmadinejad proclaimed that he is the forerunner for the coming Mahdi, the Moslems' expected messiah, but he stood in the way of the man of lawlessness who has already been introduced to the world.

The Republic of Sudan, where Satan is activating the

beast, is a land whose motto is "Victory is Ours", and whose anthem is "We Are the Army of God and of Our Land." Once, in 1885, it became a theocratic state after the British were driven out by a revolt led by Muhammad Ahmad, a self-proclaimed Mahdi. In 1983, Sharia Law was established in Sudan by then-Islamic president Gaafar Nimeiry, and since then many Christians have been taken captive and massacred. The present conflict that started in 2003 in the Darfur region of western Sudan opposes the Janjaweed, an Islamist militia backed by the Sudanese government and accused of killing innocent civilians and Moslem rebels. It is a sampling of Armageddon, where the enemies of Israel will come against each other. Its activities are already being felt in the surrounding countries like the Republic of Chad and Somalia. Closely watch what is happening in those nations, because God has chosen them as a living stage to show to all of those who accept Jesus as their personal Savior and openly declare themselves His children what is coming their way in the days ahead. Do not be troubled. Most of you will live to witness and endure, as John recounted, "If anyone is to be taken captive, to captivity he goes; if anyone is to be slain with the sword, with the sword must he be slain. Here is a call for the endurance and faith of the saints" (Revelation 13:10).

There is hope, since Jesus declared to John in his visions, "I am coming soon. Hold fast what you have, so that no one may seize your crown. The one who conquers, I will make him a pillar in the temple of my God. Never shall he go out of it, and I will write on him the name of my God, and the name of the city of my God, the new Jerusalem, which comes down from my God out of heaven, and my own new name. He who has an ear, let him hear what the Spirit says to the churches" (Revelation 3:11-13).

Jordan's King Abdullah II proposed, in September 2006, his country as the first one to chair a one-year rotating post of secretary general of a new economic entity of lower-middle income countries known as the G-11, which he created. This group's mission would be to encourage wealthier countries to provide specific economic assistance to lower-middle-income countries to help them meet targeted economic growth. Member countries are Croatia, Ecuador, Georgia, Honduras, Indonesia, Morocco, Pakistan, Paraguay, Tunisia, and Sri Lanka. His country has also hosted a party of three: U.S. president George W. Bush, Israeli prime minister Ariel Sharon, and Palestinian prime minister Mahmoud Abbas, who met at Aqaba on June 4, 2003, to discuss a means of finding a peaceful solution to the Israeli-Palestinian conflict in the implementation of the Quartet's Road Map for peace. And on November 30, 2006, he invited U.S. president George W. Bush and Iraqi

Prime Minister Nouri al-Maliki to meet in Amman to discuss the volatile situation in Iraq. Could this king be the beast, the little horn of Daniel 7:8 according to Revelation 17:12 mentioned above?

Many would be inclined to assert that the king of Jordan fits the profile of the Antichrist according to his role in the Israeli-Palestinian peace process and the creation of the new G-11 grouping. But he is in no way an outlaw, as revealed in the scriptures about the Antichrist.

Bin Laden escaped from the Tora Bora region in eastern Afghanistan, near the Pakistan border, after he was wounded and was not heard of over several months. From that point on, I was no more given access in the spirit to anything concerning him and came to the conclusion that he was either in a comatose state or dead. When he resurfaced, I understood that he was none other than the man of lawlessness who was spared to fulfill the prophecies of John. Now he is a fugitive, a man hiding in dark caves with a substantial bounty over his head. If he appears to be fearful for his life, although he has no respect for the lives of others, even for the peaceful people of the Islamic faith, do not be duped. He is the one God has revealed twice to me as the man of whom it is said, "And you know what is restraining him now so that he may be revealed in his time. For the mystery of lawlessness is already at work. Only he who now restrains it will do so until he is out of the way. And then the lawless one will be revealed, whom the Lord Jesus will kill with the breath of his mouth and bring to nothing by the appearance of his coming" (2 Thessalonians 2:6-8).

Judas, the twelfth apostle, is hosting Satan a second time. "Then Satan entered into Judas called Iscariot, who was of the number of the twelve" (Luke 22:3).

He is coming from the bottomless pit as described to John by one of the seven angels who had the seven bowls, and said "The beast that you saw was, and is not, and is about to rise from the bottomless pit and go to destruction. And the dwellers on earth whose names have not been written in the book of life from the foundation of the world will marvel to see the beast, because it was and is not and is to come" (Revelation 17:8).

Beware, he has come back to rule the world, to do Satan's bidding, and to establish a global religion and world order where those who resist conversion will be decapitated or will be sent to labor camps. He will extend an olive branch to Europe, the U.S., and Israel. He will propose a peaceful and prosperous world. His plans for a better world will sound very attractive to many who are already tired of escalating violence in the Middle East, mainly in Iraq. The world will view him as a savior, the only one capable of curbing terrorism and bringing lasting peace to earth. Paul explained it this way, "The coming of the lawless one is by the activity of Satan with all power and false signs and wonders, and with all wicked deception for those who are perishing, because they refused to love the truth and so be saved. Therefore God sends them a strong delusion, so that they may believe what is false, in order that all may be condemned who did not believe the truth but had pleasure in unrighteousness" (2 Thessalonians 2:9-12).

At the beginning of 2001, before the event of September 11, in a night vision, I found myself in a city being terrorized by a raging bull, and after I took refuge with my sister behind a not-too secure door, I stepped outside to confront it and grabbed it by the horns and hurled it to the ground, where it remained. I then walked past ferocious-looking bulldogs, on their belly and with their heads up. Suddenly I found myself on the other side of a wide chasm, as soon as I had reached the end of a collapsed bridge where they were lining up side-by-side on both sides. This vision was to indicate the beginning of a new wave of attacks by terror groups and their eventual demise. The ongoing violence that Al-Qaeda has been fueling in different parts of the world will finally subside, because the quick and strong response to its vile and despicable acts followed by relentless offensives carried out by the U.S. and allies will shake up its foundation, weaken its strength, and bring it down to its knees by decimating its ranks and depriving it of strongholds.

In the morning of August 19, 2007, in a night vision, I was shown a raging bull roaming and terrorizing a city and then the world, looking for victims, and it was not seen for a time. Then I woke up. This vision is to indicate that Al-Qaeda will finally slow down for a while as the man of lawlessness rethinks its battle plan. This head of the beast will be severely wounded, but even as mortal as it will be; it will survive and regain strength. John reporting what he was shown in his visions wrote, "One of its heads seemed to have a mortal wound, but its mortal wound was healed, and the whole earth marveled as they followed the beast" (Revelation 13:3).

The man of lawlessness and his cohorts will understand their first strategy did not work to its fullest and that it will only take them down the road of defeat; then he will try to use subterfuge as its new approach, and since many have been yearning for peace, they will fall for it. The Bible says, "And they worshiped the dragon, for he had given his authority to the beast, and they worshiped the beast, saying, 'Who is like the beast, and who can fight against it?' " (Revelation 13:4).

Al-Qaeda's acts of terror around the world, the sectarian war in Iraq, and the Israeli-Palestinian conflict had intensified to a point where hope for peace had become a utopia. But Israel will soon sign a peace treaty with the Palestinians. And the man of lawlessness will then propose a peace plan because attacks either in the U.S. and European countries, or Iraq will fail to create the psychological impact expected. Major world powers, eager to end a senseless and prolonged conflict, will quickly accept his peace plan, cessation of all hostilities and amnesty for him and his cohorts, and then he will recall his hordes, declaring himself a friend.

When peace is finally restored and people start enjoying life with less fear, then Satan will give his authority to the man of lawlessness and his assistant, a false prophet who will use it to mesmerize the world with great signs, making fire to come down from heaven, declaring that their religion is the true one. Many, who have been already looking for such signs, will be quick at becoming believers and their followers. These two may then receive invitations from religious and lay organizations to lecture their members, from governments of many nations, to entertain them with their wise advice. All those who are not in the book of life will be listening to their promise of a new and brighter future, economic stability, a better distribution of the planet resources among nations and people, a more equitable, crimeless, and peaceful world where poverty and its woes would be things of the past. The world will be apt at responding positively to his rhetoric and utopian propositions, preferring peace to war and terror. But it will be just the beginning. Many will rebel and refuse indoctrination into a world order incompatible with their belief system. Many will prefer imprisonment, torture, and death by firing squads or decapitation instead of departing from their faith and obedience to Jesus Christ our Lord and Savior. John reporting his vision of the man of lawlessness and his false prophet wrote, "And it was allowed to give breath to the image of the beast, so that the image of the beast might even speak and might cause those who would not worship the image of the beast to be slain. (Revelation 13:15).

The whole earth will submit to his rules; from the Scriptures we read, "His power shall be great—but not by his own power; and he shall cause fearful destruction and shall succeed in what he does, and destroy mighty men and the people who are the saints" (Daniel 8:24).

He may put an end to the Papacy, and the Church will suffer violence. "And the ten horns that you saw, they and the beast will hate the prostitute. They will make her desolate and naked, and devour her flesh and burn her up with fire, for God has put it into their hearts to carry out his purpose by being of one mind and handing over their royal power to the beast, until the words of God are fulfilled. And the woman that you saw is the great city that has dominion over the kings of the earth" (Revelation 17:16-18).

But as soon as the beast regains strength, its leader will become bold and arrogant, and they will turn against the Church and its Christ. It will unleash its furor on Jerusalem, the saints, and their leaders, which will last three years and a half. But two messengers will stand against the Antichrist's rules until the prophecy concerning the end of their mission on the earth will be fulfilled. He will hate them and finally kill them. "And I will grant authority to my two witnesses, and they will prophesy for 1,260 days, clothed in sackcloth. These are the two olive trees and the two lampstands that stand before the Lord of the earth. And if anyone would harm them, fire pours from their mouth and consumes their foes. If anyone would harm them, this is how he is doomed to be killed. They have the power to shut the sky, that no rain may fall during the days of their prophesying, and they have power over the waters to turn them into blood and to strike the earth with every kind of plague, as often as they desire. And when they have finished their testimony, the beast that rises from the bottomless pit will make war on them and conquer them and kill them, and their dead bodies will lie in the street of the great city that symbolically is called Sodom and Egypt, where their Lord was crucified. For three and a half days some from the peoples and tribes and languages and nations will gaze at their dead bodies and refuse to let them be placed in a tomb, and those who dwell on the earth will rejoice over them and make merry and exchange presents, because these two prophets had been a torment to those who dwell on the earth. But after the three and a half days a breath of life from God entered them, and they stood up on their feet, and great fear fell on those who saw them. Then they heard a loud voice from heaven saying to them, 'Come up here!' And they went up to heaven in a cloud, and their enemies watched them. And at that hour there was a great earthquake, and a tenth of the city fell. Seven thousand people were killed in the earthquake, and the rest were terrified and gave glory to the God of heaven" (Revelation 11:3-13).

Who are these two messengers? Could they be Moses and Elijah whom the apostles witnessed talking to Jesus? The Bible says, "And after six days Jesus took with him Peter and James, and John his brother, and led them up a high mountain by themselves. And he was transfigured before them, and his face shone like the sun, and his clothes became white as light. And behold, there appeared to them Moses and Elijah, talking with him" (Matthew 17:1-3).

When the beast of Revelation and its allies, which are the kings of the east, will be invading Jerusalem, then the remnant of the Holy City will escape by the way of a valley God will form for them as He comes to deliver them. Concerning this episode, the word of the LORD came to the prophet Zechariah, the son of Berechiah, son of Iddo, saying, "For I will gather all the nations against Jerusalem to battle, and the city shall be taken and the houses plundered and the women raped. Half of the city shall go out into exile, but the rest of the people shall not be cut off from the city. Then the LORD will go out and fight against those nations as when he fights on a day of battle. On that day his feet shall stand on the Mount of Olives that lies before Jerusalem on the east, and the Mount of Olives shall be split in two from east to west by a very wide valley, so that one half of the Mount shall move northward, and the other half southward. And you shall flee to the valley of my mountains, for the valley of the mountains shall reach to Azal. And you shall flee as you fled from the earthquake in the days of Uzziah king of Judah. Then the LORD my God will come, and all the holy ones with him" (Zechariah 14:2-5).

WORLD WAR III: WILL IT ALSO BE GALACTIC?

Unlike previous global conflicts, the next one will be different. Satan will give his authority to the beast, and the fallen angels, the demons, will fight side-by-side with the enemy's armies. Modern weapons will not be very effective against them, but we should not worry, because the Lord is coming with the holy angels to fight on the side of Israel and those who believe in Christ as their Savior. From Revelation we read, "Then I saw heaven opened, and behold, a white horse! The one sitting on it is called Faithful and True, and in righteousness he judges and makes war. His eyes are like a flame of fire, and on his head are many diadems, and he has a name written that no one knows but himself. He is clothed in a robe dipped in blood, and the name by which he is called is The Word of God. And the armies of heaven, arrayed in fine linen, white and pure, were following him on white horses. From his mouth comes a sharp sword with which to strike down the nations and he will rule them with a rod of iron. He will tread the winepress of the fury of the wrath of God the Almighty. On his robe and on his thigh he has a name written, King of kings and Lord of lords" (Revelation 19:11-16).

And the end of the enemies of Israel will be swift as the Lord described it to the prophets. God will cause many nations to come against Israel in a place of his choosing, where He will reveal on whose side He is. The Lord speaking to Ezekiel the priest and son of Buzi, declared, "Therefore, son of man, prophesy, and say to Gog, Thus says the

Lord GOD: On that day when my people Israel are dwelling securely, will you not know it? You will come from your place out of the uttermost parts of the north, you and many peoples with you, all of them riding on horses, a great host, a mighty army. You will come up against my people Israel, like a cloud covering the land. In the latter days I will bring you against my land, that the nations may know me, when through you, O Gog, I vindicate my holiness before their eyes. "Thus says the Lord GOD: Are you he of whom I spoke in former days by my servants the prophets of Israel, who in those days prophesied for years that I would bring you against them? But on that day, the day that Gog shall come against the land of Israel, declares the Lord GOD, my wrath will be roused in my anger" (Ezekiel 38:14-18).

John reporting what he has witnessed wrote, "And I saw, coming out of the mouth of the dragon and out of the mouth of the beast and out of the mouth of the false prophet, three unclean spirits like frogs. For they are demonic spirits, performing signs, who go abroad to the kings of the whole world, to assemble them for battle on the great day of God the Almighty" (Revelation 16:13-14), and further declared, "And they assembled them at the place that in Hebrew is called Armageddon" (Revelation 16:16).

There they will destroy each other with their weapons

and their nuclear arsenals, bringing an end to the greatest world conflict, WWIII. The holy angels would have already brought order in the heavens, throughout the galaxies, after chasing the evil ones to our planet, their last refuge, where they will be finally captured along with Satan, the dragon, and thrown down into the bottomless pit. From the Scriptures we read, "And this shall be the plague with which the LORD will strike all the peoples that wage war against Jerusalem: their flesh will rot while they are still standing on their feet, their eyes will rot in their sockets, and their tongues will rot in their mouths. And on that day a great panic from the LORD shall fall on them, so that each will seize the hand of another, and the hand of the one will be raised against the hand of the other" (Zechariah 14:12-13). From the Scripture we read, "I will summon a sword against Gog on all my mountains, declares the Lord GOD. Every man's sword will be against his brother. With pestilence and bloodshed I will enter into judgment with him, and I will rain upon him and his hordes and the many peoples who are with him torrential rains and hailstones, fire and sulfur. So I will show my greatness and my holiness and make myself known in the eyes of many nations. Then they will know that I am the LORD" (Ezekiel 38:21-23).

This last battle will take place in the valley of the mountain region of Meggido near the River Kishon, which was the scene of a decisive battle between Israel and the army of Jabin the king of Canaan. The Lord gave Sisera, the general of the king's army, his chariots and his troops into the hand of Barak the son of Abinoam and his men from the tribes of Naphtali and Zebulun. The Bible says, "The Lord's sword was against Sisera and his army. And the LORD routed Sisera and all his chariots and all his army before Barak by the edge of the sword. And Sisera got down from his chariot and fled away on foot. And Barak pursued the chariots and the army to Harosheth-hagoyim, and all the army of Sisera fell by the edge of the sword; not a man was left" (Judges 4:15-16).

The prophetess Deborah reminded Barak the Lord had told him that he would win that day and went with him to battle. After his victory, to give glory to the Lord, she sang these words that he too sang with her: 'The kings came, they fought; then fought the kings of Canaan, at Taanach, by the waters of Meggido; they got no spoils of silver. From heaven the stars fought, from their courses they fought against Sisera'" (Judges 5:19-20).

It will be the costliest war in term of human lives. John, describing his vision of the battlefield and the beast's armies marching against Israel, wrote, "The number of mounted troops was twice ten thousand times ten thousand; I heard their number. And this is how I saw the horses in my vision and those who rode them: they wore breastplates the color of fire and of sapphire and of sulfur, and the heads of the horses were like lions' heads, and fire and smoke and sulfur came out of their mouths. By these three plagues a third of mankind was killed, by the fire and smoke and sulfur coming out of their mouths" (Revelation 9:16-18).

Paul referring to this glorious day of our Lord to the Thessalonians wrote, "And may the Lord make you increase and abound in love for one another and for all, as we do for you, so that he may establish your hearts blameless in holiness before our God and Father, *at the coming of our Lord Jesus with all his saints*" (1 Thessalonians 3:12-13).

The fallen angels, called also "stars of heaven," inhabited all the galaxies after they rebelled against God and were thrown out of His kingdom; some of them even inhabited earth until they disobeyed God and took the daughters of man for wives and were sent to hell. *When Jesus opened the fifth seal*, those who were killed and tortured for his sake demanded vengeance, and John wrote, "When he opened the sixth seal, I looked, and behold, there was a great earthquake, and the sun became black as sackcloth, the full moon became like blood, and the stars of the sky fell to the earth as the fig tree sheds its winter fruit when shaken by a gale. The sky vanished like a scroll that is being rolled up, and every mountain and island was removed from its place. Then the kings of the earth and the great ones and the generals and the rich and the powerful, and everyone, slave and free, hid themselves in the caves and among the rocks of the mountains, calling to the mountains and rocks, 'Fall on us and hide us from the face of him who is seated on the throne, and from the wrath of the Lamb' " (Revelation 6:12-16).

Then will come the moment when God will send His angels to destroy the kingdom of the man of lawlessness with all kinds of plagues. John described what he was shown this way, "*When the Lamb opened the seventh seal, there was silence in heaven for about half an hour.* Then I saw the seven angels who stand before God, and seven trumpets were given to them. And another angel came and stood at the altar with a golden censer, and he was given much incense to offer with the prayers of all the saints on the golden altar before the throne, and the smoke of the incense, with the prayers of the saints, rose before God from the hand of the angel. Then the angel took the censer and filled it with fire from the altar and threw it on the earth, and there were peals of thunder, rumblings, flashes of lightning, and an earthquake. Now the seven angels who had the seven trumpets prepared to blow them" (Revelation 8:1-6).

And He will put an end to the reign of the man of lawlessness. John further wrote, "Then I saw an angel standing in the sun, and with a loud voice he called to all the birds that fly directly overhead, 'Come, gather for the great supper of God, to eat the flesh of kings, the flesh of captains, the flesh of mighty men, the flesh of horses and their riders, and the flesh of all men, both free and slave, both small and great.' And I saw the beast and the kings of the earth with their armies gathered to make war against him who was sitting on the horse and against his army" (Revelation 19:17-19). To Ezekiel the priest and son of Buzi, the Lord pronounced an irrevocable sentence against those who will come against Israel: "You shall fall on the mountains of Israel, you and all your hordes and the peoples who are with you. I will give you to birds of prey of every sort and to the beasts of the field to be devoured. You shall fall in the open field, for I have spoken, declares the Lord GOD." (Ezekiel 39:4-5). He further declared, "On that day I will give to Gog a place for burial in Israel, the Valley of the Travelers, east of the sea. It will block the travelers, for there Gog and all his multitude will be buried. It will be called the Valley of Hamon-gog. For seven months the house of Israel will be burying them, in order to cleanse the land. All the people of the land will bury them, and it will bring them renown on the day that I show my glory, declares the Lord GOD" (Ezekiel 39:11-13).

War broke out also in the heavens and on the earth. John reporting his vision of this event wrote, "Now war arose in heaven, Michael and his angels fighting against the dragon. And the dragon and his angels fought back, but he was defeated and there was no longer any place for them in heaven. *And the great dragon was thrown down, that ancient serpent, who is called the devil and Satan*, the deceiver of the whole world—he was thrown down to the earth, and his angels were thrown down with him" (Revelation 12:7-9). This is what the Lord revealed to the prophet Isaiah the son of Amoz, and he wrote, "On that day the LORD will punish the host of heaven, in heaven, and the kings of the earth, on the earth. They will be gathered together as prisoners in a pit; they will be shut up in a prison, and after many days they will be punished. Then the moon will be confounded and the sun ashamed, for the LORD of hosts reigns on Mount Zion and in Jerusalem, and his glory will be before his elders" (Isaiah 24:21-23).

The man of lawlessness and his assistant, the false prophet, will be thrown alive in the lake of fire and sulfur, where they will remain for eternity. John who witnessed this final episode wrote, "*And the beast was captured, and with it the false prophet* who in its presence had done the signs by which he deceived those who had received the mark of the beast and those who worshiped its image.

These two were thrown alive into the lake of fire that burns with sulfur. And the rest were slain by the sword that came from the mouth of him who was sitting on the horse, and all the birds were gorged with their flesh" (Revelation 19:20-21).

Then those who will follow the beast and who will receive his mark will be also sent to the lake of fire. John wrote, "And another angel, a third, followed them, saying with a loud voice, 'If anyone worships the beast and its image and receives a mark on his forehead or on his hand, he also will drink the wine of God's wrath, poured full strength into the cup of his anger, and he will be tormented with fire and sulfur in the presence of the holy angels and in the presence of the Lamb. And the smoke of their torment goes up forever and ever, and they have no rest, day or night, these worshipers of the beast and its image, and whoever receives the mark of its name' " (Revelation 14:9-11).

During the reign of the man of lawlessness many will be killed by one of the worst volcanic eruptions ever, which may cause deadly freezing temperatures similar to those during the last ice age. The Bible says, "He opened the shaft of the bottomless pit, and from the shaft rose smoke like the smoke of a great furnace, and the sun and the air were darkened with the smoke from the shaft" (Revelation

9:2). Many more will be decimated by superbugs, which will devour human flesh and against which there will no vaccine or cure, by natural disasters such as destructive earthquakes, fire, and floods, by hailstones and winds not yet known of this generation, by windless seasons and extreme heat from the sun that will cause their skin to roast and fall off their bones, by polluted water caused by the fall of celestial matters and the resulting death of all fish and mammals in the rivers and the seas, and from pollution of the air caused by all above-mentioned extreme climatic conditions and cataclysmal events. Those who do not receive the mark of the beast will be spared. The Bible says, "Then from the smoke came locusts on the earth, and they were given power like the power of scorpions of the earth. They were told not to harm the grass of the earth or any green plant or any tree, *but only those people who do not have the seal of God on their foreheads.* They were allowed to torment them for five months, but not to kill them, and their torment was like the torment of a scorpion when it stings someone. And in those days people will seek death and will not find it. They will long to die, but death will flee from them. (Revelation 9:3-6). John wrote, "So the first angel went and poured out his bowl on the earth, and harmful and painful sores came upon the people who bore the mark of the beast and worshiped its image" (Revelation

16:2).

Satan will be captured and thrown down in the bottom-less pit for a thousand years. John wrote, "Then I saw an angel coming down from heaven, holding in his hand the key to the bottomless pit and a great chain. And he seized the dragon, that ancient serpent, who is the devil and Satan, and bound him for a thousand years, and threw him into the pit, and shut it and sealed it over him, so that he might not deceive the nations any longer, until the thousand years were ended. After that he must be released for a little while" (Revelation 20:1-3).

Those who remain faithful to the Lord will take part in the first resurrection or will change in the blink of an eye into angels of light to meet Jesus in space and to be with Him. The Bible says, "For this we declare to you by a word from the Lord, that we who are alive, who are left until the coming of the Lord, will not precede those who have fallen asleep. For the Lord Himself will descend from heaven with a cry of command, with the voice of an archangel, and with the sound of the trumpet of God. And the dead in Christ will rise first. *Then we who are alive, who are left*, will be caught up together with them in the clouds to meet the Lord in the air, and so we will always be with the Lord" (1 Thessalonians 4:15-17). This is what was revealed to John, who penned it this way, "And I heard a voice from heaven saying, 'Write this: Blessed are the dead who die in the Lord from now on.' 'Blessed indeed,' says the Spirit, 'that they may rest from their labors, for their deeds follow them!' Then I looked, and behold, a white cloud, and seated on the cloud one like a son of man, with a golden crown on his head, and a sharp sickle in his hand. And another angel came out of the temple, calling with a loud voice to him who sat on the cloud, 'Put in your sickle, and reap, for the hour to reap has come, for the harvest of the earth is fully ripe.' So he who sat on the cloud swung his sickle across the earth, and the earth was reaped" (Revelation 14:13-16).

And after that they will reign with Him on this earth for a thousand years. "Blessed and holy is the one who shares in the first resurrection! Over such the second death has no power, but they will be priests of God and of Christ, and they will reign with him for a thousand years" (Revelation 20:6).

One day, when I was 17 years old, I watched a very long and green serpent pass me, crawling very fast on the hot asphalt of my street, while I was standing at one of the gates of my house. I took off after it, as I was gaining ground, it turned around, and counterattacked without slowing down, holding its head and almost half of its body up. As it was closing in, I bent down, grabbed a flat and sharp-edged stone that happened to be the only one there, and targeting the head, I threw it in a swift move. In slow motion, I watched it fly pass the serpent as the sectioned head flew away from the body that was stopped dead in its track. Was not this a prelude to a future event?

In a night vision on February 1, 2006, I was shown the defeat of Satan. As I was resisting temptation, I watched a baby turn into a gigantic lizard standing on its hind legs, and knew it was Satan; he tried to attack me, but I rebuked him, and he fell backward to the ground and turned into a small lizard among several smaller ones that surrounded me. I fought him and them, and they fell into small parts, and then a dog swallowed their remains and came and vomited them at my feet and they disintegrated. Relieved, I cried out, "It is finished."

For several nights I dreamed of small green serpents crawling in my small bedroom and of a larger one that swallowed them. Then, one day, as I went to bed and after I turned to my right, which I do rarely, a big shelf laden with books came crashing down hitting the bed at the exact place where my feet were seconds before.

The following day, as I was at my desk completing the last chapters of this book, all a sudden, the atmosphere of my bedroom changed and, as though a portal to Hell had been opened, I could hear of lamentations of those destined

to eternal damnation. I heard the squeaking of a stable two-foot-wide shelf that was behind me as though someone was pushing it toward me and a thud when it hit the wall that it abutted. I sprang up and spun on one leg thrusting my right hand three times toward an invisible enemy crying out at each instance, "By the blood of Jesus"; the same way I did it in the night vision when I was shown that epic fight with Satan as described above. Total calm suddenly replaced that cacophony that filled the room seconds before. The evil one and his demons were defeated by the precious holy blood of Jesus.

The same week, another night, standing by the head of my bed, a narrow cot, I watched the grey hands of the angel of death firmly grabbed my wrists, trying to tug my body away. All of a sudden, small green serpents were crawling very fast toward me and a larger one met them half way and swallowed them, and the vision ended. I have not been subjected to such attacks since.

The Bible says, "The seventh angel poured out his bowl into the air, and a loud voice came out of the temple, from the throne, saying, 'It is done!' And there were flashes of lightning, rumblings, peals of thunder, and a great earthquake such as there had never been since man was on the earth, so great was that earthquake. *The great city was split into three parts*, and the cities of the nations fell, and God remembered Babylon the great, to make her drain the cup of the wine of the fury of his wrath. And every island fled away, and no mountains were to be found. And great hailstones, about one hundred pounds each, fell from heaven on people; and they cursed God for the plague of the hail, because the plague was so severe" (Revelation 16:17-21).

Jesus and His Father will come to dwell among us as John described it: "Then the seventh angel blew his trumpet, and there were loud voices in heaven, saying, 'The kingdom of the world has become the kingdom of our Lord and of his Christ, and he shall reign forever and ever'" (Revelation 11:15). And he further wrote, "And I saw the holy city, New Jerusalem, coming down out of heaven from God, prepared as a bride adorned for her husband. And I heard a loud voice from the throne saying, 'Behold, the dwelling place of God is with man. He will dwell with them, and they will be his people, and God himself will be with them as their God' " (Revelation 21:2-3). Some might argue that this event will not take place at the beginning of the millennium reign of Christ Jesus, but the Bible says, "Let us rejoice and exult and give him the glory, for the marriage of the Lamb has come, and his Bride has made herself ready; it was granted her to clothe herself with fine linen, bright and pure'—for the fine linen is the righteous deeds of the saints. And the angel said to me, 'Write this:

Blessed are those who are invited to the marriage supper of the Lamb.' And he said to me, 'These are the true words of God' " (Revelation 19:7-9)

Why would angel declare to John, in his vision: "Blessed are those who wash their robes, so that they may have the right to the tree of life and that they may enter the city by the gates. *Outside are the dogs and sorcerers and the sexually immoral and murderers and idolaters*, and everyone who loves and practices falsehood" (Revelation 22:14-15), If it were not so and if he were not referring to the Millennium era?

After the last judgment there will be no more wickedness on the earth since those who will not be found in the Book of life will join Satan and cohort in the lake of fire where they will remain for ever. The Bible says, "And when the thousand years are ended, Satan will be released from his prison and will come out to deceive the nations that are at the four corners of the earth, Gog and Magog, to gather them for battle; their number is like the sand of the sea. And they marched up over the broad plain of the earth and surrounded the camp of the saints and the beloved city, but fire came down from heaven and consumed them, and the devil who had deceived them was thrown into the lake of fire and sulfur where the beast and the false prophet were, and they will be tormented day and night forever and ever" (Revelation 20:7-10).

Then will play the last chapter of the history of mankind and this planet as we know it. And the end will come with the last judgment. John sitting in front row, watching it unfolding on his visionary screen, described it for us: The Bible says, "Then I saw a great white throne and him who was seated on it. *From his presence earth and sky fled away, and no place was found for them.* And I saw the dead, great and small, standing before the throne, and books were opened. Then another book was opened, which is the book of life. And the dead were judged by what was written in the books, according to what they had done. And the sea gave up the dead who were in it, Death and Hades gave up the dead who were in them, and they were judged, each one of them, according to what they had done. Then Death and Hades were thrown into the lake of fire. This is the second death, the lake of fire. And if anyone's name was not found written in the book of life, he was thrown into the lake of fire" (Revelation 20:11-15).

The events described above in (Revelation 20:11) might explain the functions of black holes as being there by design to be receptacles God has created to dispose of the universe or rearrange it, in due time, as John put it: "The sky vanished like a scroll that is being rolled up, and every mountain and island was removed from its place" (Revelation 6:14), and he further wrote, "Then I saw a new heaven and a new earth, for the first heaven and the first earth had passed away, and the sea was no more" (Revelation 21:1). Before John, the prophet Isaiah, the son of Amoz, reporting what the Lord spoke to him, wrote, "All the host of heaven shall rot away, and the skies roll up like a scroll. All their host shall fall, as leaves fall from the vine, like leaves falling from the fig tree" (Isaiah 34:4).

On June 4, 1998, around 7 p.m., in Coral Gables, Florida, as the sun was setting, in my spirit I was told to step outside and to look up. As I did without hesitation, I saw right above head, at that very second, three skywriters that had started writing a message that I could not read because it was written in an alphabet that I could not understand, and then I was reminded in my spirit that it was the Hebrew message that my Lord had showed me in a night vision in 1981. He announced to me then, "When you see this sign, you shall know that my coming is near." The next day listening to the radio, I learned that the Jewish community was celebrating the fiftieth anniversary of the State of Israel, and later in the afternoon, around 7 p.m., I saw the planes writing the same message across the setting sun as I was standing in front of a window looking west. If I hadn't been at the right location, at the right minute and second, I would have missed that event. On the third day, I started sending my first message to the Church, announcing the good news that our Lord's coming was near. The eighth anniversary of that day fell on Tuesday, June 6, 2006, which can be written interchangeably as 06/06/06 or 6/6/6 or, after the 999 pattern, as 666, the mystery code that has allowed us to learn more about the character and modus operandi of the man of lawlessness, while 999 was 9/11, his calling card, a day that will remain etched for a very long time in our mind.

Only God can put together something as complex as this with so many independent entities and events along a time-line in a tri-dimensional environment. I have humbly applied myself to being just a servant, reporting faithfully what was given to me in dreams and visions, by word of knowledge or spoken words, and I have carried my burden, heavy at times but made light by my Lord. Paul wrote, "For I am already being poured out as a drink offering, and the time of my departure has come. I have fought the good fight, I have finished the race, I have kept the faith. Henceforth there is laid up for me the crown of righteousness, which the Lord, the righteous judge, will award to me on that Day, and not only to me but also to all who have loved his appearing" (2 Timothy 4:6-8).

LETTERS TO CHURCH LEADERS

WAKE UP! THE BEAST IS ABOUT TO RULE THE WORLD

Are you ready to lead under the new system where no one will be able to transact, buy or sell unless one receives the mark of the beast? Think about it for a moment, what have you done to prepare the church to be self-sufficient?

Now that I have revealed to you who he is, it should be evident to you that this ruler, a religious extremist, will establish Sharia Law with the help of the Taliban and their blind leader Mullah Omar. He will try to coerce everyone into accepting his religion. He will take over all those multimillion dollar houses of worship you have built and will forbid Christians to practice their faith. His followers and he will burn all Bibles they can put their hands on and whoever will be caught with one will surely die.

You might say "Well we won't have to buy anything from him because many of us are farmers and own most of the crops, others own most of the stores selling everything we consume." You are dead wrong; he will take over control of all countries' natural resources, production of goods and their movement, and their banking system.

Many Christians will survive the plagues because they will not be harmed. The Bible says, "They were told not to harm the grass of the earth or any green plant or any tree, but only those people who do not have the seal of God on their foreheads" (Revelation 9:4). Paul to the faithful wrote, "For the Lord himself will descend from heaven with a cry of command, with the voice of an archangel, and with the sound of the trumpet of God. And the dead in Christ will rise first. Then we who are alive, who are left, will be caught up together with them in the clouds to meet the Lord in the air, and so we will always be with the Lord" (1 Thessalonians 4:16-17).

This is a call to tighten your belt, to preach the truth and lead the sheep to good pasture. Jesus said, "By *your endurance* you will gain your lives" (Luke 21:19). And to John the angel said, "Here *is a call for the endurance* of the saints, those who keep the commandments of God and their faith in Jesus" (Revelation 14:12).

A prominent minister, surrendering to the beast denied Christ three times on a syndicated TV show watched by millions globally. Many among you and your flock will defect the same way.

Stop bickering between you, be of one mind, and in secret, start preparing for what is to come. Form a battle plan on how church members will use technology as well as primitive means to keep sharing the word, move to and fro, grow food, and make their cloths and other basic necessities that will become tomorrow's luxuries. Remember how the first Christians, living in the manner of the Hittites, survived persecutions. The Bible says, "Women received back their dead by resurrection. Some were tortured, refusing to accept release, so that they might rise again to a better life. Others suffered mocking and flogging, and even chains and imprisonment. They were stoned, they were sawn in two, and they were killed with the sword. They went about in skins of sheep and goats, destitute, afflicted, mistreated-- of whom the world was not worthy--wandering about in deserts and mountains, and in dens and caves of the earth" (Hebrews 11:35-38).

Because the two witnesses will refuse to bear the mark of the beast as well as many others among us, they will have to improvise to cover themselves. The Bible says, "And I will grant authority to my two witnesses, and they will prophesy for 1,260 days, clothed in sackcloth" (Revelation 11:3).

LETTER TO CARDINALS BEFORE PAPAL ELECTION?

A Letter Released in April 2005

You and other cardinals are gathering for a conclave to elect a new pope, and as you pray for guidance, open your heart and remain silent so you may hear His (The Lord's) voice.

Our Lord Jesus Christ, who sent me to prepare His coming, is already at the door, and there may not be a third pontiff before He comes. The new one must be stronger than the departed one and bring the lost sheep back to the fold.

The Church has been walking away from the Lord's way because those in authority have indulged in idolatry, fornication, adultery, gay life, and other immoralities and have not preached according to the Word, misleading the sheep that the Lord has entrusted to their care. The prophet Jeremiah warning the religious leaders of Israel of God's discontent with them, declared, "Woe to the shepherds who destroy and scatter the sheep of my pasture!' declares the LORD" (Jeremiah 23:1).

The new Pope must remove from the house of the Lord and from the neck of the Lord's sheep all carved images of Him or anyone else in heaven or on earth, all those they have been bowing down to, kissing, praying to. He must promulgate a clear ruling that forbids those practices so the people may turn back to their true God and stop the worship of anyone else but Jesus Christ who is Lord, the first and only one who has risen from the dead, and who sits at the right hand of his father and intercedes for us as an eternal priest. From the Scriptures we read, "You shall not make for yourself a carved image, or any likeness of anything that is in heaven above, or that is in the earth beneath, or that is in the water under the earth. You shall not bow down to them or serve them, for I the LORD your God am a jealous God, visiting the iniquity of the fathers on the children to the third and the fourth generation of those who hate me" (Exodus 20:4-5).

Church leaders may try to argue they never did kneel and bow down to worship the statue of Mary and other servants who have passed away, or crosses of wood or metal with or without the carving of Christ, and they never did burn incense, but they know those instances and practices are recorded on earth and in heaven.

If they were to argue instead that they were right to practice and teach the Lord's sheep those things kindling his anger, do they then pray to or worship Abraham, Isaac, and Jacob, and Moses, who are already in heaven? Don't they serve God by living according to their own rules and not his commands? In no way can they escape judgment if they do not change their course when they still can. The Lord spoke to Jeremiah saying, "The children gather wood, the fathers kindle fire, and the women knead dough, to make cakes for the queen of heaven. And they pour out drink offerings to other gods, to provoke me to anger" (Jeremiah 7:18).

Whoever would argue that Mary, the mother of Jesus, is to be prayed to or to be worshipped is contradicted by the following verses, where Jesus, who knew that many would be misled into committing such sin, established clearly that she was a servant as anyone else, provided that she keep doing the will of God. The Bible says, "And a crowd was sitting around him, and they said to him, 'Your mother and your brothers are outside, seeking you.' And he answered them, 'Who are my mother and my brothers?' And looking about at those who sat around him, he said, 'Here are my mother and my brothers! Whoever does the will of God, he is my brother and sister and mother" (Mark 3:32-35).

Jesus, the Word made flesh, our Creator and Savior, has chosen Mary to do His will just the same way He has called you to priesthood, and speaking to His disciples He emphasized, "You did not choose me, but I chose you and appointed you that you should go and bear fruit and that your fruit should abide, so that whatever you ask the Father in my name, he may give it to you" (John 15:16).

Only our Lord Jesus Christ is holy. Worship belongs only to Him and the Father. John wrote, "Who will not fear, O Lord, and glorify your name? For you alone are holy. All nations will come and worship you, for your righteous acts have been revealed" (Revelation 15:4).

Jesus is the only mediator between man and His Father. Paul to the Thessalonians wrote, "For there is one God, and there is one mediator between God and men, the man Christ Jesus" (1 Timothy 2:5).

Church leaders must fear the Lord and turn away from their abominations while they still can, because He is coming soon with His retribution. He spoke to me more than once and showed me signs in the heavens about those things. He raised me up for such a time as this. You might not believe me, but what would I gain at sending you this message, other than the fulfillment of a mission, since I am a mere servant and only the Lord is Judge? The Lord said, "I will seek the lost, and I will bring back the strayed, and I will bind up the injured, and I will strengthen the weak, and the fat and the strong I will destroy. I will feed them in justice" (Ezekiel 34:16). And from the Scriptures we read, "Both prophet and priest are ungodly; even in my house I have found their evil, declares the LORD. Therefore their way shall be to them like slippery paths in the darkness, into which they shall be driven and fall, for I will bring disaster upon them in the year of their punishment, declares the LORD" (Jeremiah 23:11-12).

Do not resent the rebuke. To the contrary, accept it as a blessing, and may the will of God be known. From the Scriptures we read, "My son, do not despise the LORD's discipline or be weary of his reproof, for the LORD reproves him whom he loves, as a father the son in whom he delights. Blessed is the one who finds wisdom, and the one who gets understanding" (Proverbs 3:11-13).

A JUDAS IN YOUR MIDST

A Letter Released in February 2005

I am sending this message, the sixth one, to a handful of you because it concerns mainly those who have the means to reach the whole earth with the Gospel of Jesus in an instant, having great authority over many.

Early on the morning of February 15, 2005, in a vision succeeding, as a continuum, another one in which it was revealed to me the meaning of a certain End-Time mystery, I realized that I was aware that the knowledge that I was given was about to be erased, and I struggled to access it, but when it was over, all that remained was enough to alarm me. I opened my Bible, and the Lord took me to 2

Peter 2, which He had once put in my heart to warn Church leaders. Only then did the understanding of the vision come to light.

One of you is among the false teachers, and with his great knowledge of the Word, he has mesmerized many but has skillfully hidden his evil side. Now, emboldened by his popularity, he is openly promoting a man who worships a queen of heaven and who has caused many to commit idolatry in the manner of those who have preceded him.

They have established a cult of themselves, declaring that it is only through them that one can benefit fully from the means of salvation. Peter wrote, "But false prophets also arose among the people, just as there will be false teachers among you, who will secretly bring in destructive heresies, even denying the Master who bought them, bringing upon themselves swift destruction. And many will follow their sensuality, and because of them the way of truth will be blasphemed" (2 Peter 2:1-2).

Through Jesus we have access to the Father, who made His Holy Spirit, a Helper, available to all, and speaking to His disciples He said, "If you then, who are evil, know how to give good gifts to your children, how much more will the heavenly Father give the Holy Spirit to those who ask him!" (Luke 11:13).

The apostle Luke commenting on the day of Pentecost

to his friend Theophilus wrote, "And they were all filled with the Holy Spirit and began to speak in other tongues as the Spirit gave them utterance" (Acts 2:4).

Beware of the beast that is to be revealed soon, since the Bible says, "One of its heads seemed to have a mortal wound, but its mortal wound was healed, and the whole earth marveled as they followed the beast" (Revelation 13:3).

THE ANCHORED GALLEON

A Letter Released in November 2004

For the past few years I have been communicating, to most of you messages that our Lord Jesus Christ has placed in my heart or that He has given me in dreams and visions. He has raised me up for such a time as this. Because of other aspects of my mission, I have received a great number of messages of a different nature, which clearly indicate that this one might be the indication of a quick unfolding of End-Time prophecies.

I woke up troubled by a dream I had on that Saturday morning, November 27, 2004. I was in charge of an anchored galleon, and I was there to help onboard Christians rowing away from evil pursuers. Then arrived on the last boat a young ebony bride in white attire, a veil covering her face, and an escort of groomsmen walking in pairs, forming two rows, was following her, and behind them a horse-drawn carriage. They stopped in an orderly fashion on the opposite side of the pier, as if waiting to be called. The enemy was catching up fast; I woke up when I was about to motion the bride's party to board quickly. Jesus said to his disciples, "Just as it was in the days of Noah, so will it be in the days of the Son of Man. They were eating and drinking and marrying and being given in marriage, until the day when Noah entered the ark, and the flood came and destroyed them all" (Luke 17:26-27).

Who are those who made it onboard? Many generations of Christians are already in the presence of the Lord and are to return with the King of kings to reign with Him in the New Jerusalem. The works of the flesh are manifest in today's Church, which is being overrun by the enemy. The sheep are still wandering and being misled. A great number of them act after the followers of satanic and voodoo priests and priestesses who write their wishes on sheets of paper, which they place under their pillow, sleeping on them, hoping to receive messages in their dreams, or burning them on altars. Those servants of Satan in the church attach pieces of fabrics considered to have received power transferred by their priests under their bed sheets and inside their clothing to receive favors or protection from the spirit world. They delve into animism and worship a queen of heaven along with the canonized element whom they give strange names; on saint's day, many demonic spirits indwell some of them and cause them to wear black attire, to use profane words and get drunk. Their confusion has caused them to lose faith, as though God is incapable of knowing the desire of their heart or of hearing them when they call upon Him, forgetting that their body is His temple, because many shepherds have departed from Jesus' teachings.

What is the good of being in charge of a mammoth flock and not really having time for the sheep mainly when the enemy is on the prowl and traps are being set at every corner of your towns and cities? What is the good of boasting about worldly possessions that Jesus did not care about when He could have, in the blink of an eye, built the tallest, biggest, most beautiful, and best ornate house of worship or could have turned every ordinary stone on the ground where He walked into precious ones more brilliant and heavier than any of those the world is quick at showing off?

Which one of you would give a man fifteen thousand sheep and expect him to properly take care of each one of them or to effectively protect them against packs of hungry wolves? I sincerely believe that, savvy as you are, none of you would because you know it would be a senseless and costly decision. You would probably say to this man, "I am putting you in charge of my herd, and I want you to find honest and capable men to help you. Let them report to you, and let each of them take care of a reasonable number of sheep." Why should you conduct the affairs of God differently?

Moses, listening to the advice of Jethro, his father-in-law, picked a number of God-fearing, trustworthy, and able young men to help him in his daily tasks. The Scriptures say, "Moses chose able men out of all Israel and made them heads over the people, chiefs of thousands, of hundreds, of fifties, and of tens" (Exodus 18:25).

Jesus spoke of a shepherd with a manageable number of sheep and how much each one of them deserved his unconditional attention. To the Pharisees and the scribes He told this parable: "What man of you, having a hundred sheep, if he has lost one of them, does not leave the ninety-nine in the open country, and go after the one that is lost, until he finds it?" (Luke 15:4).

Jesus showed His disciples how to effectively provide for a large group of followers. The Bible says, "For there were about five thousand men. And he said to his disciples, 'Have them sit down in groups of about fifty each'" (Luke 9:14).

THE LORD'S COMMAND

A Letter Released in April 2004

On a Thursday morning, the twenty-second day of the fourth month of 2004, in a vision I became aware that I was about to receive the Lord's command and that I had in my possession a certain container. And after what seemed to be a few minutes, the Lord came to me just like He came to me when I was a child. In a loud voice He ordered me to go pour out the contents of the vessel on the earth. I knew it was fire and other means to affect humankind. I was resolute to go fulfill what He had commanded me, and the vision came to an end. I opened my eyes, troubled by it, got out of bed, and felt the urge to tell someone about it. As I was about to do so, I felt an irresistible thirst from my soul to go first to the Word. I opened my Bible and the Lord took me to the right page. My eyes fell on Revelation 15:5-8, which says, "After this I looked, and the sanctuary of the tent of witness in heaven was opened, and out of the sanctuary came the seven angels with the seven plagues, clothed in pure, bright linen, with golden sashes around their chests. And one of the four living creatures gave to the seven angels seven golden bowls full of the wrath of God who lives forever and ever, and the sanctuary was filled with smoke from the glory of God and from his power, and no one could enter the sanctuary until the seven plagues of the seven angels were finished."

I avidly read up to Revelation 16:1, which says, "Then I heard a loud voice from the temple telling the seven angels, 'Go and pour out on the earth the seven bowls of the wrath of God.'" Later I read repeatedly that command which was also given to me in the vision.

Brother, there is no doubt in my mind that the time of the last tribulations has arrived. This is the fourth time the Lord has communicated his message to me in that manner, although it comes to me by all the other means that most of you experience everyday. I know that when He does, it is to announce to me a command in direct connection with Bible prophecies and whose fulfillment I will witness or execute. Before 9/11, the Lord never gave me a date, except when He had given me, through his servant my sister, knowledge of the day, encoded as 999, concerning that violent attack against the towers, which caused the whole world to mourn their dead. But it took more or less forty years to fulfill the first mission because He had to raise me up. It took almost seventeen years to witness the second one concerning His second coming because they were both linked to the fiftieth anniversary of the state of Israel. And it took just a few weeks for the third one because a chosen servant was soon to rule this land amid strife.

The following is about the "chosen servant" I referred to in the above epistle to the Church. It was a letter addressed to the press in a sealed envelope inside another one with the recommendation not to open it until after the presidential election ended. I wrote, "*In the morning of October 11, 2000, around 9:00 a.m., as I was relaxing in bed, all of a sudden in a vision, an illustrated children's history book opened in front of me. My eyes wandered at the top of the first page. On the left, two words grabbed my attention: 'BUSH' and 'PRESIDENT.' As I was about to read the whole sentence, a loud voice said something that came out like the following: 'ALAS! BUSH BECAME PRESIDENT.'*" In fact, he won the presidency amid deep sorrow from the opposition. God has spoken loudly to the nation that he was the chosen one. Indeed, he was the one for a time such as this. He has been a thorn in the enemy's side, and he is wearing them out. After everything is over, because of his tenacity and his faith, the man of lawlessness will have no other option but to extend the olive branch, even though it will be a tactical gesture to come back even stronger in due time, as the Lord meant it to be.

RISE, CHURCH LEADERS, HEAD-ON!

A Letter Released in March 2004

I have to warn you that terrible dangers are looming at the horizon. The enemy, enraged and frustrated because it is being defeated and has been incapable of intimidating the leadership of this country into withdrawing from present theaters of operations overseas, is preparing itself to deliver everything it has in its arsenal to bring to our shores destruction of cataclysmal proportion. I have been writing to you, Church leaders, warning you about what may become of those who are misleading the sheep of the Lord and of this land if they do not change course. It is up to the very few of you receiving this message to take the lead. I cannot write to every one of you, because time is of the essence.

I told you how the Lord has been using me to warn the leadership of evil plots by the enemy against this country, which has been chosen by Him to be the springboard for the Gospel and as one that would stand by Israel. In February 2004, as I was ministering to churches in other parts of the world, because of what I was shown, I felt compelled to stop for a moment and warn of the new faces of danger. Three days before the recent event train attacks in Europe, I was given knowledge of new developments but could not prevent the one of March 11, 2004, when bombs on commuter trains in Madrid, Spain, killed almost two hundred people and wounded many more. Just as the previous event that shook the world, this one of a lesser proportion is to be taken as a warning that the real protection can come only if we cover ourselves in the armor or the Lord by conforming to His Word.

Since a very large sector of this country is willing to turn it into Sodom and Gomorrah, Church leaders ought to stand up against this new wave of attacks by Satan and mobilize the whole nation, challenging the body of Christ to walk in holiness, the only way that pleases the Lord. The Bible says, "For whoever shall keep the whole law, and yet stumble in one point, he has become guilty of all" (James 2:10 EMTV).

The new danger I was shown made me tremble, not of fright but of fear that the curse of Babylon may be near because of the corruption, the inaction, the complacence, and complaisance of many in charge of the sheep of this land. Many are diluting the Word, because they are still preaching according to their needs, transforming themselves into mere merchants peddling their wares, promoting idolatry (Jeremiah 7:18-20, Luke 8:20-21) and sexual immorality, (2 Peter 2:11-22). Blessed are those who are faithful to the Word and are taking the sheep to the right pasture. Many will be caught in their wrongdoing and will not be given any last minute chance to repent as they have come to expect.

I am urging Church leaders to set apart specific moments for praise and prayer at a national and even international level, not just after upheaval or because of imminent danger but as a permanent feature in the context of the fight against evil. "Watch ye therefore, and pray always, that ye may be accounted worthy to escape all these things that shall come to pass, and to stand before the Son of man" (Luke 21:36 KJV).

THE LORD'S REBUKE

A Letter Released in 2003

Dear brothers in Christ, I am writing to you to encourage you in staying firm in your ministry. I was under tremendous attacks and was subjected to ridicule and to the most ignominious lies and treason when I wrote to most of you several years ago to share with you the good news that Christ was at the door on the fourth day of the sixth month of the year 1998, as the Jewish community was celebrating the fiftieth anniversary of the State of Israel. I had seen, being written in the sky, the Hebrew message that many years earlier the Lord had shown me as He announced then, "When you see this sign you shall know that my coming is near." Five years later, on that very same day, four world leaders met at Aqaba, Jordan, to find a peaceful solution to the Israeli-Palestinian conflict. As I am addressing you, the enemy, which is Satan, is still on the offensive, but I know that it is because of the nature of my work. He does not want me to share with you what the Lord has placed in my heart.

The world is walking away from the Lord's way, as fornication, adultery, gay life, and other immoralities have become rampant and widely supported. His name has been removed from the mouth of the children and blotted out of their books, and His commands have been taken down by those in authority because you have misled the sheep the Lord has entrusted to your care. It is now your responsibility more than ever to undo the wrong that was done and to restore what is to be restored for fear that the cities of your land will be delivered into the hands of the enemy. I cannot be complaisant. I have to tell you the truth and warn you of what may befall you and the people of your land. Even though I was shown what was about to occur on that fatidic day, the Lord had revealed it to me many years earlier. I was not allowed to warn the leadership a second time because it was to be a more convincing warning of things that might come your way if you do not bring His scattered sheep back to the fold. Do not let the curse of Babylon

(Revelation 18:1-24) visit you and the people of your land. Time is running out. From the Scriptures we read, "Woe to the shepherds who destroy and scatter the sheep of my pasture!' declares the LORD. Therefore thus says the LORD, the God of Israel, concerning the shepherds who care for my people: 'You have scattered my flock and have driven them away, and you have not attended to them. Behold, I will attend to you for your evil deeds, declares the LORD' " (Jeremiah 23:1-2). And the Lord spoke again saying, "For the land is full of adulterers; because of the curse the land mourns, and the pastures of the wilderness are dried up. Their course is evil, and their might is not right. 'Both prophet and priest are ungodly; even in my house I have found their evil, declares the LORD. Therefore their way shall be to them like slippery paths in the darkness, into which they shall be driven and fall, for I will bring disaster upon them in the year of their punishment, declares the LORD' " (Jeremiah 23:10-12).

I am a living witness of your misconduct, and you have transformed the house of the Lord into a house of commerce and fornication, glorifying yourselves of having conquered the wives of those who have come to you for counsel. You preach according to your needs, developing a materialistic cult, and you are competing among yourselves to acquire the bigger and better of everything. Those who are diluting the Word to sell their wares are of the kind Jesus angrily drove out of the temple. But those who are faithful to the Word and who use their entrepreneurial skills for the good of the kingdom are surely blessed. You concern yourselves more with your affairs than with leading the flock, but you can await what shall come your way if you do not change course. Of you it is said, "They have eyes full of adultery, insatiable for sin. They entice unsteady souls. They have hearts trained in greed. Accursed children! Forsaking the right way, they have gone astray. They have followed the way of Balaam, the son of Beor, who loved gain from wrongdoing, but was rebuked for his own transgression; a speechless donkey spoke with human voice and restrained the prophet's madness. These are waterless springs and mists driven by a storm. For them the gloom of utter darkness has been reserved. For, speaking loud boasts of folly, they entice by sensual passions of the flesh those who are barely escaping from those who live in error. They promise them freedom, but they themselves are slaves of corruption. For whatever overcomes a person, to that he is enslaved. For if, after they have escaped the defilements of the world through the knowledge of our Lord and Savior Jesus Christ, they are again entangled in them and overcome, the last state has become worse for them than the first. For it would have been better for them never to have known the way of righteousness than after knowing it to turn back from the holy commandment delivered to them. What the true proverb says has happened to them: 'The dog returns to its own vomit, and the sow, after washing herself, returns to wallow in the mire' " (2 Peter 2:14-22).

Clean up your act. Because of your misconduct, your negligence, and your complaisance, you are calling upon yourselves the wrath of the Lord, because your flock has gone astray and is profoundly divided. Because of the bad example you have set, they have lost faith and live in fear, relying more on man instead of the Lord. And the enemy has taken over their lives. If you were firm in your teaching, they would have been more careful. Why are they indulging in fornication, adultery, and extravagance? Isn't it because you do the same? Clean up your act before it is too late. This land has suffered enough because of you, because you have made a mockery of God and have taken his sheep to the wrong pasture. You have created an adulterated version of the Word since you preach according to your needs and your manner of living. To the Galatians Paul wrote, "Now the works of the flesh are evident: sexual immorality, impurity, sensuality" (Galatians 5:19).

Because, contrary to the Word, you've made God's forgiveness unconditional, there is no more fear of sins and retribution. John wrote, "Jesus stood up and said to her, 'Woman, where are they? Has no one condemned you?' She said, 'No one, Lord.' And Jesus said, 'Neither do I condemn you; go, and from now on sin no more' " (John 8:10-11). "Again Jesus spoke to them, saying, 'I am the light of the world. Whoever follows me will not walk in darkness, but will have the light of life.' So the Pharisees said to him, 'You are bearing witness about yourself; your testimony is not true.' Jesus answered, 'Even if I do bear witness about myself, my testimony is true, for I know where I came from and where I am going, but you do not know where I come from or where I am going' "(John 8:10-14).

You're even preaching that believing is all one needs to be saved. The Bible says, "And behold, a man came up to him, saying, 'Teacher, what good deed must I do to have eternal life?' And he said to him, 'Why do you ask me about what is good? There is only one who is good. If you would enter life, keep the commandments.' He said to him, 'which ones?' And Jesus said, 'You shall not murder, you shall not commit adultery, You shall not steal, You shall not bear false witness, Honor your father and mother, and, You shall love your neighbor as yourself' " (Matthew 19:16-19) (see also James 2:10, James 2:19-20, 2 Peter 2:9).

Divorce has plagued your congregations, and families are being destroyed because of your complacent attitude. How long this will last? Until calamity knocks at your door! The Bible says, "And he said to them, 'Whoever divorces his wife and marries another commits adultery against her, and if she divorces her husband and marries another, she commits adultery'" (Mark 10:11-12) (see also Mark 10:11-12; Matthew 5:27-28).

You live with no respect for God's established order, and you take upon yourself to do what Christ did not teach you. Did He not show you how to pray to His Father and ask for help in the fight against principalities? He said, "And forgive us our sins, for we ourselves forgive everyone who is indebted to us. And lead us not into temptation" (Luke 11:4).

Because of your arrogant attitude, Peter wrote the following: "And especially those who indulge in the lust of defiling passion and despise authority. Bold and willful, they do not tremble as they blaspheme the glorious ones, whereas angels, though greater in might and power, do not pronounce a blasphemous judgment against them before the Lord. But these, like irrational animals, creatures of instinct, born to be caught and destroyed, blaspheming about matters of which they are ignorant, will also be destroyed in their destruction, suffering wrong as the wage for their wrongdoing. They count it pleasure to revel in the daytime. They are blots and blemishes, reveling in their deceptions, while they feast with you" (2 Peter 2:10-13).

Your churches are still much divided. Some think they deserve the best place or the greatest honor. Stop this foolishness; do not let them play in the hands of Satan. The Bible says, "But many who are first will be last, and the last first" (Matthew 19:30) (see also Matthew 19:30, James 2:1-9, Acts 10:34).

Why not consider the elders first? The following establishes the type of precedence that should take place in the congregation: "Likewise, you who are younger, be subject to the elders. Clothe yourselves, all of you, with humility toward one another, for 'God opposes the proud but gives grace to the humble' " (1 Peter 5:5) (see also Psalms 107:32, James 5:14).

Do not impose undue financial burden on your flock. Do not encourage them to enslave themselves to usury, which is Satan's plan as the premise to another form of enslavement, as described in the following: "And he causes all, small and great, rich and poor, free and bond, that they should receive marks on their right hand, or on their foreheads, and that no one may buy or sell except he that has the mark, the name of the beast, or the number of his name. Here is wisdom. Let him that has understanding calculate the number of the beast, for it is the number of man—his number is 666" (Revelation 13:16-18 EMTV).

Was not Jesus a good enough example to you? Change your course and lead your flock according to His Word. Peter wrote, "Shepherd the flock of God that is among you, exercising oversight, not under compulsion, but willingly, as God would have you; not for shameful gain, but eagerly; not domineering over those in your charge, but being examples to the flock. And when the chief Shepherd appears, you will receive the unfading crown of glory" (1 Peter 5:2-4).

You have caused the sheep not to recognize their master because yourself you have not. The Bible says, "Beware lest anyone captures you through philosophy and empty deceit, according to the tradition of men, according to the basic principles of the world, and not according to Christ. For in Him dwells all the fullness of the Godhead bodily" (Colossians 2:8-9 EMTV) (see also Genesis 1:1, Deuteronomy 32:39, Isaiah 43:10, Isaiah 44:6, Isaiah 45:15, Isaiah 45:22, Hosea 13:4, John 1:1-13, John 8:18-19, John 10:1-2, John 10:9, John 10:15, John 10:30, John 10:37-38, John 12:26, John 14:13-21, Colossians 1:18-19, Colossians 2:8-9).

Because you have led the sheep into idolatry, into utter destruction you are walking. From the Scriptures we read,

"The children gather wood, the fathers kindle fire, and the women knead dough, to make cakes for the queen of heaven. And they pour out drink offerings to other gods, to provoke me to anger. Is it I whom they provoke? declares the LORD. Is it not themselves, to their own shame? Therefore thus says the Lord GOD: behold, my anger and my wrath will be poured out on this place, upon man and beast, upon the trees of the field and the fruit of the ground; it will burn and not be quenched" (Jeremiah 7:18-20) (see also Ezekiel 23:37, Luke 8:20-21).

But the Lord will deliver his sheep from evil hands. From the Scriptures we read, "Therefore, you shepherds, hear the word of the LORD: Thus says the Lord GOD, Behold, I am against the shepherds, and I will require my sheep at their hand and put a stop to their feeding the sheep. No longer shall the shepherds feed themselves. I will rescue my sheep from their mouths, that they may not be food for them. 'For thus says the Lord GOD: Behold, I, I myself will search for my sheep and will seek them out'" (Ezekiel 34:9-11) (see also Ezekiel 34:1-16).

Every time you address your audience, you misquote the Lord. All you care about is self-aggrandizement and the profit thereof. The Lord said, "I did not send the prophets, yet they ran; I did not speak to them, yet they prophesied. But if they had stood in my council, then they would have proclaimed my words to my people, and they would have turned them from their evil way, and from the evil of their deeds. 'Am I a God at hand, declares the LORD, and not a God afar off? Can a man hide himself in secret places so that I cannot see him? declares the LORD. Do I not fill heaven and earth? declares the LORD. I have heard what the prophets have said who prophesy lies in my name, saying, 'I have dreamed, I have dreamed!' How long shall there be lies in the heart of the prophets who prophesy lies, and who prophesy the deceit of their own heart, who think to make my people forget my name by their dreams that they tell one another, even as their fathers forgot my name for Baal?" (Jeremiah 23:21-27).

Guard yourself against doing those things the Lord hates because you are bringing His judgment upon yourselves and this land. He spoke again saying, "Let the prophet who has a dream tell the dream, but let him who has my word speak my word faithfully. What has straw in common with wheat? declares the LORD. Is not my word like fire, declares the LORD, and like a hammer that breaks the rock in pieces?" (Jeremiah 23:28-29)

Exhort one another, the Bible says: "Brothers, if a man is overtaken in any trespass, you who are spiritual restore such a person in a spirit of gentleness, looking out for yourself lest you also be tempted" (Galatians 6:1 EMTV).

Brother! Because time is of the essence and because of the urgency of the matter at hand, it is imperative that this truth, which no man can keep hidden, reaches every one of you. The Church must rise up to face terrible dangers looming at the horizon, while consciences are stirred up for repentance. Do not resent the rebuke to the contrary; accept it as a blessing, and may the will of God be known. From the Scriptures we read, "My son, do not despise the LORD's discipline or be weary of his reproof, for the LORD reproves him whom he loves, as a father the son in whom he delights. Blessed is the one who finds wisdom, and the one who gets understanding" (Proverbs 3:11-13).

Those of you who are really sincere and are telling the truth, leading the sheep to good pasture, have no fear and keep up the good work. Your share of the kingdom one day will be shown to you. From the Scriptures we read, "You will walk safely and never stumble; you will rest without a worry and sleep soundly. So don't be afraid of sudden disasters or storms that strike those who are evil. You can be sure that the LORD will protect you from harm" (Proverbs 3:23-26 CEV).

WHO WAS JESUS?

God is spirit. To be visible to the angels before they were created, He made Himself a celestial body He called a soul. Jesus, the visible expression of God, whom He called his begotten son, is the first of all creations. He came down from heaven with the good news of His grace and our salvation. To achieve that, God chose a human body for His celestial one through a chosen virgin called Mary and sent the angel Gabriel to speak to her, to announce that she was going to be pregnant and bear a son. And since Mary was betrothed to Joseph with whom she did not have any sexual relationship, she expressed doubt. "And Mary said to the angel, 'How will this be, since I am a virgin?' And the angel answered her, 'The Holy Spirit will come upon you, and the power of the Most High will overshadow you; therefore the child to be born will be called holy—the Son of God'" (Luke 1:34-35).

The story of His life has been told to people of all race, creed, and tongue. He was threatened, arrested, humiliated, flogged, and crucified, where He shed His precious blood to the last drop for our justification. He was buried and resurrected on the third day, as He told his disciples. The Bible says, "And taking the twelve, he said to them, 'See, we are going up to Jerusalem, and everything that is written about the Son of Man by the prophets will be accomplished. For he will be delivered over to the Gentiles and will be mocked and shamefully treated and spit upon. And after flogging him, they will kill him, and on the third day he will rise' " (Luke 18:31-33).

COULD JESUS MARRY AND HAVE CHILDREN?

Jesus was a man, and his cells had the X and Y chromosomes as well as the gene responsible for His being born a boy, but He was different from the rest of us. Since He did not receive his Y chromosome from a man but from the Holy Spirit's intervention, it was impossible for Him to have inherited specific genes involved in procreation, which definitely invalidate the assertion that He had sexual relationships with women and had children.

His abode is a Kingdom, at the end of the heavens, where He went up bodily and is awaiting the preset day and hour to return to earth with a celestial army to defeat Satan and the fallen angels and to destroy those who will dare attack Israel, at Armageddon, in the valley of Meggido. This is what He said of His celestial army: "They come from a distant land, from the end of the heavens, the LORD and the weapons of his indignation, to destroy the whole land. Wail, for the day of the LORD is near; as destruction from the Almighty it will come! Therefore all hands will be feeble, and every human heart will melt. They will be dismayed: pangs and agony will seize them; they will be in anguish like a woman in labor. They will look aghast at one another; their faces will be aflame. Behold, the day of the LORD comes, cruel, with wrath and fierce anger, to make the land a desolation and to destroy its sinners from it. For the stars of the heavens and their constellations will not give their light; the sun will be dark at its rising, and the moon will not shed its light. I will punish the world for its evil, and the wicked for their iniquity; I will put an end to the pomp of the arrogant, and lay low the pompous pride of the ruthless. I will make people more rare than fine gold, and mankind than the gold of Ophir. Therefore I will make the heavens tremble, and the earth will be shaken out of its place, at the wrath of the LORD of hosts in the day of his fierce anger" (Isaiah 13:5-13).

To those who would doubt that the preceding verses are referring to Jesus and his mighty angels coming from a definite location at the outer limits of the universe God called "the end of the heavens," where His kingdom lies trillions and trillions of light years away, Paul, trying to comfort the Thessalonians persecuted because of their faith, wrote, "Since indeed God considers it just to repay with affliction those who afflict you, and to grant relief to you who are afflicted as well as to us, when the Lord Jesus is revealed from heaven with his mighty angels in flaming fire, inflicting vengeance on those who do not know God and on those who do not obey the Gospel of our Lord Jesus. They will suffer the punishment of eternal destruction, away from the presence of the Lord and from the glory of his might, when he comes on that day to be glorified in his saints, and to be marveled at among all who have believed, because our testimony to you was believed" (2 Thessalonians 1:6-10). The Bible says, "They will say, "Where is the promise of his coming? For ever since the fathers fell asleep, all things are continuing as they were from the beginning of creation." For they deliberately overlook this fact, that the heavens existed long ago, and the earth was formed out of water and through water by the word of God, and that by means of these the world that then existed was deluged with water and perished. But by the same word the heavens and earth that now exist are stored up for fire, being kept until the day of judgment and destruction of the ungodly" (2 Peter 3:4-7).

If this exercise is not enough for the doubters, here is how God revealed again his intentions concerning the day when his anger will be made manifest to men: "On that day the LORD will punish the host of heaven, in heaven, and the kings of the earth, on the earth. They will be gathered together as prisoners in a pit; they will be shut up in a prison, and after many days they will be punished. Then the moon will be confounded and the sun ashamed, for the LORD of hosts reigns on Mount Zion and in Jerusalem, and his glory will be before his elders" (Isaiah 24:21-23).

WAS HE ALSO GOD OR JUST A PROPHET?

Many calling themselves Christians are still contesting the divine nature of Jesus Christ and do not see Him as God the Son being one with God the Father and God the Holy Spirit. To refuse to recognize Him as the physical expression of God is to refute God's own words. "Then God said, 'Let us make man in our image, after our likeness. And let them have dominion over the fish of the sea and over the birds of the heavens and over the livestock and over all the earth and over every creeping thing that creeps on the earth' " (Genesis 1:26).

Isn't it true that we have a body, a soul, and a spirit and still function as one, because all of them interact flawlessly? Furthermore why would God declare to the prophet Zechariah, "And I will pour out on the house of David and the inhabitants of Jerusalem a spirit of grace and pleas for mercy, so that, when they look on me, on him whom they have pierced, they shall mourn for him, as one mourns for an only child, and weep bitterly over him, as one weeps over a firstborn" (Zechariah 12:10), if He were not one with His son?

Why would Jesus say to one of the criminals next to Him, "Truly, I say to you, today you will be with me in Paradise" (Luke 23:43)? Why three days later, speaking to Mary Magdalena, if He were not God the Son, one with God the Father, did Jesus say to her, "Do not cling to me, for I have not yet ascended to the Father; but go to my brothers and say to them, 'I am ascending to my Father and your Father, to my God and your God.' " (John 20:17)?

Why would He say, "And I will ask the Father, and he will give you another Helper, to be with you forever, even the Spirit of truth, whom the world cannot receive, because it neither sees him nor knows him. You know him, for he dwells with you and will be in you. 'I will not leave you as orphans; I will come to you' " (John 14:16-18), if He were not God the Son and God the Holy Spirit? If one cannot ignore these words spoken by Jesus Christ, one cannot deny his Divine nature. We have proof of that in our time, because hundreds of Christians and non-Christians alike are being healed in no other name than that of Jesus, publicly, in the many crusades and other religious events being held daily around the globe and privately.

A committee of a certain denomination composed of twelve elders, according to their own belief system, declares that they are of the 144,000 Jews who will follow Jesus around at his second coming. Aren't they married? Or are they virgins? John wrote, "Then I looked, and behold, on Mount Zion stood the Lamb, and with him 144,000 who had his name and his Father's name written on their foreheads. And I heard a voice from heaven like the roar of many waters and like the sound of loud thunder. The voice I heard was like the sound of harpists playing on their harps, and they were singing a new song before the throne and before the four living creatures and before the elders. No one could learn that song except the 144,000 who had been redeemed from the earth. It is these who have not defiled themselves with women, for they are virgins. It is these who follow the Lamb wherever he goes. These have been redeemed from mankind as firstfruits for God and the Lamb, and in their mouth no lie was found, for they are blameless" (Revelation 14:1-5).

Are they of the twelve tribes of Israel? John wrote, "And I heard the number of the sealed, 144,000, sealed from every tribe of the sons of Israel" (Revelation 7:4).

If they are not, they are counted among those of us who

are not Jews. There should not be any doubt that anyone who would not be of the twelve tribes of Israel will not be counted among these 144, 000. John further wrote, "After this I looked, and behold, a great multitude that no one could number, from every nation, from all tribes and peoples and languages, standing before the throne and before the Lamb, clothed in white robes, with palm branches in their hands, and crying out with a loud voice, 'Salvation belongs to our God who sits on the throne, and to the Lamb!' " (Revelation 7:9-10 ESV).

Of those who are not Jews and are trying to pass for such, this is what Jesus said, "I know your tribulation and your poverty (but you are rich) and the slander of those who say that they are Jews and are not, but are a synagogue of Satan" (Revelation 2:9).

It is enough said that it should be clear to everyone that the following passage should be taken literally: "It is these who have not defiled themselves with women, for they are virgins" (Revelation 14:4).

This religious think-tank is undoubtedly made up of the greatest minds of our time in matters of the Scriptures, but can they really prevent the truth from coming out concerning the deity of Christ? I can say emphatically, "No!" Their congregants hear the true word of God from others preaching the truth, even though these leaders have gone the extra mile at hiding it from them. Like many of other religions, they believe in the God of Abraham, and also believe that Jesus was born of Mary and that He is a prophet. They are not true Jesus' witnesses because they reject the trinity of God.

Jesus, trying to convince His apostles that the Son was God the Spirit in a human body, patiently explained, "If you had known me, you would have known my Father also. From now on you do know him and have seen him.' Philip said to him, 'Lord, show us the Father, and it is enough for us.' Jesus said to him, 'Have I been with you so long, and you still do not know me, Philip? Whoever has seen me has seen the Father. How can you say, 'Show us the Father'?'" (John 14:7-9).

Patient, comparative research has in fact revealed that one can use this denomination's own Bible version to prove that Jesus is one with the Father who is Spirit. John 10:30 and Colossians 2:9 in their Bible version are similar to the following ones: "I and my Father are one" (John 10:30 KJV) and "For in Him dwells all the fullness of the God-head bodily" (Colossians 2:9 EMTV). In the following passage, Jesus is proven to possess the fullness of God's Holy Spirit, and their version even written differently has the same meaning. John wrote, "And between the throne and the four living creatures and among the elders I saw a

Lamb standing, as though it had been slain, with seven horns and with seven eyes, which are the seven spirits of God sent out into all the earth" (Revelation 5:6).

If the Lamb, who is our Purchaser, our Redeemer Jesus Christ, possesses all the seven Spirits of God, isn't it proof enough that Jesus is God the Son, being one with the Father, both having the same level of power. If it were not so, then Jesus would have been a second God, but since God, whose name is also Jehovah according to Exodus 6:3, has always declared of Himself that there is no other than Him, we must declare undoubtedly that when we say God the Father, God the Son, and God the Holy Spirit, we are talking of the three characteristics of one unique God.

They use the following biblical passages to declare that Christ is God's son and is inferior to Him: Matthew 3:17, John 8:42, John 14:28, John 20:17, 1 Corinthians 1:15, and 1 Corinthians 15:28. But they cannot disprove that Jesus the Son is one with God the Father; they only bring forth the fact that His begotten Son Jesus, which is the human body that God gave to His heavenly one, was sent by Him who is Spirit. He created them to hold His seven Spirits and to be the vehicles by which He made Himself visible first to the angels and then to man. In Capernaum, speaking to a crowd that was looking for Him and responding to one of their questions, Jesus said, "For I have come down from heaven, not to do my own will but the will of him who sent me" (John 6:38), and further added, "I am the living bread that came down from heaven. If anyone eats of this bread, he will live forever. And the bread that I will give for the life of the world is my flesh" (John 6:51). Who in heaven could come down and say such thing but God Himself?

Speaking to the Pharisees, "Jesus said to them, 'If God were your Father, you would love me, for I came from God and I am here. I came not of my own accord, but he sent me' " (John 8:42).

Speaking to His apostles He further said, "You heard me say to you, 'I am going away, and I will come to you.' If you loved me, you would have rejoiced, because I am going to the Father, for the Father is greater than I" (John 14:28).

He spoke the truth because the Spirit God has created the Son of man whom He called Jesus to receive His Soul, which is His Heavenly body that was the first of his creations as reported by Paul in the following passage: "He is the image of the invisible God, the firstborn of all creation" (Colossians 1:15).

The Son of God is also the creator of everything that exists on the earth and the heavens. The Bible says, "For by him all things were created, in heaven and on earth, visible and invisible, whether thrones or dominions or rulers or authorities—all things were created through him and for him. And he is before all things, and in him all things hold together" (Colossians 1:16-17 ESV). If He were not also God the Father, the Word of God would contradict itself, therefore canceling the entire Bible, or there would have been two creators or Gods, since the Scriptures says, "In the beginning, God created the heavens and the earth" (Genesis 1:1 ESV). John wrote, "In the beginning was the Word, and the Word was with God, and the Word was God" (John 1:1). And he further declared, "And the Word became flesh and dwelt among us, and we have seen his glory, glory as of the only Son from the Father, full of grace and truth" (John 1:14).

Who has ever heard that the creation is greater than the Creator? Jesus was God's physical body. God spoke to Jesus' disciples through his earthly body because He is Spirit. Before Jesus was born, He addressed man through His angels. After He had suffered as Jesus who died on the cross to redeem us, and after He had given back His soul, which was His celestial body, to Jesus, His human body, which was resurrected three days after He died, He retrieved both as one and sat back in heaven on His throne, as the lamb that was slain.

We should not dismiss the work of God because we do not understand the mystery behind it, since no one can if

He does not reveal it Himself. He spoke of His soul in the following biblical passage: "And I will destroy your high places and cut down your incense altars and cast your dead bodies upon the dead bodies of your idols, and my soul will abhor you" (Leviticus 26:30).

Can we limit God's power? Jesus reassured the twelve disciples whom He chose, that with his Father's help they would make it through the narrow door leading to His Father's kingdom, since they expressed doubt, understanding that it would be humanly impossible, "But he said, 'What is impossible with men is possible with God' " (Luke 18:27).

John who received the testimony of Jesus Christ wrote, "Behold, he is coming with the clouds, and every eye will see him, even those who pierced him, and all tribes of the earth will wail on account of him. Even so. Amen" (Revelation 1:7).

The Scriptures say, "On that day the mourning in Jerusalem will be as great as the mourning for Hadad-rimmon in the plain of Megiddo. (Zechariah 12:11)

Since His ascension to heaven, it was the first time Jesus Christ confirmed to John that He was the Eternal, the Almighty God, declaring, "I am the Alpha and the Omega," says the Lord God, "who is and who was and who is to come, the Almighty" (Revelation 1:8).

Jesus, who sent His angel to testify to John concerning

those things that have been revealed to him as he was taken in the spirit to the heavenly realm, declared "And he said to me, "It is done! I am the Alpha and the Omega, the beginning and the end. To the thirsty I will give from the spring of the water of life without payment. The one who conquers will have this heritage, and I will be his God and he will be my son." (Revelation 21:6-7).

To those who deny that that Jesus and the Father are one, I would say farewell; they cannot inherit the promise of becoming His son, even less, quenching their thirst from the spring of the water of life if they reject Him as being their God and Father because it is reserved only for those who are willing to except this truth and become his children. To John He declared, "Behold, I am coming soon, bringing my recompense with me, to repay everyone for what he has done" (Revelation 22:12), and further confirmed of His Eternal and Divine nature by declaring for the third time, "I am the Alpha and the Omega, the first and the last, the beginning and the end" (Revelation 22:13).

Are you willing to accept Him as your God and Father and become His child? Or do you prefer to be a child of the devil, lose your life for the sake of man and false teachings, and be thrown in hell as He warned? Speaking to His disciples and a large crowd, He said, "The field is the world, and the good seed is the children of the kingdom. *The weeds are the sons of the evil one,* and the enemy who sowed them is the devil. The harvest is the close of the age, and the reapers are angels. *Just as the weeds are gathered and burned with fire, so will it be at the close of the age.* (Matthew 13:38-40).

You may argue that you are saved because you believe in Him as being the Son who has given His life at the cross for you, but do not accept him as being God and the Father. Well, you would be right if you could choose and pick just a portion of His Word. Foolish who would think that God compromises with man; it is either you accept it in its entirety or you don't. Jesus warned you, "Whoever is not with me is against me, and whoever does not gather with me scatters" (Matthew 12:30). But you still may argue that you are on His side even though you agree with Him on one thing and disagree on another. Foolish who would believe so, since He made it clear that it is not so; He again warned you, "So, because you are lukewarm, and neither hot nor cold, I will spit you out of my mouth." (Revelation 3:16).

Remember, you will be judged by the Word whole as it is, and not by just the small portion that pleases you or taught to you. Your false teachers are mere human having to face judgment, like you will, alone with no right to speak in their own defense or have someone else to do so. The one chance we all have is when we are still breathing. If

you really desire to be saved, seek the truth. Because several denominations carries their own Bible translation and
because many of them, unfortunately, allegedly alter the
meaning of a particular passage or verse to steer their congregation in the direction of their own belief, it is best for
one to compare verses of one Bible to another or of one
language to another for those who are multilingual, by either looking online for sites offering such capabilities e.g.
www.e-sword.net, or buying more than one version. When
the majority of them agree on a particular passage or verse,
it must be true, and abide by it. The book of Revelation
contains riddles and passages not understood by the casual
reader, but the rest of the New Testament is written to be
understood by all. What Jesus said in parable to the crowds,
in private, He would explain it in plain language to his
apostles because He wanted us all to know what He meant.
To Hosea, the son of Beeri, the Lord declared, "My people
are destroyed for lack of knowledge" (Hosea 4:6).

DID JESUS DRINK WINE?

Jesus often spoke of wine, which is mentioned more than
two hundred times in the Bible, but a great number of ministers refuse to say the word "wine." They prefer to call it
"the juice," either from fear that congregants would take it

as an invitation to get drunk, or to be religiously correct instead of preaching the truth. Wine is, by definition, a beverage containing ten to fifteen percent alcohol by volume and made of the fermented juice of grapes. Now let us go to the verses where it appears for the first time in the Bible. From the Scriptures we read, "Noah began to be a man of the soil, and he planted a vineyard. He drank of the wine and became drunk and lay uncovered in his tent" (Genesis 9:20-21). It is evident that Noah knew how to make wine by first pressing grapes and then allowing the juice to undergo fermentation.

Some Pharisees questioned Jesus as to why His disciples were always eating and drinking instead of fasting and praying, and He explained in parables to them that as long as He was with them, they would not have to fast; in the same manner, no guests would fast while they would be celebrating with a bridegroom if they were invited to his wedding. He continued saying, "And no one puts new wine into old wineskins. If he does, the new wine will burst the skins and it will be spilled, and the skins will be destroyed" (Luke 5:37).

Isn't it evident that He was referring to the pressure exerted by carbon dioxide gas formed during fermentation, confirming that whenever He spoke of wine He meant an alcoholic beverage made from pressed grapes?

He further said, "For John the Baptist has come eating no bread and drinking no wine, and you say, 'He has a demon.' The Son of Man has come eating and drinking, and you say, 'Look at him! A glutton and a drunkard, a friend of tax collectors and sinners!'" (Luke 7:33-34). This verse confirms that He drank wine as well.

Jesus had turned water into wine at a wedding in Cana of Galilee when it ran out and after his mother has insisted that He do something, and "When the master of the feast tasted the water now become wine, and did not know where it came from (though the servants who had drawn the water knew), the master of the feast called the bridegroom and said to him, 'Everyone serves the good wine first, and when people have drunk freely, then the poor wine. But you have kept the good wine until now' " (John 2:9-10).

Why did the master of ceremony find the one He made better than the one they had if it were not real wine?

Paul to his friend Timothy wrote the following: "No longer drink only water, but use a little wine for the sake of your stomach and your frequent ailments" (1 Timothy 5:23). And further to Titus, whom he loved as a son, he wrote, "For an overseer, as God's steward, must be above reproach. He must not be arrogant or quick-tempered or a drunkard or violent or greedy for gain" (Titus 1:7). Isn't it evident that while recommending the use of wine to Timothy, he wrote to Titus to prohibit the excessive use of it by those teaching the faithful, and condemned drunkenness, which God forbids?

At Passover, on the first day of the Unleavened Bread, Jesus had dinner with His disciples at the house of a certain man. "Now as they were eating, Jesus took bread, and after blessing it broke it and gave it to the disciples, and said, 'Take, eat; this is my body.' And he took a cup, and when he had given thanks he gave it to them, saying, 'Drink of it, all of you, for this is my blood of the covenant, which is poured out for many for the forgiveness of sins. I tell you I will not drink again of this fruit of the vine until that day when I drink it new with you in my Father's kingdom' " (Matthew 26:26-29). On Sunday August 6, 2006, while talking to my sister, I wondered why Jesus used wine to represent His shed blood, and then at the very moment that I said, "One day the Lord will reveal this mystery to someone." Suddenly, the Lord revealed to me that in the same manner fermentation (the process) allows the juice of grapes (the old state) to turn into wine (the new state) for a long shelf life, the shed blood of Jesus at the cross (the process) brings salvation for an everlasting life (the new state) from the original sin (the old state). We should not discard the Word of God even though it does not make sense to us. He reveals biblical mysteries in due time through whomever He desires.

Finishing His thought while answering the Pharisees' question as to why His disciples were not fasting, He said, "And no one after drinking old wine desires new, for he says, 'The old is good.'" (Luke 5:39). Isn't it true that the process is what produces new wine over and over, as the spiritual one makes new vessels to receive what is new? Isn't it true that the alcohol in the wine is what reveals the chemical process in the same manner that the characteristics of the new vessel reveal the spiritual one?

When we drink wine in remembrance of Him, isn't it true that we are testifying of His sacrifice that led to our salvation? The apostle Paul to the faithful put it this way: "For as often as you eat this bread and drink the cup, you proclaim the Lord's death until he comes" (1 Corinthians 11:26). Should we do it in any manner we wish? Paul went on penning his epistle to declare, "Whoever, therefore, eats the bread or drinks the cup of the Lord in an unworthy manner will be guilty of profaning the body and blood of the Lord. Let a person examine himself, then, and so eat of the bread and drink of the cup. For anyone who eats and drinks without discerning the body eats and drinks judgment on himself. That is why many of you are weak and ill, and some have died" (1 Corinthians 11:27-30).

We can illustrate again the symbolism attached to wine

where it exemplifies the end result of a process. Let us read from the writings of the apostle John where he prophesied the fate of those who are unwilling to submit to the Lord. He wrote, "And another angel, a third, followed them, saying with a loud voice, 'If anyone worships the beast and its image and receives a mark on his forehead or on his hand, he also will drink the wine of God's wrath, poured full strength into the cup of his anger, and he will be tormented with fire and sulfur in the presence of the holy angels and in the presence of the Lamb' " (Revelation 14:9-10). Isn't it true that these will endure the punishment brought about by the Lord's anger against them as a result of their disobedience? In other terms, won't the punishment they will endure (the wine they will drink) be a testimony (the end result) of the wrath of God (the process) directed at them for misconduct? All sins deserve punishment (the wine of His anger), but His shed blood brings salvation (the wine of His compassion for us).

WHAT DID JESUS LOOK LIKE?

In the morning of July 31, 2005, as I was writing what has become this book, I had a very peculiar dream. I became aware that I was in the presence of a young man of medium build who was in his thirties. With him was a young girl, and he explained to me that she was one he had rescued. The Middle Eastern facial features of this man remained etched in my mind as clear as the day I saw them. He had black curly hair and his complexion was a medium burnt umber hue. He was gentle and it felt as though he could read my mind. Without asking me what I wanted, he promised that he would reserve me a place on his soon-to-depart ship, which was adorned with a golden molding running along its white hull. In a continuum, I saw myself running down a pier, and I saw the young man's ship departing, and a few feet away, my children in a small white boat with a molding similar to the one on the side of the ship, and without any hesitation, I swam toward it. When I climbed on board, I noticed that my clothes were dry. The ship stopped after I shouted, asking him to wait for me. When we arrived, he climbed down a rope into the boat to welcome and invite us onboard, and with him was the girl, and next to her stood one covered, whose face and feet I did not see. They went back up as easily as they came down. Then my eldest son offered to help me climb up, but I assured him that I would be all right. I grabbed the rope and with both feet on the side of the ship, like in a standing position, started my ascension. But I got stuck in that position when I reached the edge, and as I was trying to move my right foot to step onboard, two men rushed to help. My host went back to taking control of the ship, and with him were the girl and the invisible one. My eldest son and I were directed to a large unfurnished room, and my two daughters remained behind. On that boat there were none of the things we would normally find in a modern cruise ship, and I can assume that we had no need of them since we were about to take the fastest trip we had ever experienced, one that was going to take us, in the blink of an eye, to God's abode, the place we call Heaven. The Lord's return is approaching, and His ship is soon to come to take away those who have remained faithful to Him. First, the two witnesses will be caught up and the others at the last trumpet. The Bible says, "For three and a half days some from the peoples and tribes and languages and nations will gaze at their dead bodies and refuse to let them be placed in a tomb, and those who dwell on the earth will rejoice over them and make merry and exchange presents, because these two prophets had been a torment to those who dwell on the earth. But after the three and a half days a breath of life from God entered them, and they stood up on their feet, and great fear fell on those who saw them. Then they heard a loud voice from heaven saying to them, 'Come up here!' And they went up to heaven in a cloud, and their enemies watched them" (Revelation 11:9-12).

The young girl whom He told me that He has rescued is

none other than His earthly mother Mary. He wanted everyone to know that He was also her Savior and that He shed
blood on the cross for her as He did for us all. The invisible
one standing next to her, in a dark grey hooded outer garment is the angel of death, master of the abode of the dead,
where she is still sleeping, awaiting the first resurrection
because she did not ascend to heaven as claimed by the
Vatican. She appeared chubby and of very short stature; she
appeared to be no more than four feet tall, and she was of a
light, yellowish complexion. Her small round face was just
plain, not close to resembling the many artistic renditions
of her either on canvas, print, or in a sculptured representation.

Jesus showed me His physical appearance when He was
walking among us, because He wants to end the controversy concerning it. Describing the boy named Jesus, the
prophet Isaiah wrote, "For he grew up before him like a
young plant, and like a root out of dry ground; he had no
form or majesty that we should look at him, and no beauty
that we should desire him" (Isaiah 53:2).

Once, after returning from a summer vacation, a teen-
age friend who happened to see me and who was about my
age, marveled at the miraculous temporary transformation
of my naturally wavy hair into curly locks. Over many
years I wondered why that had happened and could never

understand until a ten-year-old event has brought some light to my long-time quest. One day a young Christian man stated that there were three gods and continued on saying that they were "God the Father, God the Son, and God the Holy Spirit." I convinced him that there was only one God by quoting Isaiah, "I am the LORD, and there is no other, besides me there is no God; I equip you, though you do not know me" (Isaiah 45:5).

A few days later we were conversing, and all of a sudden, he declared to me "If Jesus were here on earth, He would look like you." For a few seconds, I remained silent and perplexed, and the conversation resumed. I know now that the Holy Spirit put that in his heart.

Our Lord, willing to end the controversy that He knew would exist in our time concerning His physical appearance by the attempt of many who would try to portray Him other than how He chose to appear among His children, being the Redeemer of all mankind, sent many with physical characteristics resembling His, as a means to let us all know the truth concerning this very object of contention.

A young man whose friends, girlfriend, and close family members could hardly tell us apart, failed, one evening, to deliver to his grandmother a gift that one of his uncles who had traveled with him that day had charged him with. The irate man would not stop blaming me for the mistake of his nephew and kept arguing with his mom, who was trying to tell him that I was a family friend, until he finally left, still angry at me. This young man looks like Jesus as He showed Himself to me.

Many have told me that they either have a friend or a family member who looks like me. In truth, we all share the same origin, which is traced back to Noah and his sons, and then to Adam and Eve. No one can disprove this assertion, while scientists can only concur to it. How much fun would we have if we all looked alike, as though we were dolls from the same mold? Who would prefer God to have created one kind of animal, one kind of insect, one kind of fish, one kind of bird, one kind of flower, and one kind of fruit, and all of them to be of a medium olive green hue? Who would like to live in a world where "choice" was an unknown concept or not allowed?

My ancestors were from all parts of the world. They spoke most of the European languages and many dialects and languages of Africa and Asia, as far as India, China and beyond. Some came to North America, centuries ago, probably fleeing religious persecution. Others went to South America and the Caribbean. Some were of noble descent; others were of humble origin. Some were among the wealthiest; others were among the poorest.

I am an islander, born and raised on the island of Hispaniola, on the western portion colonized by the French and once called the Pearl of the Antilles. Haiti is considered to be one of the poorest countries. In his infinite wisdom, God wanted to give Satan the opportunity to verify that I was indeed a chosen one, who would precede the King of kings, the Lord of lords. I grew up among people with deep knowledge of the secrets of Satan, who sent many of them to destroy me by all means, and never succeeded. One came to Christ because he finally understood that God was the Almighty after he witnessed how powerfully He has delivered me from their hands. Paul also wrote, "Oh, the depth of the riches and wisdom and knowledge of God! How unsearchable are his judgments and how inscrutable his ways!" (Romans 11:33).

I was raised by parents who were servants of the Lord. My mother's maternal grandmother was a woman with so much wisdom and knowledge of the word of God that many religious leaders would visit her often. Her mother, a young American Baptist girl, set foot on the landing dock of a small town on the west coast of the island, called St. Marc, while in America, the North and the South were engaged in a civil war; she had sailed from New Orleans on her family's ship accompanied by her elder sister and her brother-in-law, a physician. She finally married a physician whose wealthy family settled there long before she arrived.

They fell in love with the nice climate of the island and never left. My paternal grandfather was the son of a French businessman who also loved the island, married an islander, and remained. Other branches of his family tree count a well-known theologian who wrote several books, among which two concern the manners of the Israelites and Christians, and at least a king. And each successive generation has expanded the cultural tree even further.

God chose the Jews to be protagonists in a setting with real rebellion and punishment, with real laughter and weeping, with real pleasure and suffering, where our existence on earth is lived by them, from the moment we became slaves to sin until we will be either banished eternally to the lake of fire or inherit the promised land, a new earth, versus a drama played by actors on the silver screen or at an off-Broadway theatre. He hardened their heart and made them rebel against Him. He dispersed them among all nations, customs, and tongues, to be brought back as one nation when the End-Time would approach as a sign that the pre-set time for their salvation has arrived after He has used them for the sake of His kingdom and salvation of others. Paul wrote, "Lest you be wise in your own conceits, I want you to understand this mystery, brothers: a partial hardening has come upon Israel, until the fullness of the Gentiles has come in" (Romans 11:25), and he further wrote, "Just as you were at one time disobedient to God but now have received mercy because of their disobedience, so they too have now been disobedient in order that by the mercy shown to you they also may now receive mercy. For God has consigned all to disobedience, that he may have mercy on all" (Romans 11:30-32).

As all these nations have come together to form the physical entity that I am, so it was of Jesus, a Jew, who came to be one for all humanity, and so it is of the Jews, who are now one nation from all those among which they were. The curtain is about to close on a realistic demonstration of the dynamic relationship between God, Creator and Redeemer, and His children, who were doomed because of the original sin.

Those faithful to The Lord will reign with Him as angels of light, and no one among them will look upon another and ask, "Are you an angel?" even though one may shine more intensely than another. Jesus in response to questions from the Sadducees said, "For in the resurrection they neither marry nor are given in marriage, but are like angels in heaven" (Matthew 22:30).

For those who might wonder whether all angels shine with the same intensity and have the same level of power, this is what John wrote, "After this I saw another angel coming down from heaven, having great authority, and the earth was made bright with his glory" (Revelation 18:1).

In a vision I had in 2004 and have mentioned at the beginning of the letter, to Church leaders, titled "The Lord's Command," God instructed me to go pour out the bowl of His anger on the earth, and when I woke up, He then took me to Revelation 16:1, where He has given such an order to the seven angels with the seven bowls of His wrath. By this vision, God showed me my future involvement with the last plagues.

The two witnesses, who are believed to be Elijah and Moses, will also have the power to call all manner of destructions and plagues upon mankind. John wrote, "These are the two olive trees and the two lampstands that stand before the Lord of the earth. And if anyone would harm them, fire pours from their mouth and consumes their foes. If anyone would harm them, this is how he is doomed to be killed. They have the power to shut the sky, that no rain may fall during the days of their prophesying, and they have power over the waters to turn them into blood and to strike the earth with every kind of plague, as often as they desire" (Revelation 11:4-6).

Those who will be thrown in the lake of fire because of their unbelief and wickedness will neither reflect nor project light just like the fallen angels, Satan and the demons, who will share their fate. Peter wrote, "These are waterless springs and mists driven by a storm. For them the gloom of utter darkness has been reserved" (2 Peter 2:17).

God is spirit: "God is spirit, and those who worship him must worship in spirit and truth" (John 4:24), but He gave Himself a form to be visible to the angel among whom He desired to live. Daniel described Him as an elder, "As I looked, thrones were placed, and the Ancient of days took his seat; his clothing was white as snow, and the hair of his head like pure wool; his throne was fiery flames; its wheels were burning fire" (Daniel 7:9). John reported a similar vision, and he wrote, "Then I turned to see the voice that was speaking to me, and on turning I saw seven golden lampstands, and in the midst of the lampstands one like a son of man, clothed with a long robe and with a golden sash around his chest. The hairs of his head were white like wool, as white as snow. His eyes were like a flame of fire, his feet were like burnished bronze, refined in a furnace, and his voice was like the roar of many waters. In his right hand he held seven stars, from his mouth came a sharp two-edged sword, and his face was like the sun shining in full strength" (Revelation 1:12-16), and again he described the Lord from another vision he had, "At once I was in the Spirit, and behold, a throne stood in heaven, with one seated on the throne. And he who sat there had the appearance of jasper and carnelian, and around the throne was a rainbow that had the appearance of an emerald" (Revelation 4:2-3), where jasper stands for an opaque stone that may be red, yellow, or brown, and the carnelian is a reddish-brown one.

After He had created man, He made Himself a body, in His begotten son, born of a woman, and became our Redeemer; *"When they look on me, on him whom they have pierced"* as we read from Zechariah 12:10. He is to finally dwell among us, the Bible says, "And I heard a loud voice from the throne saying, 'Behold, the dwelling place of God is with man. He will dwell with them, and they will be his people, and God himself will be with them as their God'" (Revelation 21:3).

Paul writing to the believers of Philippi summed it well for us; he wrote, "And think the same way that Christ Jesus thought: Christ was truly God. But he did not try to remain equal with God. Instead he gave up everything and became a slave, when he became like one of us. Christ was humble. He obeyed God and even died on a cross. Then God gave Christ the highest place and honored his name above all others. So at the name of Jesus everyone will bow down, those in heaven, on earth, and under the earth. And to the glory of God the Father everyone will openly agree, 'Jesus Christ is Lord!'" (Philippians 2:5-11 CEV).

HAS JESUS YET RETURNED?

Beware! The thief is in the fold to take away the sheep. Be attentive to the Shepherd's voice that you may recognize it and not fall for the counterfeit; after the release of the identity of the man of lawlessness, after Jesus opens the seventh seal, after Israel is delivered, after the beast and the false prophet are seized and thrown in the lake of fire, and after Satan and the fallen angels are captured and thrown down into the bottomless pit, with the sound of the last trumpet, the gathering to Christ shall occur. Paul offered reassurance to the Thessalonians as to the expectation of the second coming of the Lord: "Now concerning the coming of our Lord Jesus Christ and our being gathered together to him, we ask you, brothers, not to be quickly shaken in mind or alarmed, either by a spirit or a spoken word, or a letter seeming to be from us, to the effect that the day of the Lord has come. Let no one deceive you in any way. For that day will not come, unless the rebellion comes first, and the man of lawlessness is revealed, the son of destruction" (2 Thessalonians 2:1-3).

Paul to the faithful wrote, "For the Lord himself will descend from heaven with a cry of command, with the voice of an archangel, and with the sound of the trumpet of God. *And the dead in Christ will rise first. Then we who are alive, who are left*, will be caught up together with them in the clouds to meet the Lord in the air, and so we will always be with the Lord" (1 Thessalonians 4:16-17).

The Church of Christ shall suffer persecution and violence before the gathering takes place. John wrote, "When he opened the fifth seal, I saw under the altar the souls of those who had been slain for the word of God and for the witness they had borne. They cried out with a loud voice, 'O Sovereign Lord, holy and true, how long before you will judge and avenge our blood on those who dwell on the earth?' Then they were each given a white robe and told to rest a little longer, until the number of their fellow servants and their brothers should be complete, who were to be killed as they themselves had been" (Revelation 6:9-11).

The rapture will not occur before the sound of the seventh trumpet resonates in the heavens and before the conclusion of the Tribulation. Jesus speaking to His disciples concerning His Father's Kingdom said, "When the Son of Man comes in his glory, and all the angels with him, then he will sit on his glorious throne. Before him will be gathered all the nations, and he will separate people one from another as a shepherd separates the sheep from the goats. And he will place the sheep on his right, but the goats on the left. Then the King will say to those on his right, 'Come, you who are blessed by my Father, inherit the kingdom prepared for you from the foundation of the world' " (Matthew 25:31-34). The disciples asked Him later about the parable of the weeds of the fields. "He answered, 'The one who sows the good seed is the Son of Man. The field is the world, and the good seed is the children of the kingdom. The weeds are the sons of the evil one, and the enemy who sowed them is the devil. *The harvest is the close of the age*, and the reapers are angels' " (Matthew 13:37-39). Paul in his letter to the faithful of Corinth wrote, "Behold! I tell you a mystery. We shall not all sleep, but we shall all be changed, in a moment, in the twinkling of an eye, *at the last trumpet*. For the trumpet will sound, and the dead will be raised imperishable, and we shall be changed" (1 Corinthians 15:51-52). A mighty angel whose face shone like the sun spoke to John in his visions, "And swore by him who lives forever and ever, who created heaven and what is in it, the earth and what is in it, and the sea and what is in it, that there would be no more delay, *but that in the days of the trumpet call to be sounded by the seventh angel*, the mystery of God would be fulfilled, just as he announced to his servants the prophets" (Revelation 10:6-7).

For three years and a half, the beast's troops will be allowed to fight Israel, to occupy, ransack, and take prisoners from many parts of the region, but will never be allowed to take over Jerusalem. After the two witnesses are killed by the antichrist, and after they resuscitate and go up to heaven as the world's major TV networks and satellites cameras capture the event, *then will the seventh angel blow the trumpet.* John described to us what he saw in his vision concerning this episode: "But after the three and a half days a breath of life from God entered them, and they stood up on their feet, and great fear fell on those who saw them. Then they heard a loud voice from heaven saying to them, "Come up here!" And they went up to heaven in a cloud, and their enemies watched them. And at that hour there was a great earthquake, and a tenth of the city fell. Seven thousand people were killed in the earthquake, and the rest were terrified and gave glory to the God of heaven. *The second woe has passed; behold, the third woe is soon to come*" (Revelation 11:11-14).

Not to leave any doubt in our mind as to when the rapture will occur, the Lord gave John a compelling vision of the beginning of the third and last woe. The Bible says, "Then *the seventh angel blew his trumpet*, and there were loud voices in heaven, saying, 'The kingdom of the world has become the kingdom of our Lord and of his Christ, and he shall reign forever and ever.' And the twenty-four elders who sit on their thrones before God fell on their faces and worshiped God, saying, 'We give thanks to you, Lord God

Almighty, who is and who was, for you have taken your great power and begun to reign. *The nations raged, but your wrath came, and the time for the dead to be judged, and for rewarding your servants, the prophets and saints, and those who fear your name, both small and great*, and for destroying the destroyers of the earth'" (Revelation 11:15-18).

The Bible says, "Then I saw an angel coming down from heaven, holding in his hand the key to the bottomless pit and a great chain. And he seized the dragon, that ancient serpent, who is the devil and Satan, and bound him for a thousand years, and threw him into the pit, and shut it and sealed it over him, so that he might not deceive the nations any longer, until the thousand years were ended. After that he must be released for a little while. *Then I saw thrones, and seated on them were those to whom the authority to judge was committed.* Also I saw the souls of those who had been beheaded for the testimony of Jesus and for the word of God, and who had not worshiped the beast or its image and had not received its mark on their foreheads or their hands. They came to life and reigned with Christ for a thousand years. The rest of the dead did not come to life until the thousand years were ended. This is the first resurrection. Blessed and holy is the one who shares in the first resurrection! Over such the second death has no power, but they will be priests of God and of Christ, and they will reign with him for a thousand years" (Revelation 20:1-6).

Some would argue that long after the seventh angel blew the trumpet, the apostle John had the visions of the seven angels and the seven bowls and that they were a second series of plagues to affect humanity up to the seventh bowl being poured out, but the following passages show near simultaneity, where after each trumpet blast some events take place and others are to follow with higher intensity, or one set of successive events are to take place.

The first blast announces the judgments against the earth and its inhabitants, for the Bible says, "The first angel blew his trumpet, and there followed hail and fire, mixed with blood, and these were thrown upon the earth. And a third of the earth was burned up, and a third of the trees were burned up, and all green grass was burned up" (Revelation 8:7). And the Bible says, "So the first angel went and poured out his bowl on the earth, and harmful and painful sores came upon the people who bore the mark of the beast and worshiped its image" (Revelation 16:2).

The second blast announces the judgments against the sea, for the Bible says, "The second angel blew his trumpet, and something like a great mountain, burning with fire, was thrown into the sea, and a third of the sea became blood. A third of the living creatures in the sea died, and a third of the ships were destroyed" (Revelation 8:8-9). And the Bible says, "The second angel poured out his bowl into the sea, and it became like the blood of a corpse, and every living thing died that was in the sea" (Revelation 16:3).

The third blast announces the judgments against the rivers and the springs, for the Bible says, "The third angel blew his trumpet, and a great star fell from heaven, blazing like a torch, and it fell on a third of the rivers and on the springs of water. The name of the star is Wormwood. A third of the waters became wormwood, and many people died from the water, because it had been made bitter" (Revelation 8:10-11). And the Bible says, "The third angel poured out his bowl into the rivers and the springs of water, and they became blood. And I heard the angel in charge of the waters say, 'Just are you, O Holy One, who is and who was, for you brought these judgments. For they have shed the blood of saints and prophets, and you have given them blood to drink. It is what they deserve!' And I heard the altar saying, 'Yes, Lord God the Almighty, true and just are your judgments!' " (Revelation 16:4-7)

The fourth blast announces the judgments against the heavens, for the Bible says, "The fourth angel blew his trumpet, and a third of the sun was struck, and a third of the moon, and a third of the stars, so that a third of their light might be darkened, and a third of the day might be kept from shining, and likewise a third of the night. Then I looked, and I heard an eagle crying with a loud voice as it flew directly overhead, '*Woe, woe, woe* to those who dwell on the earth, at the blasts of the other trumpets that the three angels are about to blow!' " (Revelation 8:12-13). And the Bible says, "The fourth angel poured out his bowl on the sun, and it was allowed to scorch people with fire" (Revelation 16:8).

The fifth blast announces the judgments against those who have received the mark of the beast and have worshiped his image as the wrath of God intensifies, for the Bible says, "And the fifth angel blew his trumpet, and I saw a star fallen from heaven to earth, and he was given the key to the shaft of the bottomless pit. He opened the shaft of the bottomless pit, and from the shaft rose smoke like the smoke of a great furnace, and the sun and the air were darkened with the smoke from the shaft. Then from the smoke came locusts on the earth, and they were given power like the power of scorpions of the earth. *They were told not to harm the grass of the earth or any green plant or any tree, but only those people who do not have the seal of God on their foreheads.* They were allowed to torment them for five months, but not to kill them, and their torment was like the torment of a scorpion when it stings someone. And in those days people will seek death and will not find it. They will long to die, but death will flee from them. In appearance the locusts were like horses prepared for battle: on their heads were what looked like crowns of gold; their faces were like human faces, their hair like women's hair, and their teeth like lions' teeth; they had breastplates like breastplates of iron, and the noise of their wings was like the noise of many chariots with horses rushing into battle. They have tails and stings like scorpions, and their power to hurt people for five months is in their tails. They have as king over them the angel of the bottomless pit. His name in Hebrew is Abaddon, and in Greek he is called Apollyon. The first woe has passed; behold, two woes are still to come" (Revelation 9:1-12). Then the Bible says, "The fifth angel poured out his bowl on the throne of the beast, and its kingdom was plunged into darkness. People gnawed their tongues in anguish" (Revelation 16:10).

The sixth blast announces the judgments against the river Euphrates to dry it up and against those who have received the mark of the beast but did not die by the previous plagues, for the Bible says, "Then the sixth angel blew his trumpet, and I heard a voice from the four horns of the golden altar before God, saying to the sixth angel who had the trumpet, 'Release the four angels who are bound at the great river Euphrates.' So the four angels, who had been prepared for the hour, the day, the month, and the year, were released to kill a third of mankind. The number of mounted troops was twice ten thousand times ten thousand; I heard their number. And this is how I saw the horses in my vision and those who rode them: they wore breastplates the color of fire and of sapphire and of sulfur, and the heads of the horses were like lions' heads, and fire and smoke and sulfur came out of their mouths. By these three plagues a third of mankind was killed, by the fire and smoke and sulfur coming out of their mouths. For the power of the horses is in their mouths and in their tails, for their tails are like serpents with heads, and by means of them they wound. The rest of mankind, who were not killed by these plagues, did not repent of the works of their hands nor give up worshiping demons and idols of gold and silver and bronze and stone and wood, which cannot see or hear or walk, nor did they repent of their murders or their sorceries or their sexual immorality or their thefts" (Revelation 9:13-21). And the Bible says, "The sixth angel poured out his bowl on the great river Euphrates, and its water was dried up, to prepare the way for the kings from the east. And I saw, coming out of the mouth of the dragon and out of the mouth of the beast and out of the mouth of the false prophet, three unclean spirits like frogs. For they are demonic spirits, performing signs, who go abroad to the kings of the whole world, to assemble them for battle on the great day of God the Almighty. ('Behold, I am coming like a thief! Blessed is the one who stays awake, keeping his garments on, that he may not go about naked and be seen exposed!') And they assembled them at the place that in Hebrew is called Armageddon" (Revelation 16:12-16).

The seventh blast announces the judgments against Satan, the beast and his false prophet, and Babylon the great, and also announces the triumph of the Christ, for the Bible says, "Then the seventh angel blew his trumpet, and there were loud voices in heaven, saying, 'The kingdom of the world has become the kingdom of our Lord and of his Christ, and he shall reign forever and ever.' And the twenty-four elders who sit on their thrones before God fell on their faces and worshiped God, saying, 'We give thanks to you, Lord God Almighty, who is and who was, for you have taken your great power and begun to reign. The nations raged, but your wrath came, and the time for the dead to be judged, and for rewarding your servants, the prophets and saints, and those who fear your name, both small and great, and for destroying the destroyers of the earth.' Then God's temple in heaven was opened, and the ark of his covenant was seen within his temple. There were flashes of lightning, rumblings, peals of thunder, an earthquake, and heavy hail" (Revelation 11:15-19). And the Bible says, "The seventh angel poured out his bowl into the air, and a loud voice came out of the temple, from the throne, saying, 'It is done!' And there were flashes of lightning, rumblings, peals of thunder, and a great earthquake such as there had never been since man was on the earth, so great was that earthquake. The great city was split into three parts, and the cities of the nations fell, and God remembered Babylon the great, to make her drain the cup of the wine of the fury of his wrath. And every island fled away, and no mountains were to be found. And great hailstones, about one hundred pounds each, fell from heaven on people; and they cursed God for the plague of the hail, because the plague was so severe" (Revelation 16:17-21).

WHAT DOES JESUS EXPECT OF US?

Jesus is coming a second time to judge and rule. "Then I saw heaven opened, and behold, a white horse! The one sitting on it is called Faithful and True, and in righteousness he judges and makes war. His eyes are like a flame of fire, and on his head are many diadems, and he has a name written that no one knows but himself" (Revelation 19:11-12). He wants us to keep His word and to work for the kingdom. He said, "Whoever is not with me is against me, and whoever does not gather with me scatters" (Luke 11:23). In Jerusalem as His crucifixion was soon to take place, addressing a crowd, He warned them saying, "But the one who did not know, and did what deserved a beating, will receive a light beating. Everyone to whom much was given, of him much will be required, and from him to whom they entrusted much, they will demand the more" (Luke 12:48).

He wants us to be entirely committed and not to try to serve two masters, Him and what is in this world. To this effect He declared, "No one can serve two masters, for either he will hate the one and love the other, or he will be devoted to the one and despise the other. You cannot serve God and money" (Matthew 6:24).

In a message to John for the church of Laodicea, He that has the seven Spirits of God said, "I know your works: you are neither cold nor hot. Would that you were either cold or hot! So, because you are lukewarm, and neither hot nor cold, I will spit you out of my mouth" (Revelation 3:15-16).

He is coming also with a reward for those who shall remain faithful to Him. Addressing his disciples, Jesus declared, "When the Son of Man comes in his glory, and all the angels with him, *then he will sit on his glorious throne. Before him will be gathered all the nations*, and he will separate people one from another as a shepherd separates the sheep from the goats. *And he will place the sheep on his right, but the goats on the left.* Then the King will say to those on his right, 'Come, you who are blessed by my Father, inherit the kingdom prepared for you from the foundation of the world. For I was hungry and you gave me food, I was thirsty and you gave me drink, I was a stranger and you welcomed me, I was naked and you clothed me, I was sick and you visited me, I was in prison and you came to me' " (Matthew 25:31-36).

To emphasize on the importance of remaining obedient, Jesus, from His abode in heaven, spoke again to John, saying, "The one who conquers will have this heritage, and I will be his God and he will be my son. But as for the cowardly, the faithless, the detestable, as for murderers, the sexually immoral, sorcerers, idolaters, and all liars, their portion will be in the lake that burns with fire and sulfur, which is the second death" (Revelation 21:7-8).

And those who shall overcome will sit on His throne as rulers over nations, since Jesus declared, "The one who conquers and who keeps my works until the end, to him I will give authority over the nations" (Revelation 2:26). He further revealed to John, "The one who conquers, I will grant him to sit with me on my throne, as I also conquered and sat down with my Father on his throne" (Revelation 3:21).

No one knows the hour, the minute, or the second of

His coming. To John for the angel of the church of Sardis, Jesus, the one with the seven Spirits of God and the seven stars, from His kingdom in heaven declared, "Remember, then, what you received and heard. Keep it, and repent. If you will not wake up, I will come like a thief, and you will not know at what hour I will come against you" (Revelation 3:3).

THE KINGDOM OF GOD

God is Love, and He proved it by accepting His own son as a sacrifice for our salvation. "For God so loved the world, that he gave his only Son, that whoever believes in him should not perish but have eternal life" (John 3:16).

Because of this act of love, we are citizens of the Kingdom of God and subjects of a King, on whose account John wrote, "And they sang a new song, saying, 'Worthy are you to take the scroll and to open its seals, for you were slain, and by your blood you ransomed people for God from every tribe and language and people and nation, *and you have made them a kingdom and priests to our God, and they shall reign on the earth*'" (Revelation 5:9-10), establishing clearly that whoever is subjected to Him will rise above those who are not and will be like the angels. The Bible says, "For when they rise from the dead, they neither marry nor are given in marriage, *but are like angels in heaven*" (Mark 12:25).

If we come across any rebuke, we should view it as an act of love, that of a father towards his children, reminding them that they are never out of his sight, for their good. He wants us to experience intimacy with Him who is "Love." Jesus said, "Those whom I love, I reprove and discipline, so be zealous and repent" (Revelation 3:19).

In response to a scribe's question, He said, "And you shall love the Lord your God with all your heart and with all your soul and with all your mind and with all your strength." (Mark 12:30).

Jesus said, "In my Father's house are many rooms. If it were not so, would I have told you that I go to prepare a place for you?" (John 14:2).

The Bible says, "Then came one of the seven angels who had the seven bowls full of the seven last plagues and spoke to me, saying, 'Come, I will show you the Bride, the wife of the Lamb.' And he carried me away in the Spirit to a great, high mountain, and showed me the holy city Jerusalem coming down out of heaven from God'" (Revelation 21:9-10).

This city would be bigger than the territories of Israel, Lebanon, Jordan, Egypt, Iraq, Iran, Syria, Turkey, and Greece together, or about half the size of the U.S., if we were to take its dimensions to the letter. The apostle John wrote, "Then I saw a new heaven and a new earth, for the first heaven and the first earth had passed away, and the sea was no more. And I saw the holy city, new Jerusalem, coming down out of heaven from God, prepared as a bride adorned for her husband" (Revelation 21:1-2).

The Bible says, "And I heard a loud voice from the throne saying, 'Behold, the dwelling place of God is with man. He will dwell with them, and they will be his people, and God himself will be with them as their God. He will wipe away every tear from their eyes, and death shall be no more, neither shall there be mourning nor crying nor pain anymore, for the former things have passed away.'" (Revelation 21:3-4).

John described the Holy City, "Having the glory of God, its radiance like a most rare jewel, like a jasper, clear as crystal" (Revelation 21:11).

John further describing what life will be like in the Holy City wrote, "Then the angel showed me the river of the water of life, bright as crystal, flowing from the throne of God and of the Lamb through the middle of the street of the city; also, on either side of the river, the tree of life with its twelve kinds of fruit, yielding its fruit each month. The leaves of the tree were for the healing of the nations. No longer will there be anything accursed, but the throne of God and of the Lamb will be in it, and his servants will worship him. They will see his face, and his name will be on their foreheads. And night will be no more. They will need no light of lamp or sun, for the Lord God will be their light, and they will reign forever and ever" (Revelation

22:1-5).

Heaven is a real place with better technologies than ours. The prophet Ezekiel described a flying machine that has taken up with the glory of God above it after He had come down to see the abomination that was taking place in the temple and ordered His angels to kill all the idolaters and their children found in Jerusalem. Ezekiel wrote, "And their whole body, their rims, and their spokes, their wings, and the wheels were full of eyes all around—the wheels that the four of them had. As for the wheels, they were called in my hearing 'the whirling wheels.' And every one had four faces: the first face was the face of the cherub, and the second face was a human face, and the third the face of a lion, and the fourth the face of an eagle. And the cherubim mounted up. These were the living creatures that I saw by the Chebar canal. And when the cherubim went, the wheels went beside them. And when the cherubim lifted up their wings to mount up from the earth, the wheels did not turn from beside them. When they stood still, these stood still, and when they mounted up, these mounted up with them, for the spirit of the living creatures was in them. Then the glory of the LORD went out from the threshold of the house, and stood over the cherubim. And the cherubim lifted up their wings and mounted up from the earth before my eyes as they went out, with the wheels beside them.

And they stood at the entrance of the east gate of the house of the LORD, and the glory of the God of Israel was over them" (Ezekiel 10:12-19).

On the morning of Wednesday, April 12, 2006, in a dream I was shown the armies of heaven with their dark, grayish vehicles shaped as a triangle with something like a white circle in the center of them, and they were hovering over my abode. I also saw iridescent angels wearing iridescent warrior gear standing by in combat formation. From the Scriptures we read, "The sound of a tumult is on the mountains as of a great multitude! The sound of an uproar of kingdoms, of nations gathering together! The LORD of hosts is mustering a host for battle. They come from a distant land, from the end of the heavens, the LORD and the weapons of his indignation, to destroy the whole land" (Isaiah 13:4-5).

WHO WILL MAKE IT TO THE KINGDOM OF HEAVEN?

Only those who love God and their fellow men, and who live by His Word in obedience to Him, accepting Jesus as their personal Savior will make it. The Bible says, "And behold, a man came up to him, saying, 'Teacher, what good deed must I do to have eternal life?' And he said to him,

'Why do you ask me about what is good? There is only one who is good. If you would enter life, keep the command-ments.' He said to him, 'Which ones?' And Jesus said, 'You shall not murder, You shall not commit adultery, You shall not steal, You shall not bear false witness, Honor your father and mother, and, You shall love your neighbor as yourself.' The young man said to him, 'All these I have kept. What do I still lack?' Jesus said to him, 'If you would be perfect, go, sell what you possess and give to the poor, and you will have treasure in heaven; and come, follow me' " (Matthew 19:16-21).

Many would argue that believing is enough to be saved, but the following passage dispels that. This is what Jesus said to a Pharisee named Nicodemus, "For God did not send his Son into the world to condemn the world, but in order that the world might be saved through him. Whoever believes in him is not condemned, but whoever does not believe is condemned already, because he has not believed in the name of the only Son of God. And this is the judg-ment: the light has come into the world, and people loved the darkness rather than the light because their deeds were evil. For everyone who does wicked things hates the light and does not come to the light, lest his deeds should be ex-posed. But whoever does what is true comes to the light, so that it may be clearly seen that his deeds have been carried out in God" (John 3:17-21).

Teaching a crowd and his disciples, Jesus said this: "On that day many will say to me, 'Lord, Lord, did we not prophesy in your name, and cast out demons in your name, and do many mighty works in your name?' And then will I declare to them, 'I never knew you; depart from me, you workers of lawlessness' " (Matthew 7:22-23).

Jesus told them how those who are disobedient will be allowed to prosper along with those who are faithful to Him until He comes to judge mankind and have His angels gather them and throw them in the lake of fire. "Let both grow together until the harvest, and at harvest time I will tell the reapers, Gather the weeds first and bind them in bundles to be burned, but gather the wheat into my barn" (Matthew 13:30).

And when His apostles asked Him to clarify the parable for them, He obliged them with greater detail. "Just as the weeds are gathered and burned with fire, so will it be at the close of the age. The Son of Man will send his angels, and they will gather out of his kingdom all causes of sin and all law-breakers, and throw them into the fiery furnace. In that place there will be weeping and gnashing of teeth" (Matthew 13:40-42).

Jesus also explained to His apostles how important it was for them to sacrifice what is temporal to gain what is eternal in the kingdom of heaven. "The kingdom of heaven is like treasure hidden in a field, which a man found and covered up. Then in his joy he goes and sells all that he has and buys that field. 'Again, the kingdom of heaven is like a merchant in search of fine pearls, who, on finding one pearl of great value, went and sold all that he had and bought it' " (Matthew 13:44-46).

And to make sure they understood His message, Jesus told them the parable of bad fish caught in the net of a fisherman. He said, "When it was full, men drew it ashore and sat down and sorted the good into containers but threw away the bad. So it will be at the close of the age. The angels will come out and separate the evil from the righteous and throw them into the fiery furnace. In that place there will be weeping and gnashing of teeth" (Matthew 13:48-50).

Jesus emphasized to them and for those who have been called to preach the Word how important it is to consider it a treasure to be displayed to others as they have received it. "And he said to them, 'Therefore every scribe who has been trained for the kingdom of heaven is like a master of a house, who brings out of his treasure what is new and what is old' " (Matthew 13:52).

Jude the brother of James warning about those who know the Word but fall by the wayside wrote, "But these people blaspheme all that they do not understand, and they are destroyed by all that they, like unreasoning animals, understand instinctively. Woe to them! For they walked in the way of Cain and abandoned themselves for the sake of gain to Balaam's error and perished in Korah's rebellion. These are blemishes on your love feasts, as they feast with you without fear, looking after themselves; waterless clouds, swept along by winds; fruitless trees in late autumn, twice dead, uprooted; wild waves of the sea, casting up the foam of their own shame; wandering stars, for whom the gloom of utter darkness has been reserved forever. It was also about these that Enoch, the seventh from Adam, prophesied, saying, 'Behold, *the Lord came with ten thousands of his holy ones, to execute judgment on all and to convict* all the ungodly of all their deeds of ungodliness that they have committed in such an ungodly way, and of all the harsh things that ungodly sinners have spoken against him.' These are grumblers, malcontents, following their own sinful desires; they are loud-mouthed boasters, showing favoritism to gain advantage. But you must remember, beloved, the predictions of the apostles of our Lord Jesus Christ. They said to you, 'In the last time there will be scoffers, following their own ungodly passions.' It is these who cause divisions, worldly people, devoid of the Spirit' " (Jude 1:10-19).

Further, He had comforting words and advice for those who keep the Word: "But you, beloved, build yourselves up in your most holy faith; pray in the Holy Spirit; keep yourselves in the love of God, waiting for the mercy of our Lord Jesus Christ that leads to eternal life. And have mercy on those who doubt; save others by snatching them out of the fire; to others show mercy with fear, hating even the garment stained by the flesh. Now to him who is able to keep you from stumbling and to present you blameless before the presence of his glory with great joy, to the only God, our Savior, through Jesus Christ our Lord, be glory, majesty, dominion, and authority, before all time and now and forever. Amen" (Jude 1:20-25).

IS EZEKIEL'S TEMPLE TO BE BUILT?

This is what Ezekiel the priest, the son of Buzi, wrote: "In the twenty-fifth year of our exile, at the beginning of the year, on the tenth day of the month, in the fourteenth year after the city was struck down, on that very day, the hand of the LORD was upon me, and he brought me to the city. In visions of God he brought me to the land of Israel, and set me down on a very high mountain, on which was a structure like a city to the south. When he brought me there, behold, there was a man whose appearance was like bronze, with a linen cord and a measuring reed in his hand. And he was standing in the gateway. And the man said to me, 'Son of man, look with your eyes, and hear with your ears, and set your heart upon all that I shall show you, for you were brought here in order that I might show it to you. Declare all that you see to the house of Israel.' And behold, there was a wall all around the outside of the temple area, and the length of the measuring reed in the man's hand was six long cubits, each being a cubit and a handbreadth in length. So he measured the thickness of the wall, one reed; and the height, one reed" (Ezekiel 40:1-5).

After the preceding introduction, let us read the following passage to have an understanding of the size of the temple that has caused so much controversy as to whether it will be built before the coming of Christ. "Now when he had finished measuring the interior of the temple area, he led me out by the gate that faced east, and measured the temple area all around. He measured the east side with the measuring reed, 500 cubits by the measuring reed all around. He measured the north side, 500 cubits by the measuring reed all around. He measured the south side, 500 cubits by the measuring reed. Then he turned to the west side and measured, 500 cubits by the measuring reed" (Ezekiel 42:15-19).

After we have made all necessary calculations, we realize that the size of the square temple is more than two hundred times bigger than Solomon's, according to the following verse: "The house that King Solomon built for the LORD was sixty cubits long, twenty cubits wide, and thirty cubits high" (1 Kings 6:2).

Let us now take a look at the city described by Ezekiel as given to him in his visions, and let us see if by examining it closer, and with the help of the Holy Spirit, it can be our stepping stone into understanding the mystery behind the controversy surrounding the temple as to whether or not it should be built. This is what he wrote: "The circumference of the city shall be 18,000 cubits. And the name of the city from that time on shall be, The LORD is there" (Ezekiel 48:35).

It becomes evident that Ezekiel's city is very small compared to New Jerusalem, the Holy City, which is to come down from heaven, and which is described by John, who wrote, "The city lies foursquare; its length the same as its width. And he measured the city with his rod, 12,000 stadia. Its length and width and height are equal. He also measured its wall, 144 cubits by human measurement, which is also an angel's measurement" (Revelation 21:16-17).

But both cities have two things in common: a river flowing from the temple as described in Ezekiel, "Then he brought me back to the door of the temple, and behold, water was issuing from below the threshold of the temple toward the east (for the temple faced east). The water was flowing down from below the south end of the threshold of the temple, south of the altar" (Ezekiel 47:1). And trees were growing on its banks giving fruits every month of the year, whose leaves are for healing: "And on the banks, on both sides of the river, there will grow all kinds of trees for food. Their leaves will not wither, nor their fruit fail, but they will bear fresh fruit every month, because the water for them flows from the sanctuary. Their fruit will be for food, and their leaves for healing" (Ezekiel 47:12).

John described the river flowing out of the temple of New Jerusalem, the Holy City, from heaven, "Then the angel showed me the river of the water of life, bright as crystal, flowing from the throne of God and of the Lamb through the middle of the street of the city; also, on either side of the river, the tree of life with its twelve kinds of fruit, yielding its fruit each month. The leaves of the tree were for the healing of the nations" (Revelation 22:1-2).

In New Jerusalem, the Holy City, built by the angels, there is no temple but God and the Lamb, and John wrote, "And I saw no temple in the city, for its temple is the Lord God the Almighty and the Lamb" (Revelation 21:22).

The apostle John received instructions concerning a

certain temple, and he wrote, "Then I was given a measuring rod like a staff, and I was told, 'Rise and measure the temple of God and the altar and those who worship there, but do not measure the court outside the temple; leave that out, for it is given over to the nations, and they will trample the holy city for forty-two months" (Revelation 11:1-2).

If the temple described in Ezekiel were the same one of Revelation 11:1-2, it might represent the Church of Christ, His saints, the ones He made holy because they have received His free gift of salvation, and collectively the temple of God, as Paul wrote to the church of Ephesus saying, "So then you are no longer strangers and aliens, but you are fellow citizens with the saints and members of the household of God, built on the foundation of the apostles and prophets, Christ Jesus himself being the cornerstone, in whom the whole structure, being joined together, grows into a holy temple in the Lord. In him you also are being built together into a dwelling place for God by the Spirit" (Ephesians 2:19-22).

The exceptionally greater size of Ezekiel's temple in comparison to Solomon's, the precise description and measurements of each area of the temple and of the altar, and the intricate carving on walls and on the double doors of the Holy Place and on either sides of windows of the temple described in Ezekiel 41:18-26 indicate that it was to foreshadow the coming of another type of priesthood, greater than the one of the first covenant, to be replaced by another one with the house of Israel and with the house of Judah that surpasses the one He had with their fathers. The Scriptures say, "Thus says the LORD: If you can break my covenant with the day and my covenant with the night, so that day and night will not come at their appointed time, then also my covenant with David my servant may be broken, so that he shall not have a son to reign on his throne, and my covenant with the Levitical priests my ministers. As the host of heaven cannot be numbered and the sands of the sea cannot be measured, so I will multiply the offspring of David my servant, and the Levitical priests who minister to me" (Jeremiah 33:20-22).

This priesthood, which is the ministry of Jesus, shall last forever; His servants through His Gospel will be countless. The Bible says, "But this one was made a priest with an oath by the one who said to him: "The Lord has sworn and will not change his mind, 'You are a priest forever.'" This makes Jesus the guarantor of a better covenant. The former priests were many in number, because they were prevented by death from continuing in office, but he holds his priesthood permanently, because he continues forever. Consequently, he is able to save to the uttermost those who draw near to God through him, since he always lives to make intercession for them. For it was indeed fitting that we should have such a high priest, holy, innocent, unstained, separated from sinners, and exalted above the heavens. He has no need, like those high priests, to offer sacrifices daily, first for his own sins and then for those of the people, since he did this once for all when he offered up himself. For the law appoints men in their weakness as high priests, but the word of the oath, which came later than the law, appoints a Son who has been made perfect forever" (Hebrews 7:21-28). John, who has received the testimony of Jesus Christ, wrote, "And one of the elders said to me, 'Weep no more; *behold, the Lion of the tribe of Judah, the Root of David, has conquered*, so that he can open the scroll and its seven seals.' And between the throne and the four living creatures and among the elders I saw a Lamb standing, as though it had been slain, with seven horns and with seven eyes, which are the seven spirits of God sent out into all the earth. And he went and took the scroll from the right hand of him who was seated on the throne. And when he had taken the scroll, the four living creatures and the twenty-four elders fell down before the Lamb, each holding a harp, and golden bowls full of incense, which are the prayers of the saints. And they sang a new song, saying, 'Worthy are you to take the scroll and to open its seals, for you were slain, and by your blood you ransomed people for

God from every tribe and language and people and nation, *and you have made them a kingdom and priests to our God, and they shall reign on the earth*'" (Revelation 5:5-10).

Because Jesus died on the cross, first for the Jews and then the gentiles, was resurrected, and went up to heaven to be an eternal priest interceding for us, God has no more need of a physical temple and altar on the earth. The prophet Isaiah wrote, "Measure by measure, by exile you contended with them; he removed them with his fierce breath in the day of the east wind. Therefore by this the guilt of Jacob will be atoned for, and this will be the full fruit of the removal of his sin: when he makes all the stones of the altars like chalkstones crushed to pieces, no Asherim or incense altars will remain standing" (Isaiah 27:8-9).

This is what the Lord said to Isaiah the son of Amoz: "Behold Zion, the city of our appointed feasts! Your eyes will see Jerusalem, an untroubled habitation, an immovable tent, whose stakes will never be plucked up, nor will any of its cords be broken" (Isaiah 33:20), and He further said to him, "Thus says the LORD: 'Heaven is my throne, and the earth is my footstool; what is the house that you would build for me, and what is the place of my rest? All these things my hand has made, and so all these things came to be, declares the LORD. *But this is the one to whom I will look: he who is humble and contrite in spirit and trembles at my word.* 'He who slaughters an ox is like one who kills a man; *he who sacrifices a lamb, like one who breaks a dog's neck*; he who presents a grain offering, like one who offers pig's blood; *he who makes a memorial offering of frankincense, like one who blesses an idol.* These have chosen their own ways, and their soul delights in their abominations" (Isaiah 66:1-3).

As it was also reported by one of the apostles in a conversation with the Jews, "After they finished speaking, James replied, 'Brothers, listen to me. Simeon has related how God first visited the Gentiles, to take from them a people for his name. And with this the words of the prophets agree, just as it is written, 'After this I will return, and I will rebuild the tent of David that has fallen; I will rebuild its ruins, and I will restore it, that the remnant of mankind may seek the Lord, and all the Gentiles who are called by my name, says the Lord, who makes these things known from of old" (Acts 15:13-18).

Ezekiel's temple is also to foreshadow the real one, which is in heaven. This is what John wrote after he was shown what it will be like in heaven's temple: "After this I looked, and behold, a great multitude that no one could number, from every nation, from all tribes and peoples and languages, standing before the throne and before the Lamb, clothed in white robes, with palm branches in their hands,

THE KINGDOM OF GOD

and crying out with a loud voice, 'Salvation belongs to our God who sits on the throne, and to the Lamb!' And all the angels were standing around the throne and around the elders and the four living creatures, and they fell on their faces before the throne and worshiped God, saying, 'Amen! Blessing and glory and wisdom and thanksgiving and honor and power and might be to our God forever and ever! Amen.' Then one of the elders addressed me, saying, 'Who are these, clothed in white robes, and from where have they come?' I said to him, 'Sir, you know.' And he said to me, 'These are the ones coming out of the great tribulation. They have washed their robes and made them white in the blood of the Lamb. 'Therefore they are before the throne of God, and serve him day and night in his temple; and he who sits on the throne will shelter them with his presence. They shall hunger no more, neither thirst anymore; the sun shall not strike them, nor any scorching heat. For the Lamb in the midst of the throne will be their shepherd, *and he will guide them to springs of living water*, and God will wipe away every tear from their eyes" (Revelation 7:9-17).

The Lamb spoken of above is Jesus, who was pierced on one side, who died and shed His precious blood on the cross for the salvation of all. This is what the Lord, the God of Israel, the God of Abraham, Isaac, and Jacob said to the prophet Zechariah, the son of Berechiah, son of Iddo, "And on that day I will seek to destroy all the nations that come against Jerusalem. And I will pour out on the house of David and the inhabitants of Jerusalem a spirit of grace and pleas for mercy, so that, *when they look on me, on him whom they have pierced,* they shall mourn for him, as one mourns for an only child, and weep bitterly over him, as one weeps over a firstborn" (Zechariah 12:9-10).

Paul wrote the following to the Hebrew Christians, in one of his letters as he was away, reassuring them of the superiority of the new covenant sealed by the shed blood of Christ, the only begotten son of God, over the old covenant: "For since the law has but a shadow of the good things to come instead of the true form of these realities, it can never, by the same sacrifices that are continually offered every year, make perfect those who draw near. Otherwise, would they not have ceased to be offered, since the worshipers, having once been cleansed, would no longer have any consciousness of sin? But in these sacrifices there is a reminder of sin every year. *For it is impossible for the blood of bulls and goats to take away sins.* Consequently, when Christ came into the world, he said, 'Sacrifices and offerings you have not desired, but a body have you prepared for me; *in burnt offerings and sin offerings you have taken no pleasure.* Then I said, 'Behold, I have come to do your will, O God, as it is written of me in the scroll of the book.' When he said above, 'You have neither desired nor taken pleasure in sacrifices and offerings and burnt offerings and sin offerings' (these are offered according to the law), then he added, 'Behold, I have come to do your will.' He abolishes the first in order to establish the second. And by that will we have been sanctified through the offering of the body of Jesus Christ once for all. And every priest stands daily at his service, offering repeatedly the same sacrifices, which can never take away sins. But when Christ had offered for all time a single sacrifice for sins, he sat down at the right hand of God, waiting from that time until his enemies should be made a footstool for his feet. For by a single offering he has perfected for all time those who are being sanctified. And the Holy Spirit also bears witness to us; for after saying, 'This is the covenant that I will make with them after those days, declares the Lord: I will put my laws on their hearts, and write them on their minds,' then he adds, 'I will remember their sins and their lawless deeds no more.' Where there is forgiveness of these, there is no longer any offering for sin. Therefore, brothers, since we have confidence to enter the holy places by the blood of Jesus, by the new and living way that he opened for us through the curtain, that is, through his flesh, and since we have a great priest over the house of God, let us draw near with a true heart in full assurance of faith, with our hearts sprinkled clean from an evil conscience and our bodies washed with pure water. Let us hold fast the confession of our hope without wavering, for he who promised is faithful" (Hebrews 10:1-23).

Out of Jesus' holy temple will flow a spring of living water, as He declared to the Samaritan woman, "But whoever drinks of the water that I will give him will never be thirsty forever. The water that I will give him will become in him a spring of water welling up to eternal life" (John 4:14), and as He further added, "Whoever believes in me, as the Scripture has said, 'Out of his heart will flow rivers of living water'" (John 7:38).

This seems to be a depiction of the perpetuation of His love through believers to those living in unbelief so as to transform their hearts. And Paul wrote, "But as it is, Christ has obtained a ministry that is as much more excellent than the old as the covenant he mediates is better, since it is enacted on better promises. For if that first covenant had been faultless, there would have been no occasion to look for a second. For he finds fault with them when he says: 'Behold, the days are coming, declares the Lord, when I will establish a new covenant with the house of Israel and with the house of Judah, not like the covenant that I made with their fathers on the day when I took them by the hand to bring them out of the land of Egypt. For they did not continue in my covenant, and so I showed no concern for them, declares the Lord. For this is the covenant that I will make with the house of Israel after those days, declares the Lord: I will put my laws into their minds, and write them on their hearts, and I will be their God, and they shall be my people. And they shall not teach, each one his neighbor and each one his brother, saying, 'Know the Lord,' for they shall all know me, from the least of them to the greatest. For I will be merciful toward their iniquities, and I will remember their sins no more'" (Hebrews 8:6-12).

Ezekiel's temple represents the Church, the only one meeting God's expectation because of Jesus, His only begotten son being its cornerstone. Jesus preaching in the temple answered many questions fielded by the chief priests and the Pharisees. "Jesus said to them, 'Have you never read in the Scriptures: "The stone that the builders rejected has become the cornerstone; this was the Lord's doing, and it is marvelous in our eyes"? Therefore I tell you, the kingdom of God will be taken away from you and given to a people producing its fruits. And the one who falls on this stone will be broken to pieces; and when it falls on anyone, it will crush him'" (Matthew 21:42-44).

To show His willingness to dwell with man, according to John's Revelation 21:3 cited earlier, God made recommendation concerning a specific portion to be reserved for

His sanctuary. The Scriptures say, "When you allot the land as an inheritance, you shall set apart for the LORD a portion of the land as a holy district, 25,000 cubits long and 20,000 cubits broad. It shall be holy throughout its whole extent. Of this a square plot of 500 by 500 cubits shall be for the sanctuary, with fifty cubits for an open space around it. And from this measured district you shall measure off a section 25,000 cubits long and 10,000 broad, in which shall be the sanctuary, the Most Holy Place. It shall be the holy portion of the land. It shall be for the priests, who minister in the sanctuary and approach the LORD to minister to him, and it shall be a place for their houses and a holy place for the sanctuary. Another section, 25,000 cubits long and 10,000 cubits broad, shall be for the Levites who minister at the temple, as their possession for cities to live in. 'Alongside the portion set apart as the holy district you shall assign for the property of the city an area 5,000 cubits broad and 25,000 cubits long. It shall belong to the whole house of Israel'" (Ezekiel 45:1-6).

By allotting the portion to His prince parallel to those of the tribes, and on both sides of the holy portion having the sanctuary in its midst, and on both sides of the property of the city, the Lord proclaimed that His prince is chosen and worthy to impart justice in the land. From the Scriptures we read, "And to the prince shall belong the land on both sides of the holy district and the property of the city, alongside the holy district and the property of the city, on the west and on the east, corresponding in length to one of the tribal portions, and extending from the western to the eastern boundary of the land. It is to be his property in Israel. And my princes shall no more oppress my people, but they shall let the house of Israel have the land according to their tribes" (Ezekiel 45:7-8).

The princes, who are sons of His prince and who will uphold his commands, are those who believe in His Son and who will return with Him to reign over nations. To them He spoke as to tell them that they will be different from those who have preceded them. From the Scriptures we read, "Thus says the Lord GOD: Enough, O princes of Israel! Put away violence and oppression, and execute justice and righteousness. Cease your evictions of my people, declares the Lord GOD. 'You shall have just balances, a just ephah, and a just bath" (Ezekiel 45:9-10).

As for the water trickling out eastward from under the south end of the threshold of the temple, it is the Word of God, His Gospel pouring out of His collective temple, the Church of Christ. It also foreshadows Jesus baptizing with the Holy Spirit and with fire that has come down from the heavenly temple. Ezekiel wrote, "Then he brought me back to the door of the temple, and behold, water was issuing from below the threshold of the temple toward the east (for the temple faced east). The water was flowing down from below the south end of the threshold of the temple, south of the altar. Then he brought me out by way of the north gate and led me around on the outside to the outer gate that faces toward the east; and behold, the water was trickling out on the south side" (Ezekiel 47:1-2). Speaking of Jesus John the Baptist said, "I baptize you with water for repentance, but he who is coming after me is mightier than I, whose sandals I am not worthy to carry. *He will baptize you with the Holy Spirit and with fire*" (Matthew 3:11).

The Lord is the source of this living water, and it is free to those who are willing to receive it. The prophet Jeremiah wrote, "O LORD, the hope of Israel, all who forsake you shall be put to shame; those who turn away from you shall be written in the earth, for they have forsaken the LORD, the fountain of living water" (Jeremiah 17:13), and teaching a crowd in the temple, "On the last day of the feast, the great day, Jesus stood up and cried out, 'If anyone thirsts, let him come to me and drink. Whoever believes in me, as the Scripture has said, 'Out of his heart will flow rivers of living water'" (John 7:37-38).

This living water Jesus spoke about originated from His own heart as He started announcing the good news of His Father's kingdom, the Gospel that spread through His disciples from Galilee, then to other regions, and countries, to the Jews first and then the Gentiles, to become deep rivers of living waters flowing to all the corners of the earth, and to the most remote hamlets. It is what the Lord's angel demonstrated to Ezekiel as he was leading farther and farther downstream until Ezekiel could no more advance because the water was becoming deeper and deeper. He wrote, "Going on eastward with a measuring line in his hand, the man measured a thousand cubits, and then led me through the water, and it was ankle-deep. Again he measured a thousand, and led me through the water, and it was knee-deep. Again he measured a thousand, and led me through the water, and it was waist-deep. Again he measured a thousand, and it was a river that I could not pass through, for the water had risen. It was deep enough to swim in, a river that could not be passed through. And he said to me, 'Son of man, have you seen this?' Then he led me back to the bank of the river" (Ezekiel 47:3-6).

The water trickling out eastward from under the south end of the threshold of the temple is also the great multitude of believers who have welcomed the good news of Salvation from the Lord and who have washed themselves in the precious blood of Christ and come out clean and refreshed. They are like the Dead Sea, cleansed by this flowing water with the beneficial property to render it as fresh as it was meant to be. They are like the fish that frolic in it and multiply. The angel spoke to Ezekiel, "And he said to me, 'This water flows toward the eastern region and goes down into the Arabah, and enters the sea; when the water flows into the sea, the water will become fresh. And wherever the river goes, every living creature that swarms will live, and there will be very many fish. For this water goes there, that the waters of the sea may become fresh; so everything will live where the river goes. Fishermen will stand beside the sea. From Engedi to Eneglaim it will be a place for the spreading of nets. Its fish will be of very many kinds, like the fish of the Great Sea'" (Ezekiel 47:8-10), and went on saying, "But its swamps and marshes will not become fresh; they are to be left for salt" (Ezekiel 47:11).

The Gospel is being announced to all, but some will receive it, and like seeds in good soil, they will grow spiritually, blossom, and bear fruit. They are those who labor, not in vain, for the kingdom of God. They are like the fruit trees by the river bank that Ezekiel saw as he was coming out of the river: "Now when I had returned, behold, at the bank of the river were very many trees on the one side and on the other" (Ezekiel 47:7 KJV).

Many hear the good news of the kingdom but will prefer to ignore it and will neither benefit from it nor change course. They will remain unchanged, like marshy land, and being unproductive and incapable of bearing fruits, they will be thrown into the lake of fire in the manner John the Baptist warned the Pharisees and Sadducees, saying, "Even now the axe is laid to the root of the trees. Every tree therefore that does not bear good fruit is cut down and thrown into the fire" (Matthew 3:10).

HOW SHOULD WE HONOR OUR GOD?

After Moses had broken the two tablets of stone of the Ten Commandments, God ordered him to come alone to meet Him on top of Mount Sinai with a new set of tablets. He did as God commanded, and as he was waiting, "The LORD descended in the cloud and stood with him there, and proclaimed the name of the LORD. The LORD passed before him and proclaimed, 'The LORD, the LORD, a God merciful and gracious, slow to anger, and abounding in steadfast love and faithfulness, keeping steadfast love for thousands, forgiving iniquity and transgression and sin, but who will by no means clear the guilty, visiting the iniquity of the fathers on the children and the children's children, to the third and the fourth generation' " (Exodus 34:5-7).

And the Lord spoke to him again and told him, "Take care, lest you make a covenant with the inhabitants of the land to which you go, lest it become a snare in your midst. You shall tear down their altars and break their pillars and cut down their Asherim (for you shall worship no other god, *for the LORD, whose name is Jealous, is a jealous God*), lest you make a covenant with the inhabitants of the land, and when they whore after their gods and sacrifice to their gods and you are invited, you eat of his sacrifice, and you take of their daughters for your sons, and their daughters whore after their gods and make your sons whore after their gods" (Exodus 34:12-16).

After Moses had read to the Israelites all that God had commanded, he spoke to them recommending, "Hear, O Israel: The LORD our God, the LORD is one. You shall love the LORD your God with all your heart and with all your soul and with all your might" (Deuteronomy 6:4-5).

Responding to the question of a lawyer, one of the Pharisees who wanted to embarrass him and asked which of the commandments was the greatest, "Jesus answered, 'The most important is, 'Hear, O Israel: The Lord our God, the Lord is one. And you shall love the Lord your God with all your heart and with all your soul and with all your mind and with all your strength'" (Mark 12:29-30).

After the ark of the Lord was brought up to Jerusalem, from the Scriptures we read, "David also commanded the chiefs of the Levites to appoint their brothers as the singers who should play loudly on musical instruments, on harps and lyres and cymbals, to raise sounds of joy" (1 Chronicles 15:16).

From the Scriptures we read, "Exalt the LORD our God, and worship at his holy hill; for the LORD our God is holy" (Psalms 99:9 KJV).

And Isaiah the son of Amoz reminded Israel of the holiness of the Lord: "But the LORD of hosts is exalted in justice, and the Holy God shows himself holy in righteousness" (Isaiah 5:16).

The apostle John witnessed true worship in heaven from the angels and those who have come from the great tribulation, "Saying, 'Amen! Blessing and glory and wisdom and thanksgiving and honor and power and might be to our God forever and ever! Amen'" (Revelation 7:12), and from the four creatures and the elders, and he wrote, "And the four living creatures, each of them with six wings, are full of eyes all around and within, and day and night they never cease to say, 'Holy, holy, holy, is the Lord God Almighty, who was and is and is to come!' And whenever the living creatures give glory and honor and thanks to him who is seated on the throne, who lives forever and ever, the twenty-four elders fall down before him who is seated on the throne and worship him who lives forever and ever. They cast their crowns before the throne, saying, 'Worthy are you, our Lord and God, to receive glory and honor and power, for you created all things, and by your will they existed and were created' " (Revelation 4:8-11).

Isn't it enough said to understand that our Lord, our God, deserves the greatest honor and respect and that we cannot associate His name with anything derogatory, vile, demeaning, and offensive, words that we should not even use towards our fellowman? This is what Jesus commanded to his disciples and the crowds He was preaching to. "But I say to you that everyone who is angry with his brother will be liable to judgment; whoever insults his brother will be liable to the council; and whoever says, 'You fool!' will be liable to the hell of fire" (Matthew 5:22).

It is even forbidden to insult principalities, which are Satan and the fallen angels. Peter wrote, "Then the Lord knows how to rescue the godly from trials, and to keep the unrighteous under punishment until the Day of Judgment, and especially those who indulge in the lust of defiling passion and despise authority. Bold and willful, they do not tremble as they blaspheme the glorious ones, whereas angels, though greater in might and power, do not pronounce a blasphemous judgment against them before the Lord. But these, like irrational animals, creatures of instinct, born to be caught and destroyed, blaspheming about matters of which they are ignorant, will also be destroyed in their destruction" (2 Peter 2:9-12).

We ought to love and honor our God and worship Him at all times and use only names that testify of His holiness, righteousness, might, and power, such as all the names by which He calls Himself: "The Lord, God Almighty, Jehovah (the Eternal), Lord of Hosts, the Holy One of Israel, the Fountain of Living Water," and many more. He is called "the Righteous One" and His spirit is "Holy." He is our Banner, our Deliverer, our Father, our Healer, our Helper, our King, our Provider, our Refuge, our Rock, our Redeemer, our Shepherd, our Shield, our Strength, and many more to us.

If we are found guilty and deserve to be thrown into hell and the lake of fire for offending man, even the fallen angels, unless we repent of such sin, how much more will it be for such behavior towards God? Jesus warned those who would be found guilty of such an act: "And whoever speaks a word against the Son of Man will be forgiven, but whoever speaks against the Holy Spirit will not be forgiven, either in this age or in the age to come" (Matthew 12:32).

Let us bless the name of the Lord and ask Him to protect us against such offense! Let us repeat this payer after Jesus, as He taught His disciples saying, "Pray then like this: 'Our Father in heaven, hallowed be your name' (Matthew 6:9), and further He added, 'And lead us not into temptation, but deliver us from evil' " (Matthew 6:13).

Jesus, the King of kings, has received power, wealth, wisdom, might, honor, glory, and blessing to share with His subjects. John wrote, "Then I looked, and I heard around the throne and the living creatures and the elders the voice of many angels, numbering myriads of myriads and thousands of thousands, saying with a loud voice, 'Worthy is the Lamb who was slain, to receive power and wealth and wisdom and might and honor and glory and blessing!' And I heard every creature in heaven and on earth and under the earth and in the sea, and all that is in them, saying, 'To him who sits on the throne and to the Lamb be blessing and honor and glory and might forever and ever!' And the four living creatures said, 'Amen!' and the elders fell down and worshiped" (Revelation 5:11-14).

WHAT SHOULD BE OUR PLEDGE BEFORE JESUS RETURNS?

In the early morning of Tuesday, August 23, 2005, in a dream I saw my earthly father entering a foster home, and when I asked him if he were there to adopt a certain number of children, he knelt down and with the tip of his finger drew a tall cross in the dust as he looked at me. Isn't our Lord Jesus Christ reminding me that He is at the door ready to enter at any moment to claim those who belong to Him, who were bought and paid for at the cross by His precious blood? To John He revealed, "Behold, I am coming soon, bringing my recompense with me, to repay everyone for what he has done" (Revelation 22:12).

As we wait for His coming, let us love each other as He commanded. "You have heard that it was said, 'You shall love your neighbor and hate your enemy.' But I say to you, Love your enemies and pray for those who persecute you" (Matthew 5:43-44). "Love does no wrong to a neighbor; therefore love is the fulfilling of the law. (Romans 13:10)

Let us forgive each other because we must forgive to be forgiven. He reminded us, "For if you forgive others their trespasses, your heavenly Father will also forgive you, but if you do not forgive others their trespasses, neither will your Father forgive your trespasses" (Matthew 6:14-15).

Let us not judge, since He further added, "Judge not, that you be not judged. For with the judgment you pronounce you will be judged, and with the measure you use it will be measured to you" (Matthew 7:1-2).

While we remain obedient, let us "Put on then, as God's chosen ones, holy and beloved, compassion, kindness, humility, meekness, and patience" (Colossians 3:12).

On a last note, who should we serve and please? God or our Church leaders, other Church members, our friends and lovers, who are all mere humans? We all are sinners, incapable to stand in each other defense when Judgment day comes, since none of us will escape from it. The angels will gather all of us before Jesus Christ's throne when He returns. He will order them to divide us in two groups, those who belong to Him, who have chosen to become His sons, to his right and those who belong to Satan to His left.

With our last breath ends the opportunity to either accept Jesus as Lord and Savior and live eternally on the earth, in a glorious body, like the angels or face eternal damnation in hell and the lake of fire along with Satan and vengeful demons. The angel of death may come at any moment; it is wise that we make that choice now before it is too late if we have lived so far oblivious of this truth.

Now it is time that we part! Even though my eyes are weary and all my joints are aching, my soul rejoices that you have acquired a greater thirst for the truth and that you will hold dear what you have learned so far. May our walk together, through a field filled with invaluable jewels, remain a memorable one, onwards to eternity! Father, we thank you!

NOTES

Please Use These Pages As You Are Reading This Book

INDEX

177
CSTO (Collective Security Treaty
Organization), 177
Cubits, six long. See Ezekiel's
temple, 315
Cult of themselves, a. See False
teacher, 235
Cult, a materialistic. See also
Church leaders; Priest;
Prophet, 247
Cultural tree, the. See Author's
ancestry, 284
Cunning, by his. See Beast, 159
Cup from me, remove this, 29
Cup of demons, the, 108
Cup of his anger, the. See God's
wrath; Wine, 172, 215, 277
Cup of the Lord, whoever drinks
the. See Jesus; Wine, 276
Cup she mixed, in the. See
Babylon the great, 47
Cup, for as often as you drink the.
See Jesus; Wine, 276
Cure. See also Plagues, 216
Currency, a single, 178
Curse of Babylon, the. See Sin,
244, 246
Curse the land mourns, because of
the. See also Lord, 247
Cursed be anyone who dishonors
his father, 77
Curtain is about to close, the, 285
Curtain, that he opened for us
through the. See also Way, 325
Cush, 183
Customs Union. See EurAsEC;
EAEC, 178
Cut down and thrown into the fire,
is. See also Fruit, 333
Cut off, the rest shall not be, 118,
206
Cutting edge technologies, 190
Cyclical, 59

D

Daily occurrence, a, 28
Daily tasks, his. See Moses, 239
Dangers are looming, terrible. See

Al-Qaeda; Bin Laden, 243
Daniel described Him as an elder.
See God, 287
Daniel from the lions, He had
saved, 29
Daniel revealed to king
Nebuchadnezzar, 167
Daniel, the prophet, 160, 167
Darkness and light, a, 70
Darkness came, when the sixth
hour had come. See Jesus, 120
Darkness, and its kingdom was
plunged into. See Judgments;
Satan, 297
Darkness, and people loved the.
See also Light, 310
Darkness, like slippery paths in
the. See Priest; Prophet, 233,
247
Darwin's theory, those who
support. See Evolution, 59
Das Kapital. See Karl Marx, 70
Daughters of man, the, 124, 130,
211
Daughters remained behind, my
two. See Boat, 279
David commanded to raise sounds
of joy, 335
David, I will multiply the
offspring of, 319
Day a great panic from the LORD,
on that, 209
Day I will seek to destroy, on that.
See Jerusalem, 324
Day of battle, as when He fights
on a, 118, 206
Day of God the Almighty, the. See
Armageddon; Judments, 208,
299
Day of the east wind, the, 321
Day of the LORD comes, with
wrath, the. See Celestial army,
259
Day of the Lord has come, to the
effect that the., 158, 289
Day vision, 25, 27, 49, 155
Day, that Gog comes against
Israel, on the, 208
Day, the Lord will award, on that.

Demons, a man from the city who had. See Fallen Angels, 131

Demons, along with Satan and vengeful. See also Eternal damnation, 340

Demons, son argued that there were no, 41

Denarius, 53

Denies me, whoever. See Jesus, 101

Denomination. See also Elders, 263, 265

Denomination's own Bible version, this, 265

Deny his Divine nature, one cannot. See Jesus, 262

Denying the Master. See False teacher, 235

Departure of foreign troops, an early. See Iraq, 186

Depravation. See sexual Immorality, 77

Derogatory, we cannot associate His name with anything. See God; Jesus; Lord, 336

Desolate and naked, they will make her. See Prostitute, 45, 169, 203

Despair, 29, 64

Despotic institution, 94

Despotism, 91

Destroy the city, for the LORD is about to, 83

Destroy the whole land, to. See Celestial army, 259, 309

Destroy, without warning he shall. See Beast, 159

Destroyed, you will be. See Beast, 159

Destroyer and betrayer, 159

Destroying the destroyers of the earth. See Kingdom of our Lord, 293, 299

Destruction of cataclysmal proportion. See also Al-Qaeda, 243

Destruction of the twin towers. See 9/11; Beast 155

Destruction, these will be

destroyed in their, 252

Destructive heresies. See False teacher, 235

Detestable beast, 47, 170

Devil was thrown into the lake of fire, and the, 116, 222

Devil worshipper, 11

Devil, you are of your father the. See also Liar; Lie, 76

Devil-worshipping, 38

Devil-worshipping ritual, 38

Devoid of the Spirit. See also Rebellion, 313

Devourer, I will rebuke the, 65, 142

Diadems on its horns, with ten. See Beast, 42, 162

Diadems, on his head are many. See Jesus; Faithful and True, 207, 300

Diamond. See King of Tyre, 57, 128

Die anymore, for they cannot. See Sons of God, 134

Die without knowing Jesus Christ, millions to. See also Satan's plan, 22

Die, must surely. See Reviles his father, 77

Direction from the Lord, 2

Disaster upon them, I will bring. See Priest; Prophet, 234, 247

Disciples of Christ, 98

Disciples, 'Have them sit down, He said to his. See also Sheep, 239

Discoveries, genomic, 86

Dishonors his father or his mother, who. See Cursed; also Die, 77

Dismissal from the pulpit, their, 81

Disobedience, God has consigned all to. See Jews; Gentiles, 136, 285

Disobedient than those who have, more. See Poor, 71

Disobedient, against those who are, 41

Disobedient, as you were at one

E

Kingdom, 189, 258, 259, 309
End of the millennium, 22, 58
End time, 152
End-Time prophecies, a quick
  unfolding of, 236
Endurance of the saints, for the.
  See also Plagues; Beast, 228
Endurance, By your. See also
  Plagues; Beast, 228
Enemies appeared motionless, my,
  29
Enemies should be made a
  footstool, his. See Jesus, 325
Enemy is on the prowl, the. See
  Satan, 238
Enemy was catching up fast, the.
  See Evil pursuers; also Ebony
  bride, 237
Enemy, enraged and frustrated,
  the. See Al-Qaeda, 243
Enemy, to warn the leadership of
  evil plots by the, 243
Enemy, overrun by the. See Satan,
  237
Enemy's side, a thorn in the. See
  Bush, 242
Enoch, 132, 313
Enslaved, to that he is. See Sin,
  248
Enslavement. See also Usury, 252
Entity, concerning the other, 191
Entrepreneurial skills. See Church
  leaders, 248
Entrusted much, from him to
  whom they. See Judges and
  makes war, 301
Envelope, sealed, 242
Ephah, a just. See Princes, 329
Ephraim, 183
Era, post-Antichrist, 156
Escape for your life. Do not look
  back. See Lot, 83
Escape, if I tried to, 29
E-sword.net. See Bible; Verses,
  272
Eternal damnation in hell and the
  lake of fire, or face. See Satan;
  Demons, 340
Eternal life, to have. See Deed,

250, 309
Eternal punishment, 75, 82
Ethiopia, 57
Euphrates, the angel poured out
  his bowl on the. See
  Judgments; Plagues; also
  Kings from the East, 166, 180,
  298
EurAsEC, Eurasian Economic
  Community, 178
Eurasian conflicts, 178
Europe, 176, 179, 186, 199, 243
European languages. Author's
  ancestry, 282
European Union, 178
Evangelical radio station, 19
Evil and on the good, he makes
  His sun rise on the, 18
Evil deed, I will attend to you for
  your. See Shepherds, 247
Evil entities, 40
Evil one, sons of the. See also
  Weeds, 271, 291
Evil people, 37
Evil person from among you,
  Purge the. See Church, 106
Evil plan, 24
Evil plots. See also Saddam, Al-
  Qaeda, 243
Evil pursuers. See also Christians;
  Ebony bride; Galleon, 236
Evil pursuers. See also Galleon,
  236
Evil spirit, 96, 102, 131
Evil spirits came out of them, 102
Evolution. See Charles Darwin,
  58, 59
Example you have set, the bad.
  See Church leaders, 249
Example, serve as an, 82, 100
Examples to the flock, being. See
  Church leaders, 253
Excessive eating, 88
Excommunication. See Priests, 93
Excuses to escape punishment.
  See Liar; Lie; also Devil, 75
Execute judgment on all, to, 313
Execute justice and righteousness,
  to, 329

mountains, you shall. See also
Mount of Olives, 119, 206
Flesh is true food, my, 140
Flesh, and make no provision for
the. See Sexual immorality,
101
Flesh, He was the Word made, 97
Flesh, in the likeness of sinful, 136
Flesh, the works of the. See
Church, 237, 249
Flesh, unless you eat the. See
Jesus, 140
Flesh, weakened by the, 136
Flesh, who walk not according to
the, 136
Flock from their mouth, I will
deliver my. See also
Shepherds, 106
Flock, a mammoth, 238
Flock, being examples to the, 253
Flock, many have abandoned
their, 37
Flock, you have scattered my. See
also Shepherds, 247
Flogging, others suffered. See also
Endurance, 229
Flood came, and the, 237
Floods. See also Plagues, 216
Flying machine, 133, 308
Flying machine, they have
developed. See also UFO, 133
Foes, consumes their. See
Witnesses, 204, 286
Follow their sensuality, they. See
False teacher, 235
Followers of Jesus, 74
Food is unclean, no, 68
Food sacrificed to idols, 108
Food, do not, for the sake of, 69
Food, I had preferred to sell fast,
18
Foolishness, Stop this. See
Church, 104, 252
For his mercy, 30
Forbidden to insult principalities.
See Satan; Fallen angels, 336
Forbidden zone that makes us
sinners, the. See also Abortion;
Adam; Gray areas, 87

Forced labor. See Beast; China,
168, 173
Foreheads, the seal of God on
their. See also Judgments;
Plagues, 6, 216, 228, 296
Forerunner, 8, 12, 14, 89, 195
Forgive others, if you do not, 91,
339
Forgive us our debts, and. See
Prayer, 148
Forgive, and whenever you stand
praying,, 18
Forgiven you, that the intent may
be. See Simon Magus, 150
Forgiven, do not cry. You are, 21
Forgiveness of our trespasses, 121,
139
Forgiveness, to believe they could
buy God's. See Pope Leo X,
150
Forgiveness, Where there is. See
also Offering for sin, 325
Forgiving iniquity. See Lord;
Moses, 333
Form or majesty, no. See Jesus,
280
Former things have passed away,
for the, 307
Fornication. See also Adultery, 56,
77, 79, 100, 139, 230, 246,
247, 249
Forsake you shall be put to shame,
all who. See also Fountain of
living water, 330
Foster home, entering a. See
Earthly father, 338
Fought the good fight, I. See
Author's faith and obedience,
225
Found work, I. See Author, 26
Found, but it will never be. See
Tyre, 125
Foundation of the earth, I laid the,
59, 105, 113
Foundation of the world, from the.
See Kingdom; Book of life,
159, 163, 199, 291, 302
Foundation, the Church, 30
Fountain of living water, the. See

H

K

L

M

P

will. See Day of the Lord, 259
Punished, they will be. See Kings
of the earth; Dragon, 214, 261
Punishment of eternal destruction,
the. See Day of the Lord, 260
Punishment of eternal fire, 82, 100
Punishment, in the year of their.
See Priest; Prophet, 234, 247
Puppet government. See
Antichrist, 190
Purgatory, 59
Purge the evil person from among
you. See Church, 106
Putin. See President; Russia, 9,
175, 176, 178, 179, 180, 181,
185
Pyramid, Great, 124, 132

Q

Quake, a magnitude 8.0, 116
Queen of heaven, a man who
worships a. See False teacher,
235
Queen of heaven, the women
make cakes for the. See also
Idolatry, 113, 232, 254
Queen of Heaven, they deify her
as a. See Mary, 109

R

Race, a superhuman. See Fallen
Angels, 130
Radio shows, syndicated nightly,
134
Rags. See Fabrics; Miracles, 101
Rahab the prostitute, 138
Ramallah, 180
Rapture will not occur before the
seventh trumpet, the. See
Judgments, 290
Reapers are angels, the. See also
Harvest, 271, 291
Rebel against Him, and made
them. See Jews, 284
Rebellion and punishment, with
real. See Jews, 284

Rebellion comes first, unless the.
See Day of the Lord, 158, 289
Rebellion, and perished in
Korah's, 313
Rebuke, do not resent the, 234,
256
Rebuke, If we come across any,
305
Received and heard. Keep it, and
repent, what you. See Jesus,
303
Receiver, where is the. See Beast,
165
Recompense with me, bringing
my. See Coming soon, 270,
339
Redeemed from mankind as
firstfruits. See 144,000, 263
Redeemer Jesus Christ, our. See
Lamb, 266
Redeemer of all mankind, being
the. See Jesus, 281
Redeemer, and became our. See
God; Jesus; Lord, 288
Redemption that is in Christ Jesus,
the, 1
Refuge, He is our. See God; Jesus;
Lord, 337
Regional organization. See also
CIS; CES; Russia, 178
Reign forever and ever, he shall.
See Jesus, 221, 292, 299
Reign on the earth, and they shall.
See Priests of our God, 305,
321
Reign, for you have begun to. See
Jesus, 293, 299
Relationship, dynamic. See God
and His children, 285
Religion, God does not recognize.
See Vatican; Priests, 93
Religious groups, 183
Religious events. See also Jesus,
263
Religious hypocrites, 98
Religious matters, 80
Religious militants, 191
Religious mutant, 98
Religious persecution, 282

S

U

V

Wisdom you've made wealth by your. See Prince of Tyre, 126

Wisdom, blessed is the one who finds. See also Understanding, 234, 256

Wishes on paper, who write their. See also Satanic, 237

Witchcraft, 38

With me in Paradise, today you will be. See Jesus, 262

With me, whoever is not. See Jesus, 271, 300

With pestilence I will enter into judgment with him. See Gog, 209

Witness or execute, I will. See Author; Plagues, 241

Witness, a living. See also Priest, Prophet, 247

Witness, nor shall you bear. See Lawsuit; also Devil; Liar; Lie, 77

Witness, you shall not be a malicious. See also Devil; Liar; Lie, 76

Witnesses, the two. See Elijah and Moses, 204, 229, 279, 286, 292

Witnesses, they are not true Jesus'. See also Twelve elders, 265

Wives, of having conquered the. See also Church leaders, Prophet, 247

Wizard, a medium or a, 124

Woe has passed, The second. See also Witnesses, 292

Woe is soon to come, the third, 292

Woe, the beginning of the Second, 192

Woe, woe, woe to those who dwell on the earth. See Judgments, 296

Woman in heaven, no, 113

Woman sitting on a scarlet beast, I saw a, 43, 163

Woman that you saw, and the. See Prostitute, 46, 169, 204

Woman was given the wings of the great eagle, the, 118

Woman, but the earth came to help the. See Israel; also Mary, 117

Womb a reward, the fruit of the. See Birth control, 89

Womb that bore you, the. See Jesus; Mary, 115

Womb, blessed is the fruit of your. See Mary, 89

Womb, can he enter into his mother's. See Nicodemus, 145

Womb, the fruit of your, 66, 89

Women and Mary, the, 97

Women, all hours of the day receiving scores of, 55

Women, who have not defiled themselves with. See 144,000, 263, 264

Wooden copies of the ark, 152

Wooden structure. See Old Serpent, 31, 35

Wooden thing, awake, woe to him who says to a, 110

Word became flesh and dwelt among us, and the. See Jesus, 268

Word of God, the, 39, 52, 93, 99, 268, 275, 329

Word of God, we start with the, 138

Word of knowledge. See Author's faith and obedience, 33, 225

Word of the LORD, the, 206, 254

Word, an adulterated version of the. See Church leaders, 249

Words, they would have proclaimed my. See Prophet, 255

Work is perfect, His, 135

Work of Satan, the devil, the, 113

Work of the spirit of the Antichrist, the. See Devil, 39, 150

Workers of lawlessness, 107, 311

Works is dead, faith apart from, 138

Works is useless, faith apart from, 138

Y

Z

www.ingramcontent.com/pod-product-compliance
Lightning Source LLC
Chambersburg PA
CBHW021212090426
42740CB00006B/186